# EMOTIONAL HEALTH

# The Prevention Total Health System®

# EMOTIONAL HEALTH

by Myron Brenton and
the Editors of **Prevention**® Magazine

 Rodale Press, Emmaus, Pennsylvania

**Library of Congress Cataloging in Publication Data**

Brenton, Myron.
   Emotional health.

   (The Prevention total health system)
   Includes index.
   1. Mental health.   I. Prevention
(Emmaus, Pa.)   II. Title.   III. Series.
RA790.B74   1985        158        84-27719
ISBN 0-87857-551-0 hardcover
     6  8  10  9  7  5          hardcover

## NOTICE

The Prevention Total Health System®

Series Editors: William Gottlieb, Mark Bricklin
*Emotional Health* Editor: Carol Keough
Writers: Myron Brenton (Chapters 2, 3, 4, 5, 6, 7, 8, 10, 11), with Nona Cleland and Jean Sherman; Peggy Jo Donahue (Chapter 1); Gretchen Reynolds (Chapter 9)
Research Chief: Carol Baldwin
Associate Research Chief, Prevention Health Books: Susan Nastasee
Assistant Research Chief, Prevention Health Books: Holly Clemson
Researchers: Tawna Clelan, Jan Eickmeier, Jill Polk, Carole Rapp, Kimberlee Crawford, Robert Dresdner, Stephen Heacock
Copy Editor: Jane Sherman
Copy Coordinator: Joann Williams
Series Art Director: Jerry O'Brien
Art Production Manager: Jane C. Knutila
Designers: Lynn Foulk, Alison Lee
Illustrators: Bascove, Susan Blubaugh, Susan Gray, Jerry O'Brien, Mary Anne Shea, Elwood Smith, Chris Spollen, Carl Weisser, Wendy Wray
Project Assistants: Lisa Gatti, Margot Weissman
Director of Photography: T. L. Gettings
Photo Editor: Margaret Skrovanek
Photographic Stylists: Renee R. Keith, J. C. Vera
Photo Researcher: Donna Lewis
Staff Photographers: Angelo M. Caggiano, Margaret Skrovanek
Production Manager: Jacob V. Lichty
Production Coordinator: Barbara A. Herman
Composite Typesetter: Brenda J. Kline
Production Administrator: Eileen Bauder
Office Personnel: Susan K. Lagler, Roberta Mulliner

Rodale Books, Inc.
Publisher: Richard M. Huttner
Senior Managing Editor: William H. Hylton
Copy Manager: Ann Snyder
Art Director: Karen A. Schell
Director of Marketing: Pat Corpora
Business Manager: Ellen J. Greene

Rodale Press, Inc.
Chairman of the Board: Robert Rodale
President: Robert Teufel
Executive Vice President: Marshall Ackerman
Group Vice Presidents: Sanford Beldon
                               Mark Bricklin
Senior Vice President: John Haberern
Vice Presidents: John Griffin
                       Richard M. Huttner
                       James C. McCullagh
                       David Widenmyer
Secretary: Anna Rodale

# Contents

# Preface

## Help Yourself to Happiness

When you and I were kids, the popular belief was that emotional health was something you either had or didn't have. Today there is a revolutionary new concept of mental health. In many ways, it parallels our new thinking about physical health. We now appreciate, for instance, that physical health must be evaluated not just by the absence of serious disease such as TB or polio, but also by the positive presence of strong immune function, healthy blood pressure and many other qualities.

With mental health, it's the same new approach. Today we evaluate mental health by such diverse measures as the ability to give and accept love, to change your mind or alter your habits, to take reasonable chances, to bounce back from stress. The dividends? Simple: More sheer enjoyment of being alive.

Even, perhaps, living longer. Physician Meyer Friedman maintains that "what a person feels and thinks may be as important as what he eats or inhales in respect to heart disease." That is not idle speculation on Dr. Friedman's part. For years he has studied the relationship between heart disease, our number one cause of death, and what he calls Type A personality behavior. That's the tendency to be chronically angry, aggressive, hostile—and to be driven by a constant sense of urgency. Many of us display such characteristics from time to time, while others are classic Type A's. Dr. Friedman has now shown that learning to modify such behavior can be a powerful protective step for those prone to heart trouble. And you *can* learn to change this behavior.

The ability to change your "personality" is, in fact, the keystone of the new psychology and the essence of this book. We act a certain way, even *feel* a certain way, because we have *learned* this behavior. And if we learned one way of thinking, we can learn another.

The kind of learning we are talking about isn't book learning, though. It's more like learning to dance or play tennis. You have to do things, do them over and over until they gradually work their way into the fabric of your nervous system.

Some of the things we can learn are remarkably simple. Smiling, for instance. Dr. Friedman thinks that learning to smile more is an important part of altering Type A behavior. He cites the American philosopher William James, who said that if you pretend something long enough, you become your pretense.

Some scientists agree, but they've found another reason to look with approval on smiling. They've discovered that when you smile, there is an effect on the involuntary nervous system—an alteration that probably causes an automatic elevation of mood. "Put on a happy face" may soon graduate from musical admonition to medical prescription.

This little trick is just a jimmie on the ice cream cone of happiness. *Emotional Health,* part of The Prevention Total Health System®, has many more techniques, insights and programs that will help you enjoy the deliciousness of life.

Go ahead—help yourself to happiness!

Executive Editor, **Prevention**® Magazine

**1**

# The New Science of Emotional Health

## The power to grow and change emotionally never dims. You can help yourself all through life.

Jean woke up remembering with dismay what a tension-filled day she'd had yesterday at the office. She'd had to give some bad news about a project to several clients. It hadn't gone well, and the company was in danger of losing an important account.

"Oh, well," she thought, "I really messed that one up. But it doesn't mean I'm a total failure! Last week, I won an important piece of business for the company, so I guess I'm still doing okay.

"Besides, it's a glorious Saturday morning, and I'm not going to think about work again until Monday." Jean spent the morning on a long walk, noting the lush bounty of corn and other vegetables in the fields where she walked. She spent the afternoon with some close friends and truly forgot about her workday problems.

Jean is an emotionally healthy person. Though she faces the same kinds of stresses and responsibilities most of us face in modern life, she's trying hard to keep her life in perspective— and she seems to be succeeding. True, she still worries, but she doesn't let life's problems overwhelm her.

Jean's ability to grow, adapt and cope is a capacity all of us have. That's the attitude of most emotional-health experts today. Psychologists, the scientists who study mental health, spend more and more of their time these days studying how people can become emotionally healthier, rather than focusing so much on mental illness.

And these experts have come to realize that even if we aren't suffering from serious mental illness, many of us aren't as emotionally healthy as we could be. True, we may be getting through

1

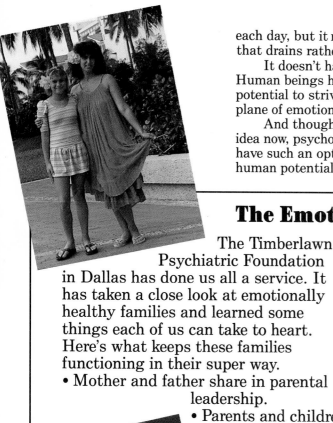

each day, but it may be a struggle that drains rather than energizes us.

It doesn't have to be that way! Human beings have enormous potential to strive toward a higher plane of emotional life.

And though they embrace the idea now, psychologists didn't always have such an optimistic view of human potential.

## IN THE BEGINNING

The beginning of psychology as a science (just a little over a hundred years ago) was based on research that focused both on the human mind and on the ability all people have to use thought and reason to grow and change.

# The Emotionally Healthy Family

The Timberlawn Psychiatric Foundation in Dallas has done us all a service. It has taken a close look at emotionally healthy families and learned some things each of us can take to heart. Here's what keeps these families functioning in their super way.

• Mother and father share in parental leadership.

• Parents and children aren't "pals"; they maintain clear generational boundaries.

• Communication among family members is clear and responsive.

• Problems are solved by negotiation.

• Family members share their feelings with each other.

The similarities among healthy families cut across economic and racial lines. The Timberlawn study began as a way to aid troubled, affluent, white adolescents, and consequently focused on their families. However, questions about how conclusions of this study could be applied to help those of other races and circumstances caused the Timberlawn group to expand its horizons.

Their latest report was done solely on working class black families, but researchers found the same two principal characteristics: The parents nurtured and supported each other, while the children were allowed to develop the independence needed to successfully enter society. Malfunctioning families, on the other hand, frequently had one dominant and domineering family member to whom the remainder of the family submitted. A second feature was the existence of alliances among certain family members against other members.

Researchers concluded that healthy families—rich or poor, black or white—value the same things: security, love, honesty, willingness to forgive, wisdom, religion and education.

Don't take any of this to mean that Timberlawn's emotionally healthy families hew to impossibly high standards. They don't. They have their faults as well as the usual number of hurts and disappointments. What makes them function so well as a unit are shared values along with a capacity and willingness to communicate openly.

The first psychology lab, set up by German physiologist Wilhelm Wundt, devoted its efforts to analyzing people's conscious thought processes. Wundt's aim was to learn as much as he could about the way human beings think and then use that information to help people better understand themselves. Psychology was studied so people could improve their own mental and emotional capabilities.

But soon the study of psychology changed. From its optimistic beginnings, it turned toward a more negative view of humankind. Leading the new movement was a psychologist whose name became a household word: Sigmund Freud.

## RULED BY THE UNCONSCIOUS

Freud disagreed with the early psychologists—he felt that human beings were helpless to change themselves. Even our best efforts to use thought and reason would come to naught, because we are somehow "ruled" by our unconscious thoughts. By unconscious, Freud meant those thoughts, feelings and attitudes that we are unaware exist in our minds.

Where do those unconscious thoughts come from, and why are we unaware that they're there? Freud believed that character and personality are formed in very early childhood, mostly by the age of six. While we are very young, we bury —or repress— some important experiences because they are painful. Once repressed, they become part of our unconscious minds, where, in adulthood, they continue to influence our entire emotional life. So, each time we try to change, Freud thought, we fail because we're helpless to fight those urges and impulses so deeply buried within us.

"If someone had set out to contrive a system to discourage people from trying to help themselves, it might have made the very assumptions that [Freud] did," writes New York therapist George Weinberg, Ph.D., in his book, *The Pliant Animal.*

Freud's method of helping people to overcome their problems was to put them in a type of therapy

## It Can Be Normal—Or Not

Many of our healthy traits become neurotic—or even psychotic—if carried to extremes. A few examples:

NORMAL TRAIT — EXTREME

LOVING — POSSESSIVE
METHODICAL — COMPULSIVE
ASSERTIVE — AGGRESSIVE
LOGICAL — UNEMOTIONAL
ENERGETIC — MANIC
SELF-CONFIDENT — GRANDIOSE
RELAXED — PASSIVE
CALM — UNCARING
RESPONSIBLE — RIGID

called psychoanalysis, where, with the help of an expert, they could eventually unlock some of their buried impulses and learn why they did what they did.

At first, Freud thought just discovering what caused their problems would be enough to help people solve them. But, in fact, it didn't. Many patients who went through psychoanalysis remained emotionally unhealthy and unhappy.

Freud eventually came to believe that our character becomes *so* fixed in childhood that there's nothing anyone or any therapy can do about it. And that was tough luck for anyone with a problem.

## BEYOND FREUD

Where could the history of psychology go from such a pessimistic and fatalistic view of humankind? Not

# How Savvy Are You about Emotional Health?

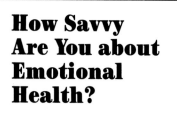

This test will help you find out. Below are 10 statements pertaining to mental health. Check each as True or False.

| | TRUE | FALSE |
|---|---|---|
| 1. Happy events don't ever cause depression. | | |
| 2. Emotionally healthy people never do anything neurotic. | | |
| 3. Only neurotic people exhibit marked mood changes. | | |
| 4. Emotional stress is always bad for us. | | |
| 5. There's a simple standard of normality that applies to everybody. | | |
| 6. Healthy people never think they're crazy. | | |
| 7. If you're hard-working and ambitious, you're at risk for a heart attack. | | |
| 8. We become happier as we grow older. | | |
| 9. If you're self-sufficient, you don't need other people. | | |
| 10. External stress is always bad for you. | | |

**SCORING:** It's very simple. If you've checked off True on any of the questions, you may have a misconception about that aspect of emotional health. If that's the case, don't be surprised. Most of us do have some misconceptions about this all-important— yet in some ways mysterious— aspect of our lives.

far. Although the second major movement in psychology was certainly different from Freud's theories, it nevertheless shared a basic tenet— that people are powerless to change emotionally.

Called behaviorism, the new movement was based on the idea that the way we act (behavior) is determined by our environment. Forget about all those unconscious thoughts and feelings, behaviorists preached. We're really controlled by external forces, which make us behave the way we do.

If a person is rewarded for doing something, he'll do it again and keep on doing it. If he's punished, he'll stop. For example, if a child is consistently punished for behavior such as mauling the family dog, he'll eventually stop doing it, believed the early behaviorists.

Behaviorists saw human beings as easily manipulated—like rats in a cage or puppets on a string. In fact, much of the early research in behaviorism was performed on rats and other animals, reinforcing the belief that human beings, like animals, could not exercise choice or control over what they do.

## THE SHIFT TOWARD MENTAL WELLNESS

Controlled by the unconscious. Controlled by our environment. Such ideas made it seem as though our freedom to grow and change, to use our own minds, was hopelessly lost. Psychology seemed obsessed with the negative —our helplessness, our lack of resourcefulness.

Finally, an optimistic new movement called humanistic psychology came to the rescue. One of its leading voices, Abraham Maslow, disagreed with both Freud and the behaviorists. Human beings are *not* controlled by mysterious unconscious impulses or their outside environments, he believed. They are free agents—not trapped robots.

Maslow chose to study the normal, healthy, creative person instead of focusing on the negative side of human nature. He believed

# How to Change Your Spots

Maybe leopards can't change their spots, but we certainly can, says Ellen Mendel, a psychotherapist at the Alfred Adler Mental Health Clinic in New York. We *can* change those facets of ourselves that we don't like or that haven't been serving us well. The transformation won't happen overnight, but if we really want to change and are willing to work at it, it will happen. Here are Ms. Mendel's tips for accomplishing change.

- Take it as an act of faith that you can't change other people, only yourself.
- Think carefully about what it is you want to change. For greater clarity, write it down.
- If you've listed a number of things, don't try to tackle everything at once. Deal with them one at a time.
- As objectively as possible, think out how this trait or behavior is destructive to you. Suppose you have a bad temper. Consider how it makes you appear to others and how it affects your relationship with them.
- Look back. Maybe you're listening to messages from the past without realizing it. One of Ms. Mendel's clients had a strong tendency to give up too quickly. Why? Her mother had constantly conveyed, in one way or another, "No matter what you do, eventually you'll fail." Isolate the message— and tell yourself how invalid it is.
- Spend a few minutes each day visualizing yourself as the changed person you want to be.
- In counseling yourself, be firm— but don't be hard on yourself. Treat yourself in a gentle, friendly way.
- Watch yourself. Whenever you behave in the way you no longer want to, consciously stop yourself. Say the word silently—"Stop!"
- Sometimes it helps if you change the focus of a troublesome situation. Suppose you're fearful of entering a room filled with strangers. Try to see it as an adventure, not an ordeal.
- Keep a journal in which you jot down good, positive things about yourself. List the times when you've behaved admirably—when you've asserted yourself, when you've overcome something. Refer to it regularly, especially when you start to put yourself down.

people are born with an inner motivation to fulfill their potential as human beings.

Those people who fulfilled their potential he called self-actualized. Maslow made a study of these people to see if he could understand how they achieved their enviable state. Once he learned how, he imparted the information to others.

Maslow described people who are self-actualized as those you have probably envied—those who enjoy life without self-consciousness. They have the courage to take risks or be individualists. And they have the courage to be honest, even if their stand may be unpopular. In other words, they feel secure and have self-esteem.

Humanistic psychology gave the impetus to a whole prevailing view in the study of psychology today. It focused on human potential rather than on human mental disease.

## THE NEW FRONTIER

One of the most effective therapies used today to help people overcome their problems and become emotionally healthier is called cognitive therapy. It endorses the ideas of humanistic psychology in that it upholds the concept—which has been proven through studies—that people *can* change and improve their emotional health.

The methods used by cognitive therapists actually hark back to the earliest research in psychology, returning to the idea that people can use thought, reason and the conscious mind to solve problems. Thus, the study of psychology has come full circle in just over 100 years.

Cognitive therapy is based on the idea that your moods are closely linked to what you are *thinking*—your perceptions of the world, your attitudes and beliefs. If you can change the way you think, you can alter your moods, deal with emotional problems and fight depression.

Say, for example, you are feeling depressed. You perceive the entire world in negative, gloomy terms. Accurate or not, these perceptions color your attitude toward life in general.

What cognitive therapists have discovered is that when you feel depressed, your perceptions of yourself and the whole world are almost always grossly distorted. These distortions are the major cause of your depression, according to one of cognitive therapy's leading proponents, David D. Burns, M.D., author of *Feeling Good*.

Cognitive therapy teaches that you can learn to recognize your distorted perceptions and *change* the way you think. In essence, you talk back to yourself, not letting negative thoughts dominate your life.

## OTHER POPULAR THERAPIES

Cognitive therapy is by no means the only modern therapy being used today to help people become emotionally healthier. According to one expert's estimate, there are about 130 different therapies currently practiced! Here are a few of the most popular.

**Gestalt Therapy.** This technique helps people focus on the "here and now" rather than dwelling on the past. In Gestalt therapy, you concentrate on releasing or getting rid of old experiences that

## How to Stop

# WORRYING WORRYING WORRYING WORRYING WORRYING WORRYING WORRYING

"Normal worries are like snapshots in the family album," says Barry Lubetkin, Ph.D., a psychologist at the Institute for Behavior Therapy in New York City. "Some of the photos may disturb you, but they're forgotten when you put the album away. Abnormal worries, however, are like upsetting home movies that can't be turned off. They run constantly in your head and become pervasive. They can take over your life," he says.

Dr. Lubetkin suggests two of the techniques he uses to help anxious and worried people. One is called *coping desensitization.* If you are worried about a problem in the future, imagine yourself in that fearful situation. Then imagine you are coping with it, or even enjoying it. The man who fears flying might replace his terror with positive images, such as the view from the window or a good in-flight meal.

The second technique is called *cognitive tracking* or *reality testing.* Ask yourself if your worries are supported by the facts. In similar situations in the past, did you cope? If you did, well, stop worrying. Or picture the "worst case." Try to imagine the worst possible outcome of a situation you're concerned about. If you're fearful of taking a long auto trip, imagine getting four flats and running out of gas. Would you somehow survive? Sure you would! Stop worrying!

# Get Hardy to Beat Stress

Why is it that some people seem able to successfully handle tremendously busy lives that are filled with responsibilities, while others cannot? One person suffers from ulcers and high blood pressure, while another, seemingly impervious to illness, walks around with a smile on his face.

Those lucky individuals who seem to thrive under stress are just "hardier" than the rest of us, say Suzanne Kobasa, Ph.D., and Salvatore Maddi, Ph.D., two job stress experts who studied countless executives on the job to find out what keeps some of them healthy.

But what does hardiness mean? In their book, *The Hardy Executive under Stress*, Dr. Kobasa and Dr. Maddi say this trait is made up of these crucial characteristics: commitment, control and challenge.

*Commitment* means making the maximum effort at whatever you are doing—involving yourself in it totally.

*Control*, the doctors write, "means that you believe and act as if you *can* influence events taking place around you. You reflect on how you can turn situations to your advantage."

*Challenge* means you consider change natural. Instead of fearing it, you anticipate it as a useful stimulus to your personal development.

Even if you're not an executive, you can use these characteristics to help you cope with stressful events before they cause enough strain to make you sick.

---

may be causing you emotional hang-ups.

Once you get back in touch with what you are *currently* feeling or perceiving, you learn how to become more aware of yourself: How you are talking and thinking at any given moment.

Gestalt therapists stress the importance of body language to help you assess your feelings, too. For instance, you learn to become more aware of your facial expressions, your posture and the way you use your hands— and what they might be saying about how you really feel.

**Transactional Analysis (T.A.).** This therapy was made popular by Eric Berne, M.D., through his book, *Games People Play.*

According to the theories of T.A., most of us have three "selves" that determine our behavior: the parent, the child and the adult. Each of these roles fulfills a necessary function in our lives. But if one role is excluded or used too much, it can throw us out of balance and especially affect our relationships with others.

For instance, you may waver between being a child and an adult in a certain relationship. At work, you try to maintain an adult demeanor with your boss, but as soon as you're reprimanded for something, you revert to acting like a child.

Or in marriage, you may try to treat your spouse as an adult but find yourself being patronizing, as though you were his or her parent.

What transactional analysis encourages you to do is get into adult-to-adult relationships with others in your life. That's the emotionally healthiest way to live.

**Reality Therapy.** This third method to help people enhance their emotional health is based on the idea that some people see themselves as successes while others constantly see themselves as failures.

Reality therapists theorize that if you're failure oriented, you'll always dwell on the obstacles and problems in your life. What reality therapy helps you develop is a "success" attitude. Armed with that, you'll come to feel good about even your smallest successes and you'll begin to strive toward goals—a key ingredient for a happy and productive life.

*(continued on page 10)*

# The Ten Happiest Things You Can Do

**M**ost mental-health professionals know there's no one formula for happiness. People are just too different. However, there is surprising agreement on what factors contribute to happiness. Here are the top 10 things that happy people do to stay happy.

## 1 Love Yourself

According to Perry W. Buffington, an Atlanta psychologist, you can begin to love yourself by waging war on negativity. "Most people's thoughts about themselves are negative," he says. "And people tend to accept the negative notions uncritically and act as though they were true. I get them to monitor what they're thinking and ask themselves if it's really true."

## 2 Seek the Loving Life

While most people think of romantic love when they consider this emotion, almost any kind of loving relationship can contribute to our happiness.

"When you focus attention on someone else, you feel better about yourself," says Buffington. "When I get patients who have no caring relationships, I usually recommend they get involved in some small group that has a definite purpose. Chances are, while they devote themselves to the group's goal, they'll get the attention they need and establish those necessary social bonds."

## 3 Join the Workaday World

Being productive is central to satisfaction. People often complain about their jobs, but most of us feel absolutely miserable when we have nothing to do for any length of time. Involve yourself in something and you'll be more involved with life.

## 4 Enjoy the Power of Touch

When you touch others you're completing a circuit that sends off sparks of well-being. In touching others you confirm that you're a part of—not apart from—the human race. Says James Hardison, Ph.D., a San Diego psychologist and the author of *Let's Touch*, "It is through touching that we are able to fulfill a large share of our human needs and, in doing so, to attain happiness. By touching someone we can affirm our friendship or approval, communicate important messages, promote health and bring about love."

Problem is, he says, people put up a lot of barriers to effective touching. "For one thing, our society tends to equate touching with either sex or violence. Consequently, many people avoid the simple acts of touching— pats on the back, heartfelt handshakes, cordial hugs—that affirm goodwill."

## 5. Live One Day at a Time

Worrying about what was or fretting about what's to come is a sure way to ruin a perfectly good day—every day. Stay in the here and now, and live it as fully as possible. You can do this by monitoring your thoughts. When you find yourself dwelling on the past or worrying about the future, put a brake on those thoughts. They're unproductive and even may be an unhealthy habit.

## 6. Turn On the Laughter

Laughing can soften the blows. As someone once said, humor is a free ride to happiness.

## 7. Move Your Muscles

Look over any of the dozens of studies on exercise and what it does for us. You'll see that in one respect all those studies draw the same conclusion. Aside from its physical benefits, exercise is a tonic for the soul—it elevates self-confidence, dissipates anxiety, chases away the blues and gives us a healthy high.

## 8. Search for Meaning

Why does one person have a zest for living while another—who's in the same boat—just drags along? No mystery. The zestful one has things to believe in, which is what makes life worthwhile.

## 9. Take Time to Waste Time

Use your leisure time for fun and relaxation. If you squander it on work you'll complain of never having enough. If you must have a goal, make it having fun.

## 10. Give to Others

Altruism is wonderful medicine—it lets you forget your own troubles and makes you feel good about yourself. It allows you to reach out to other people. As a bonus, you'll get some of that sense of purpose so essential to happiness.

## THE TRAITS OF EMOTIONAL HEALTH

All of these therapies—and dozens more—have a positive vision of emotions: that they can guide, uplift and enlighten. But what does emotional health really mean? How would an emotionally healthy person act? Well, all the experts have slightly different ideas. (That's probably why there are so many types of therapy.) Here are a few traits most of them agree on.

**The Ability to Step Back and Look at Yourself Honestly.** That's easier said than done, you may be thinking. But Ken Cinnamon, Ph.D., a clinical psychologist who works with business and industry, says it's a matter of looking for patterns in your past and present life. Patterns in choices that you've made concerning your work, your relationships and your social life should all be examined.

"You can stimulate this process in any number of ways," says Dr. Cinnamon. "Through a journal you keep, books you read and movies you see, or with a therapist. You can also ask others who know you well."

Once you've identified patterns, you're one step closer to knowing yourself and what you want and need out of life. And that can lead you forward into what Dr. Cinnamon thinks is another sign of emotional health.

**The Ability to Change.** Say you've identified a pattern in your life, such as accepting jobs that are always below your skills and abilities. Now that you've faced this pattern, what are you going to do to change it?

"Deciding to change can be scary," says Dr. Cinnamon. "People underestimate how hard it can be. Because of that, they tend to sometimes be too hard on themselves when change doesn't happen overnight." Part of the process of change and growth comes by recognizing a third trait of emotional health.

**The Ability to Increase Your Boundaries of Responsibility.** Richard B. Cohen, a mental-health expert and executive director of A Touch Of Care, an innovative individualized treatment program in Los Angeles for people with emotional problems, cites this as an important trait.

What does increasing your responsibilities mean? Cohen sees it as a process of identifying what interpersonal, vocational or educational skills you may be lacking and working toward improving them so that you can take on

## Green Achers

In comparing city living with life on the farm, country cousins are thought to be happier. This notion was seemingly given scientific confirmation on the city side when Leo Srole, Ph.D., of Columbia University's College of Physicians and Surgeons, led the Midtown Manhattan Study in 1954. This widely publicized study of Manhattan's East Side concluded that 14.2 percent of those interviewed were in need of psychiatric treatment.

But in 1974, Dr. Srole redid his study of this area of Manhattan and found that the city's health had improved.

Not only that, various studies contrasting rural with city areas have consistently shown that mental health is actually better in the big city than in sparsely populated rural areas. Those farms may not be as tranquil as they seem.

more responsibility in your life with confidence.

"So many emotional problems really aren't primary psychological problems at all. People are often depressed or lacking in confidence because they're lacking in some basic skill or experience," says Cohen.

He uses as an example a young man who couldn't get a job. The man had never been depressed before, but now he was. Cohen discovered that the man had never really learned to read—and his illiteracy was holding him back. This fellow's primary problem was not emotional, it was educational. "With someone like that, you teach him how to read. By gaining that skill, he builds up his confidence and is able to get a job," says Cohen.

Cohen's organization not only helps people identify what life skills they may be lacking, but also helps them benefit from learning various social skills, such as managing anger, anxiety and stress. "The more you learn about coping with and handling increased responsibilities by improving your skills, the more satisfied you'll feel about your life," Cohen believes.

The next trait of emotional health also has to do with responsibility, although of a more personal nature.

**The Ability to Take Responsibility for Your Own Thoughts, Feelings and Actions.** Gary Emery, Ph.D., an author and the director of the Center for Cognitive Therapy in Los Angeles, says this means not blaming others for bad things that happen to you or waiting for others to make you happier. "You accept the fact that you, ultimately, are responsible for your own happiness," says Dr. Emery. "You focus on the choices *you* have, what's within *your* power to become more successful."

In the same respect, you must not make excuses or blame others for thoughts and actions that have made you unhappy.

**The Ability to Trust and Be Open to Your Feelings.** Dr. Weinberg, the author of several books, including

*The Heart of Psychotherapy,* says, "Accept every feeling you have. If you feel anxious, don't tell yourself

# Happy Hometowns

Where you live can serve as a barometer of your happiness. If you think people are happiest where the money is—or even where it's nice and sunny—forget it! If you want to be where people really feel good, pack your bags for Oklahoma, Arkansas, Texas or Louisiana. Even with the nation's third-lowest income and education levels, this region of the country is lowest in terms of stress, according to a statistical analysis done by the magazine *Psychology Today.* That same "West South Central" region also tied for first place (with the West North Central states) in terms of residents' feelings of psychological well-being.

At the other extreme, stay away from the Middle Atlantic states of New York, New Jersey and Pennsylvania. This area ranks highest in stress and lowest in overall satisfaction with life. Its inhabitants also don't find comfort or financial rewards in their work, aren't happy with their neighborhood or friends and have the smallest number of friends to call on in an emergency.

Hurry on, then, to New England—a good refuge because it ranks highest both in overall satisfaction and in general outlook on life.

Residents of Michigan, Ohio, Indiana, Illinois and Wisconsin rank lowest in their outlook on life and highest in their negative feelings. If you keep traveling, you'll eventually wind up on the West Coast, where, its various chambers of commerce and tourist bureaus would like us to believe, you can achieve true happiness. Not so, says the *Psychology Today* analysis, for its residents place high in negative feelings and low in overall satisfaction. And they give very low marks to their family life. But you can find good things in the sunny West, too—it's a low-stress area where inhabitants feel personally competent.

If you live in a high-stress, low-satisfaction region, you may not be able to pack your belongings tomorrow and move to an area highly rated in terms of well-being. But do consider the effect of where you live on your mental health. And if you do live in a high-risk region in this respect, take special care to consider the suggestions for emotional fitness in this book.

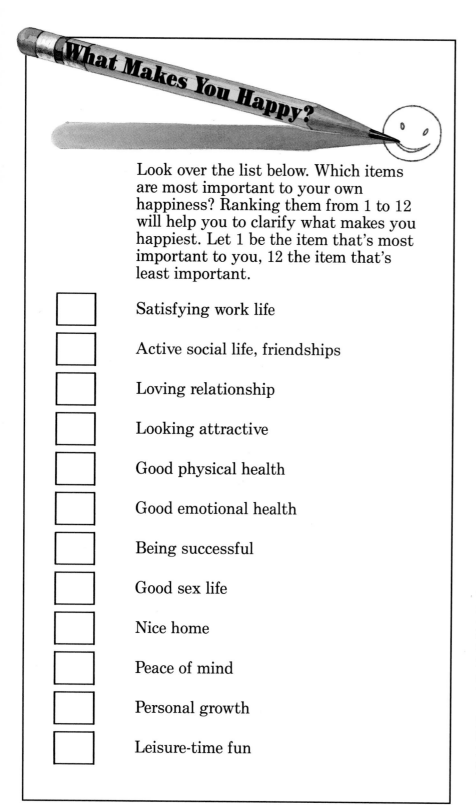

### What Makes You Happy?

Look over the list below. Which items are most important to your own happiness? Ranking them from 1 to 12 will help you to clarify what makes you happiest. Let 1 be the item that's most important to you, 12 the item that's least important.

☐ Satisfying work life

☐ Active social life, friendships

☐ Loving relationship

☐ Looking attractive

☐ Good physical health

☐ Good emotional health

☐ Being successful

☐ Good sex life

☐ Nice home

☐ Peace of mind

☐ Personal growth

☐ Leisure-time fun

there's no reason to be. There probably *is* a reason and you need to uncover it."

**The Ability to Tolerate Stress.** "And along with that, to endure frustrations," says Dr. Weinberg. Stress is here to stay, says A Touch of Care's Cohen. Stressful life situations are much more prevalent than they were 60 years ago, he believes. "We didn't have to deal with credit card bills, tax problems, increasing job responsibilities and so forth back then. Now we do. So we've got to develop the coping skills to handle all that," he says.

**The Ability to Be Flexible in Thinking.** Hendrie Weisinger, Ph.D., a California psychologist and the author of *Dr. Weisinger's Anger Work-Out Book,* says, "This means you can perceive things from many different viewpoints, and not be too rigid when dealing with a problem."

**The Ability to Recognize When You Have a Problem.** According to Dr. Weisinger, "if you're having wide fluctuations in mood, trouble sleeping, a loss of appetite, feeling constantly irritable or chronically angry or depressed, it may be time to do something about it." Recognizing that is half the battle.

Must you have all these traits to consider yourself emotionally healthy? Probably not. Abraham Maslow, one of the fathers of humanistic psychology, discovered in his studies of what it means to be emotionally healthy that striving for emotional health and self-actualization is an ongoing process throughout life.

Maslow felt that the very process of growth toward any goal *is* a sign of emotional health. So as you embark on your journey toward emotional health, keep that in mind. You'll still be having growth spurts when you're 90.

# The Self-Help Movement: Wave of the Future?

It's been called the movement to help people help themselves. Professional psychologists say, some reluctantly, that it's one of the major ways to get mental-health services to the widest group of people.

The self-help movement has attracted 15 million Americans with problems as wide-ranging as being a single parent to having epilepsy.

"Self-help groups are small groups of people with a common concern who meet regularly on a not-for-fee basis and use technical assistance such as books, magazines and recorded information from experts to help them cope," says Gerald Goodman, Ph.D., a psychologist from the California Self-Help Center at UCLA who has been developing and testing audio tape programs that give self-help groups advanced communication skills.

Self-help groups also have other characteristics in common, says Ed Madara, the founder of the first computerized statewide self-help clearinghouse in the nation, the New Jersey Self-Help Clearinghouse. They usually are made up of people who want to share experiences and help each other. Self-help groups are also run by members, which makes them very responsive to members' needs. Although groups are sometimes developed with the help of professional mental-health specialists, these experts are not running the show, says Madara.

"What self-help groups emphasize is empowerment—self-reliance and self-care, what people can do for themselves aided by group support," says Alfred H. Katz, D.S.W., a professor of public health and social welfare at UCLA who has written 4 books and more than 100 articles on self-help.

If you have a problem, how do you go about finding a self-help group? It isn't always easy, concede those in the movement. Some states have self-help clearinghouses that you can call to state your problem and be put in touch with a local group that shares it. But if you're not lucky enough to find a clearinghouse, here are a few other tips from the National Self-Help Clearinghouse, New York City.

- If you know there's a national group for your problem, such as Alcoholics Anonymous, call the national headquarters and find out where there is a group in your area.
- Contact local social agencies and ask to be referred to a group.
- Put an ad in the paper asking if a group exists nearby. You might even offer to start one yourself. The National Self-Help Clearinghouse can give you tips on how to form a self-help group.

Ed Madara also suggests that you look in your phone book under community or social services.

Here's a list of self-help clearinghouses that currently exist:

CALIFORNIA: Los Angeles—
800-222-LINK
CONNECTICUT: New Haven—
203-789-7645
DISTRICT OF COLUMBIA:
Washington area—703-536-4100
ILLINOIS: Evanston—312-328-0470
KANSAS: Wichita—316-686-1205
MICHIGAN: Berrien County—
616-983-7781
MINNESOTA: St. Paul—612-642-4060
NEBRASKA: Lincoln—402-476-9668
NEW JERSEY: Denville—
800-367-6274
NEW YORK: Long Island—
516-499-8800
PENNSYLVANIA: Philadelphia—
215-568-0860, ext. 276
TEXAS: Dallas County—214-748-7825
WISCONSIN: Milwaukee—
414-461-1466
NATIONAL: New York City—
212-840-1259

**2**

# The Body and Mind Are One

Learn to use the total you to feel happier and healthier.

Our language, so revealing, tells us a lot about how the mind and body function. You want somebody who's bothering you to "get off your back." Your response to a difficult job? "What a headache!" An unhappy love affair "breaks your heart."

With phrases such as these, we acknowledge how much of a piece we are, how closely linked are body and mind. Physiatrists (specialists in physical medicine) are among the doctors who often see that link. Tense, anxious or angry because of conflicts at home or work, patients show up with backaches, neck aches and all sorts of other aches and pains.

Thus, in the ordinary course of daily living, the body sends countless messages attesting to the power of emotions. When you're afraid, your mouth dries up. When you're furious, your stomach churns. When you're very happy, you feel light and full of energy. When you're very sad, you feel weighed down. And sometimes you cry. Significant with respect to our intimate body-mind connection, one researcher has found our emotional tears to be of a different chemical composition than tears caused by irritants.

It's not only the chemical makeup of tears that's being investigated. Exciting new research—especially ever-more-sophisticated brain, heart, and immunology studies—show how powerfully our emotions influence most, if not all, human ailments. At the same time, experiments also show how potentially powerful our own inner healing mechanisms are. It's becoming clear just how important it is for us to do our very best to take care of both body and mind.

## NEW QUESTIONS, NEW ANSWERS

It was obvious to Elliot F. Dacher, M.D., that the woman sitting in his office was in pain. Her posture showed it. So did the way she furrowed her brow. He wasn't surprised, therefore, when she told him about her headaches—the ones she'd had for a year and had discussed with a couple of other physicians, without gaining more than brief periods of relief.

A thorough physical examination revealed no overt medical problem. What the patient wanted was a strong painkiller. Instead of giving it to her, Dr. Dacher asked her to tell him something about her medical history, her marriage, her work life, her diet. It turned out that she had a teenage daughter with serious behavior problems, most of which the patient was keeping from her husband. There was conflict with her new boss. Her marriage was "okay," she said, except that recently she and her husband had been quarreling. As for her diet, most notable were the facts that she drank at least four cups of coffee a day and liked sweets.

The patient was puzzled by these personal questions, so unlike the questions most doctors ask. And she was disappointed when Dr. Dacher refused to write a pain-relieving prescription. Unperturbed, he told her to stop drinking coffee and to eliminate sugar from her diet. He also told her to start keeping a journal—jotting down when the headaches came on; when they got better; what she was doing, thinking, feeling, eating around that time. She was to keep the journal for a couple of weeks and then come back to see him. And so she did, reporting two weeks later that, indeed, the headaches were fewer in number and less severe, though they persisted.

At this point, Dr. Dacher gently talked with her about something she hadn't wanted to explore—the tremendous amount of stress she was under. He prescribed 20-minute, twice-a-day relaxation exercises and told her to go on with the journal and dietary regimen he'd prescribed on her first visit.

Nearly a year passed, and for Dr. Dacher's patient it was a memorable time. For the first time, she confronted her husband with the unpleasant details of their daughter's behavior. He took the news much better than she'd expected; in fact, he suggested getting professional help for the girl. Their marital

## Feats of Strength

A 49-year-old woman with a bad back lifts a 500-pound tombstone that's fallen on a little girl. A zoologist leaps 12 feet into the air to grasp a tree branch to escape a menacing pack of wild hyenas. A mother raises a 2-ton car to save her son.

We've all read stories like this and been amazed. But what's more amazing, say scientists, is that under conditions of stress, each and every one of us is capable of such feats. It's a matter of mind over body, and a prime example of the influence emotions can have on our physical state.

Here's how your body reacts to a

tensions lessened. Work-related pressure eased, too, when she found a new job. As for the headaches, there were far fewer of them and they were shorter in duration and less severe.

## A DIARY DIAGNOSIS

What accounted for the change? Perhaps abstaining from coffee and sugar helped. But the headaches probably would have continued if the patient hadn't kept up with and made good use of her headache journal and her relaxation regimen. The journal wouldn't let her off the hook. It made her see in black and white that her headaches were, in Dr. Dacher's words, "not apart, but a part of herself." It made her see how much conflict there was in her life and its connection with the pain inside her head. Luckily, she had the courage to change those aspects of her life that produced enough distress to hurt her physically.

Dr. Dacher belongs to a relatively small but growing group of physicians who have come to recognize that in many instances what happens in the course of patients' daily lives—what they eat and drink; whether they exercise; how they feel about their work, their families, their leisure time; where their major stresses come from—can largely determine the state of their health. So these doctors pay more attention to their patients' emotional lives than physicians usually do. These doctors practice "holistic medicine"—examining the psychological as well as the physical aspects of patients' lives.

The way Dr. Dacher handled his headache patient is a clear example of holistic medicine in practice. "There are often layers of understanding possible with regard to medical problems, whether the problem is a headache or a heart attack," Dr. Dacher says. "You—doctor and patient—may just see the headache and nothing else. But if you see the headache and underneath you also see the person, then you can recognize the headache as an expression of what's happening in

crisis—or to any emotionally charged situation. Stimulated by an emotional response, the adrenal glands pump out

adrenaline, a hormone so powerful it can flood your body with superhuman strength and electrify your system for quick action. The heart races. The liver releases stored blood sugar and your blood pressure shoots up, forcing that sugar to the muscles and brain. The pupils dilate. The intestines shut down. Breathing is short and rapid. You feel tense, apprehensive and ready. Your body has marshaled resources you didn't even know you had to deal with the emergency. You are about to perform an "impossible" act of courage and strength.

# The Anticancer Personality

This is a let's-pretend game, but one with serious intent. Suppose that scientists have succeeded in doing with cancer what they've done with coronary artery disease. Suppose they've isolated the kinds of persons who, in terms of their personality, are least (or most) likely to succumb to the disease.

While this is a let's-pretend game, it has a factual basis. Studies show that, yes, there are significant psychological differences between people who get cancer and those who don't. In general, cancer patients tend to suppress hostile feelings and to feel more lonely and alone. They tend to make a special effort to be liked, and generally try to keep up a good front. According to Lawrence LeShan, Ph.D., a highly respected researcher, they also tend to feel somewhat helpless and hopeless.

Looking at the various studies and drawing on her own 3 decades' worth of experience in treating cancer patients, New York City-based gynecologist and psychiatrist Vivian Tenney, M.D., concludes, "psychosomatic aspects play a significant role in the onset and the course of cancer. They can diminish resistance—or they can reverse the progress of the disease. An emotional uplift, for instance, can help bring about remissions."

Consider a case reported by Ainslie Meares, M.D., in the *Medical Journal of Australia.* The patient was 25, with severely advanced cancer. An amputa-tion had already been necessary. Doctors gave him just a few weeks to live when Dr. Meares first saw him. Yet he recovered; more than 2 years later he was healthy enough to resume his former occupation.

Dr. Meares's primary contribution in this instance was a special program of intensive meditation—one that, among other healing benefits, results in a very marked reduction of anxiety. Not only this young man but a number of other patients, Dr. Meares reports, experienced a regression of cancer when they practiced intensive meditation.

"If psychological factors contribute to the cause of cancer, other psychological factors may produce regression," Dr. Meares told fellow doctors in a letter published in *Lancet,* a prestigious British medical journal. Such remissions, he says, are often associated with prayer, meditation or some deep-seated psychological experience.

A diagnosis of terminal cancer can be one of those experiences. When Toronto psychotherapist Sheila Pennington, Ph.D., investigated the lives of 6 highly successful professionals, all cancer patients who had been diagnosed as terminal but who became survivors instead, she discovered that they had several patterns in common. They vowed to stand the diagnosis on its head—they vowed to live. And they vowed to make positive changes in their lifestyle.

that person's life. That recognition allows you to deal with the person and to encourage the changes that solve the medical problem."

Holistic medicine is a new term for what used to be called psychosomatic medicine. The Greek words *psyche* and *soma* translate to "mind" and "body." Psychosomatic medicine is the study of illnesses that stem from the interaction of mind and body. Until recently, many practicing physicians dismissed the emotional aspects of health and illness. But now, as new research keeps showing how interrelated body and mind really are, and as the holistic medicine movement spreads, things are starting to change.

Still, nobody knows why some people are more likely to suffer from psychosomatic disorders than others. Or why one person suffers headaches, another has stomachaches and another has palpitations of the heart.

"The feeling now is that people are constitutionally predisposed to react to emotional stress in ways that are unique to them," says Stephen Saravay, M.D., a psychiatrist at Long Island Jewish-Hillside Medical Center in New Hyde Park, New York. "One person who feels his boss is treating him unfairly might pound his desk in anger—and then confront his employer; another might keep quiet—and develop a headache, or a backache, or have an asthma attack. And the stressful situation doesn't have to be something really major—some people react to a rude stranger on the bus with somewhat the same intensity as if they were just told they were fired," the doctor says.

## STRESS POINTS

And so, our emotions can engineer changes in the body, head to toe. One of the areas most frequently and certainly most visibly affected is the skin. We blush with embarrassment. Fearful, we turn white or experience a creepy-crawly feeling. In many different ways, the skin reflects the way we feel. Certain skin disorders also are emotionally related.

For example, Debbie is allergic to her emotions. Whenever she feels frustrated or anxious or embarrassed —*really* upset—she breaks out in hives. Her doctor gave the problem a fancy name—cholinergic allergy— and told her she was extra-sensitive to the increased body temperature that accompanies her upsets.

Debbie's case seems like a rarity, but it's not. It's just an example of what happens to our bodies every time we feel a strong emotion. Often the skin problems that result are an expression of an emotion that is not expressed any other way. Debbie has a tendency to hide her feelings from others and from herself, as well. But her body knows, and it tries to let *her* know how troubled she feels.

"Emotions have to be expressed somehow, somewhere," says Domeena Renshaw, M.D., a professor in the department of psychiatry at Loyola University Medical Center. "If they're repeatedly suppressed and there is conflict about controlling

them, they then often show themselves through physical symptoms."

Emmett Miller, M.D., a California physician and specialist in psychophysiological medicine, says there is one organ in particular that commonly reacts to suppressed emotions: the skin.

"A huge number of skin problems are related to emotional factors," he says. "For instance, a woman with chronic itching may be 'itching to get out' of a relationship."

"The skin lives an emotional life of its own," agrees Ted Grossbart, Ph.D., a clinical psychologist affiliated with Beth Israel Hospital in Boston. "It remembers, rages, cries, judges and punishes for real or imagined sins. Symptoms seem to have very eloquent, personal, symbolic meanings."

Anger, says Dr. Grossbart, is the most common emotion that expresses itself through the skin. "A person is in conflict about being angry, so instead of expressing the emotion, she (and it usually is a woman) rages through the skin."

But there is an effective way to change the situation. Using a combination of psychotherapy, hypnosis, relaxation and imagery techniques, Dr. Grossbart has had success with most of the patients referred to him by dermatologists. "Of 50 patients who had completed treatment, about half experienced total or near-total skin improvement. For the other patients the improvement was partial but significant." he said.

One of his patients, Dr. Grossbart explains, "was a young woman who was preparing to leave home to work as a dental hygienist. However, she developed warts under her fingernails that forced her to stop the dental job. She took another, less demanding job close to home and remained with her parents. She was eager to grow—as a person and as a woman—but also was frightened. Her symptoms forced her to back off from her new life. Also, she was under subtle emotional pressure from her parents, who had a stake in her being at home. She functioned as an intermediary in their conflicts and acted as a kind of live-in servant. And they didn't want her to

# How Hotheaded Are You?

Researchers who've studied emotions say that hostility, cynicism and anger are health villains. To find out if you have the dangerous characteristics, answer the questions below honestly. Yes answers indicate it's time to pay some serious attention to calming down.

**1.** Do you tend to feel that other people are only out for themselves, that they make friends only to gain advantage?
**2.** Do you get angry more than once a week?
**3.** Do you turn your anger on other people rather than on yourself?
**4.** Do you get irritable when you have to wait in line?
**5.** Are you very competitive when playing games with friends?
**6.** Do you frequently talk fast and loud?
**7.** When someone asks you a question, do you usually respond quickly and emphatically?

grow up and remind them *they* were growing older. When we resolved these problems with treatment, she became comfortable with becoming an adult, and the warts went away."

Another frequent stress point is the stomach, and emotional belly-aches are common.

Frieda, about to play the female lead in a college play, has a large case of stage fright and vomits just minutes before the curtain goes up. Tom, unemployed and with a family to support, develops a peptic ulcer. Sylvia, newly yet unhappily married, finds herself with her usual reaction to emotional tension—diarrhea, gas and pain.

In Frieda's case, a complex series of physiological events originating in the brain caused her to vomit under stress. For Tom, prolonged stress caused a steady secretion of gastric acid, which in time wore down the stomach's gastric-mucosal barrier and resulted in an ulcer. Sylvia's irritable bowel syndrome is activated when an emotional response influences the autonomic nervous system, which, in turn, makes the bowels work faster and at an increased rate.

If the digestive area is your Achilles heel, so to speak, you may require medical treatment. But there's another kind of treatment that only you can provide, and that's to practice the principles of sound mental health. Learning to control anxiety will, in the long run, do more to ease distress in the digestive area than all the antacid tablets you can swallow in the course of a day.

## IT TAKES YOUR BREATH AWAY

A third area hit hard by emotions run amok is the respiratory system. According to Dr. Saravay, two respiratory disorders stand out because of their emotional origins. If you think that asthma is one, you're right. The tightness in the chest, the wheezing, the out-of-breath feeling and the coughing so painfully common to an asthma attack can be triggered by nonemotional causes—irritants in the air, infections, cold temperatures and the like. But people whose air passages are unusually sensitive (and that's all asthmatics) are often vulnerable to those terrible attacks when they're under emotional stress.

While asthma is well publicized, another dramatic, emotion-linked disorder is not. Called hyperventilation syndrome, it usually affects those men and women who respond to stress by altering their breathing.

Specifically, those who unconsciously stop using their diaphragms when they breathe. These people quickly get the scary feeling that they're smothering. This makes them breathe deeper and faster. The excessive breathing means they're eliminating too much carbon dioxide, so they become dizzy. This process changes their calcium balance and they get cramps. As if that weren't enough, Dr. Saravay says, because they're using the muscles in the chest wall so strenuously, they start to develop chest pains, which often makes them think they're having a heart attack. It's a frightening, vicious circle.

If you have a respiratory problem, try to assess whether it's affected by your emotions. Keeping a journal is the easiest way to track the onset of attacks. You may find a specific pattern related to events in your life. If the problem is one you have trouble handling alone, you might consider psychological counseling. Such counseling may also help you deal with the attacks themselves, which can generate so much fear and anxiety that they provide the fuel for more attacks.

## YOUR BEATEN HEART

There is also a somewhat controversial link between mood and blood pressure. Sure, there's a connection, but nobody knows how permanent it may be. For example, if someone sneaks up behind you and shouts "Boo!" your heart will pound and your blood will race. What we don't know is whether sustained stress can cause chronic high blood pressure. There may well be a link, but clinical studies haven't proven it. Yet a great many cases of hypertension don't seem to have any observable cause and some leading experts—for example, Herbert Benson, M.D., of the Harvard Medical School—feel that repeated stressful emotions like anger, fear and anxiety may be the culprits.

## TYPE A RECONSIDERED

With phrases like, "He's driving himself to a heart attack," so much a part of the language, can there be any doubt that our emotions have a lot to do with the health of the heart? As so often happens, science now validates common belief—and goes beyond. New research shows that certain kinds of personal conduct can be as harmful to the heart as a high-fat diet.

Two cardiologists, Meyer Friedman, M.D., and Ray H. Rosenman, M.D., some years ago excited the world with their discovery that men who are always on the go, always under time pressure, aggressive, quick to anger, ambitious and competitive make prime heart attack candidates. Such men—dubbed Type A personalities—had higher cholesterol levels and a much higher rate of coronary heart disease than other men who ate the same high-fat foods and exercised the same amount but who led a much more relaxed life.

The Type A study got an enormous amount of play both in the public press and in medical journals. Suddenly it seemed as if everyone who lived a fast-paced life was called a Type A, and those close to them warned, "Slow down, don't drive yourself so hard, give your heart a rest." The advice givers forgot that hardworking, ambitious people are what made this country great—and that most achievers don't drop dead from heart attacks.

New research gives us a clearer picture of Type A's and heart disease. What's emerging from the studies is that not all of the personality traits that make up the Type A personality are bad for the heart. Drive and ambition have been given a clean bill of health. The new picture of the coronary-prone person emerges from studies by Dr. Rosenman and colleagues, and shows someone who is very competitive, explosive in manner, impatient, irritable and angry.

As other researchers review behavior patterns that may be associated with coronary heart disease, they're coming up with a similar picture. A research team headed by Redford B. Williams, M.D., of Duke University, surveyed more than 400 patients being examined for clogged arteries. Each was given a comprehensive personality test, one that included a 50-item hostility scale. The investigators found marked differences between people who were hostile, mistrustful and vengeful and other people who had kinder feelings about their fellows. Of the patients with high hostility scores, 70 percent had at least one clogged artery. Among the less hostile folks, half had clogged arteries. Since clogged arteries are a sure sign of heart disease and a precursor of heart attacks, the conclusion is inescapable: Be loving, live longer.

In fact, a study by Dr. Friedman and Dr. Rosenman showed what a difference lifestyle change can make. Large numbers of heart attack patients who underwent a behavior modification program that changed them from Type A's had a rate of heart attack recurrence that was about half that of patients who received only medical counseling. The program is a lesson in good emotional and physical health. Participants learned to soften their anger and impatience, to make time for reflection and for their families, to avoid high-fat foods, overexertion, excessive caffeine and alcohol and to protect their extremities from extreme heat and cold.

## SETUP FOR SICKNESS

We've seen how sensitive the body and mind are in reaction to the stresses and strains of life. But it isn't only specific "target organs" like the heart or the respiratory system that are outlets for emotions. Recent research has shown that much more is at risk when we don't handle stress well—the entire immune system, one of the true keys to physical health, can be seriously affected. When a breakdown of the immune system occurs, it can lead to a range of illnesses that stretches from the common cold to cancer.

The immune system is extremely complex. Simply stated, we're defended against infection and disease by antibodies (protein molecules) that are formed by white blood cells called lymphocytes. Lymphocytes are our stalwart soldiers in the body's fight against the

bacteria, viruses, fungi and parasites that are all around us.

Those are the facts doctors have known for years. What's new and different, in terms of the research, is the recognition among clinicians that emotionally disturbing events in our lives can throw the whole immune system out of kilter and leave us vulnerable to a variety of diseases. For example, a clinical team at the Mount Sinai School of Medicine, City University of New York, studied a group of male volunteers, all of whom had wives with breast cancer. What the team did was to test the men's lymphocyte responses before and after their wives died.

What did they find? That there was a "highly significant suppression of lymphocyte stimulation [immune responses]" during these men's first months as widowers. Levels were similar regardless of whether the wife's death was long-awaited or occurred with relative speed. Within 4 to 14 months after the death, immune responses went back to normal for some—although not all—of the men.

That men whose wives die lose immunological effectiveness is more than an interesting point of information. Studies show that bereaved spouses—especially widowers— often die an early death themselves. In fact, it's estimated that about 35,000 deaths occur annually among newly widowed people—and that some 7,000 of these deaths may be blamed directly on the spouse's death. Lowered resistance to disease caused by the immensely stressful event of their spouse's death may well be responsible, the researchers believe.

But our resistance to infection and other sicknesses can be weakened by events of lesser magnitude. Something as relatively minor as college stress can do it. In one study, researchers examined dental students' secretion of immunoglobin A—an antibody that fights off respiratory infections and cavities—periodically throughout the school year. They found a decrease in immunoglobin A secretion for all students during exams, that high-stress time.

## Don't Blow Your Top

Squelching anger sends blood pressure skyrocketing. Blowing your top also sends blood pressure soaring.

So what to do? The answer, say University of Michigan researchers who've studied the dilemma, is to practice *discussing* the things that make you angry. First, learn to explore the situations that you find provoking. Examine them in a neutral manner, acknowledging your anger. For instance, you might say to yourself, "It was unjust of the boss to blame me for Tom's mistake. No *wonder* I'm angry." Then, set about solving the problem. Discuss it with, say, both the boss and Tom.

So don't let your blood—or your blood pressure—boil. Take action to solve the cause of your anger. You'll release heated feelings harmlessly or prevent them from building in the first place.

Other studies have shown that the stress of exams, basic training and sleep deprivation also can make the immune system malfunction.

These are just a few examples of a growing number of sophisticated psychoimmunological studies that tell us how exposed we are, medically speaking, as we struggle to cope with events of our lives.

Our emotions affect our bodies in an enormous variety of ways—from the silent shutdown of the immune system to a sudden burst of clumsiness caused by worry or distraction. In fact, it appears that many people become accident-prone during periods of stress, anxiety, depression or guilt.

## IT'S NO ACCIDENT

It goes without saying—but maybe it should be made clear, anyway—that we all can have an occasional accident without there being any deep psychological dynamic under-

neath the surface. Being bored or engaged in a very monotonous activity leaves us vulnerable to accidents. Carelessness can be just that—carelessness. Or we may simply be unlucky.

However, some accidents, especially when they are recurrent, are usually no accident at all, at least from a psychological point of view. When such a pattern exists, there definitely is something more going on, something emotionally rooted.

We don't need enormous conflict, either, to make us fall downstairs. A quarrel with a close friend, an unexpectedly large medical or repair bill, an overload of work in the plant or office—all these can do it. "We are all prone to accident-proneness at some time in our lives," says Dr. Saravay.

The bottom-line questions then become who and when. Who's the most likely to have accidents? When are we vulnerable to hurting ourselves? Here are the major patterns.

# Don't Be Dubbed a Hypochondriac

Suppose you've seen a doctor about those nagging, painful symptoms that just won't quit. And suppose the doctor has hemmed and hawed about diagnosing your ills—implying somehow that your problems are all in your head. If

that's ever happened to you, find another doctor.

People in medicine who have compassion for this kind of situation say that if your symptoms persist, you should persist, too. Doctors are not infallible. Misdiagnoses are sometimes made. And some physicians actually resent any challenge to their authority,

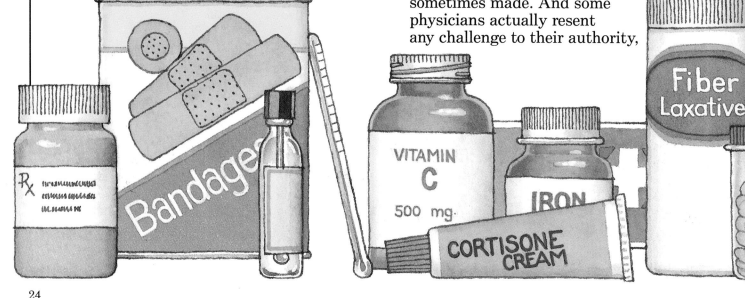

**Preoccupation with a Problem.**
Preoccupation, says Wolfgang F. Kuhn, M.D., assistant professor of psychiatry at the University of Louisville, is one of the most common causes of accident-proneness. Mental-health programs for troubled employees in both the private and public sectors recognize that a pattern of on-the-job accidents is a sure sign the employee is finding some personal or job-related problem tough going. A number of studies also reflect the role of preoccupation in accidents. A University of Michigan study, for example, found that life changes and stress are "significantly related" to traffic accidents. The researchers pinpointed the stresses most likely to cause accidents: family problems, school or job pressures or financial troubles.

**Mental Depression.** Not everyone who's feeling low goes out and smashes up the car or does something equally serious. But, notes Dr. Kuhn, "A lot of people who are depressed have a tendency toward self-punishment. It's part of their depression. Such people, rather than sit in a corner and simply be depressed, arrange for something external to happen to them." Of course, he stresses, they don't deliberately set out to do themselves harm; it's an unconscious process that prompts the self-punishment.

**Strong Guilt Feelings.** Guilt is more than a painful feeling; it sometimes makes us act in painful ways. Guilt, like depression, sometimes makes us want to punish ourselves—and, in some cases, explains accident-proneness. Mary, an Oklahoma woman, began to have accidents around the first anniversary of her mother's death. She burned her hand on the stove, poked her eye with a pencil and broke a Dresden china doll she'd prized. Mary had had a very difficult relationship with her mother, had wished her dead a number of times and felt a tremendous sense of relief when her mother

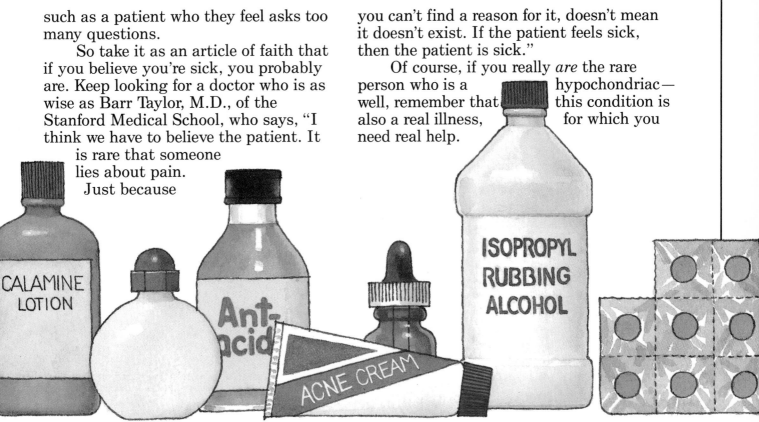

such as a patient who they feel asks too many questions.

So take it as an article of faith that if you believe you're sick, you probably are. Keep looking for a doctor who is as wise as Barr Taylor, M.D., of the Stanford Medical School, who says, "I think we have to believe the patient. It is rare that someone lies about pain. Just because

you can't find a reason for it, doesn't mean it doesn't exist. If the patient feels sick, then the patient is sick."

Of course, if you really *are* the rare person who is a hypochondriac— well, remember that this condition is also a real illness, for which you need real help.

CALAMINE LOTION

Ant-acid

ACNE CREAM

ISOPROPYL RUBBING ALCOHOL

actually died.

Mary's accident-proneness was related to a very specific situation, but that needn't be the case. We can walk around feeling very guilty in general even though we haven't really done anything to feel guilty about. In fact, some people with chronic feelings of guilt constantly victimize themselves either emotionally or physically.

**Great Anger.** Picture somebody who's gritting his teeth with anger. Now picture that person jumping into a car and driving away. You wouldn't expect such a person to drive safely, would you? You'd be right—irate drivers can be a menace on the road. But anger also affects our judgment when we're not on the road. " 'Seeing red' keeps us from being as careful as we should be no matter what we do," says New York psychotherapist Ellen Mendel. "We're so caught up in our anger we don't see potential hazards, and that gets us into trouble." Anger can make us an even greater danger to ourselves, Ms. Mendel says, "if it leads to feeling bad about being angry. Anger also may lead to impulsive, self-endangering behavior."

If you've had more than your share of accidents lately, the experts have this advice for you: See if you can relate the pattern to some event in your life. Don't drive if you're mad as a hornet about something; let some of that anger out first—relax, take deep breaths. If you're preoccupied, make a special effort to be more watchful, more aware, no matter what activity you're engaged in. Slow down. Avoid alcohol. The times when you're most accident-prone are the very times you should make a special effort to practice accident prevention.

## EMOTIONALLY TIRED

Fatigue, unlike accident-proneness, isn't necessarily connected to our emotions. Sometimes, when we've done a satisfying day's work or played hard and well, we become very tired—but feel wonderful. Being tired is one of the body's most valuable protective mechanisms, keeping us from overexertion and consequent physical collapse. It can be a warning signal—like pain or fever—that something's physically wrong, though fatigue is such a common symptom that "something" may be hard to pin down.

Emotion-caused fatigue needn't be a cause for concern, either. Sometimes we're tired because we're happy. Much of the time, though, it's not happiness but stress or depression that's the cause of emotional fatigue. Typically, then, we don't bounce back. No matter how much we try to rest, we still feel drained. We get so tired of feeling tired.

Often we can anticipate becoming emotionally fatigued, as when we're in an obvious crisis situation. But not always. Sometimes things are going on that we're not consciously aware of —strong feelings have been stirred up, perhaps, but we haven't really looked at them. The effect is the same: exhaustion.

"You see that especially with anger, anxiety and depression," Dr. Saravay observes, "and the fatigue can be quite powerful."

Anger, overt or suppressed, is especially debilitating. Stan and Karen are having difficulty in their new marriage. They're fighting a lot. Karen seems to have the stamina for their fights, but each time they quarrel intensely for more than 15 minutes or so, Stan feels completely drained and would just love to drag himself into bed. "Karen thinks I'm copping out, but I really can't function. All I want to do is sleep." Though Stan isn't aware of it, some people actually do fall asleep while quarreling.

This anger-generated fatigue is usually complex. Anger is aggression. Aggression is dangerous; it can hurt somebody. Maybe Stan's more enraged than he realizes; he'd like to hit Karen, or worse. Fatigue protects him from the act.

"Hostility or aggression is often weakened by fatigue," Dr. Saravay says, and likens the dynamics involved to those used by the great apes. When angry those huge creatures could tear each other apart, but another reaction has evolved instead—they yawn. A great

# The Doctor Who Believes in Miracles

A cancer surgeon who believes that love heals, that mental images can conquer malignant cells, who plays Willie Nelson in the operating room, hugs his patients and asks them to call him by his first name? Yes, and he teaches at Yale Medical School.

Bernard Siegel, M.D., has become widely known—respected in some circles, derided in others—for his conviction that patients, even those with so-called terminal cancer, can and sometimes do heal themselves.

How does he account for these recoveries? Are they miracles? "Yes," he says. "I see little miracles all the time. For instance, people who decide they're not going to have side effects from chemotherapy, so they don't. But, instead of 'miracles,' it would be more accurate to say 'self-induced healing.'

"One woman had this enormous tumor on her pancreas, and she went home to die. But she came back to see me, and she was well. There was no evidence of any tumor. I asked her what happened, and she said, 'I decided to live to be 100, and I left my troubles to God.'

"As this woman's experience shows, worries are absolute nonsense. I say you can help heal yourself by changing your attitudes. If you have trouble with the God concept, call it peace of mind or whatever you want. Solzhenitsyn calls it 'clear conscience.'"

To be well, Dr. Siegel says we must learn from even painful experiences. "Most of the people in the world are feeling poorly about their lives. We don't know how to love or to share. We're conditional lovers. We want something back, a thank-you.

"No one comes through life without his own pain, but we have to learn to deal with it in a positive way, grow from it. We have to learn to be able to say, 'I have a problem, and I need help with it *now*.'

"If I could deliver one message to the world, it would be that quote from the French theologian Teilhard de Chardin—'Someday after mastering the winds, the waves, the tides and gravity, we shall harness for God the energies of Love, and then, for the second time in the history of the world, man will discover fire.'"

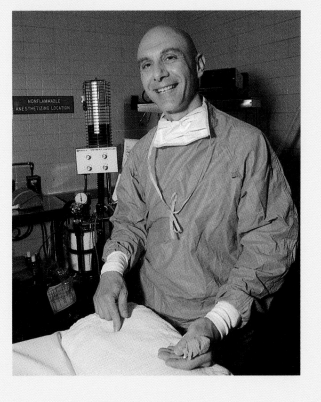

big yawn is like baring their teeth—it both symbolizes their rage and disarms it. Our fatigue may serve the same purpose. It may disarm us from acting upon our more aggressive impulses.

Dr. Kuhn touches on the fact that often our especially strong, fatiguing emotions aren't readily apparent to us. Living with an ever-increasing burden of unexpressed anger can be far more debilitating than expressing it. The same holds true for anxiety, depression, resistance to a task—anything that seethes inside us.

Take resentment, for instance. If you enjoy what you're doing, your energy seems inexhaustible. If you dislike the task intensely (even if

*(continued on page 30)*

# Alternative Methods of Healing

In the medical vanguard, along with such ultra-tech miracles as microsurgery and biocomputers, are some startling surprises—returns to ancient healing arts, some as old as written history, involving such unmeasurable mysteries as the impact of one human being on another and the dimensions of the world of the spirit. Most of all, they involve the mind as healer and the incredible influence for good or ill of what a person believes.

## Hypnosis

The image of someone being bamboozled into acting like a chicken is no longer an accurate picture of hypnosis. Though hypnosis was once primarily sideshow entertainment, its healing uses have now largely replaced the hoopla.

Recognized for a quarter of a century by the conservative American Medical Association as a "valuable therapeutic tool," hypnosis is now commonly used as a painkiller in childbirth, to treat asthma in children, to promote healing in burn patients and to ameliorate the side effects of cancer chemotherapy. It's also been found helpful in cases of obesity, sexual dysfunction and phobias, and in breaking addiction to nicotine and other drugs.

Despite its ever-increasing respectability, the mechanisms of hypnosis have been mysterious ever since an Austrian doctor named Mesmer discovered the trance state in the 18th century. What is known is that hypnosis, although the name suggests sleep, is actually a form of intense concentration during which the subject opens his or her mind to suggestion—for instance, that a certain pain will be relieved. Nor is the hypnotic state strange and foreign—all of us enter light trances occasionally, perhaps while watching a movie or a fire.

Another myth about hypnosis is that it is the person with the swinging watch, or the doctor—the hypnotist—who creates the trance. Not true. The subject makes the mental effort that creates the trance. And to be medically effective—to help relieve pain or conquer an addiction, for instance—the subject must want it to work.

## Therapeutic Touch

Therapeutic touch, an ancient practice at least as old as recorded history, has been rediscovered and is used now in some of the most prestigious hospitals and medical schools in the country.

Although the mystery of how trained touch works to heal remains unsolved, that it *does* work is fact. Temperatures drop, inflammations are reduced, pain is lessened, blood pressure falls.

What is happening? According to Dolores Krieger, R.N., Ph.D., who teaches at New York University and is the person most

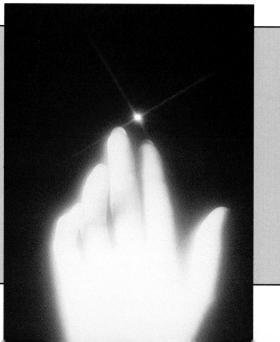

# Faith Healing

Inside the church a healing service is in progress. As a circle of people join hands in intense prayer around the person desiring a cure, one observer feels "an enormous flow of energy, like an electric shock."

No, this isn't a back-woods conclave of 50 years ago. It's the Central Presbyterian Church on Park Avenue in Manhattan, which, until recently, conducted healing services. Such services are part of a growing resurgence of interest in faith healing, the alleviation of injuries and illness through spiritual means.

Not only Presbyterians but such equally conservative faiths as the Episcopalians have begun again to heed the second half of the biblical injuction to "preach the kingdom of God, *and to heal the sick*," according to the Reverend Malcolm Marshall, formerly with St. Margaret's Church in Washington, D.C.

Even the Roman Catholic church has altered its 500-year-old stance on anointing the sick. Called the Last Rites, for centuries it was practiced only on the dying. Today this sacrament is now available for "healing the whole man," according to a church authority.

Why these changes? It may be that the growing interest in faith healing is actually a result of science's softening its hard line against mysticism. Having won its longtime battle against superstition, science's door has opened a crack to areas of human life that may not ever yield their secrets to the microscope or test tube. And faith healing, long associated with charlatanism and hokery, is actually being redeemed by its old enemy, science.

More and more, doctors have been forced to recognize the critical role expectation and belief have on healing. If someone holds a positive belief and has faith in getting better, that is likely to be what happens. Doubt and despair have just the opposite results. And the effects are so marked that some surgeons, for instance, refuse to operate on patients who believe they will die as a result of the surgery, because all too frequently they do.

Faith has even been given the ultimate scientific accolade—it has become the subject of investigation. Even researchers at the National Institute of Mental Health (NIMH) have looked for brain mechanisms associated with beliefs that affect healing.

Few doubt today that a belief in healing—whether it's by act of divine intervention, reliance on prayer or a belief in a particular doctor or medicine—does have a positive influence.

But how far can faith go? What of miracle cures? Of the millions of people who have visited the Lourdes healing shrine (shown above) —30,000 each year—the Catholic church has documented only 100 cures. Still, there *are* those 100.

responsible for the current acceptance of touch as therapy, it mobilizes the patient's own healing powers by redistributing energy. The first step of the treatment consists of passing the hands over the sick person's body to detect energy "imbalances." Touch therapists maintain that they must be calm and "centered" for the healing to work. Other touch healers believe that the energy of the practitioners themselves—such as the electrical fields said to be shown in Kirlian photographs—influences the healing.

One thing does seem certain. Belief that touch can heal is important to the results, and that belief should be shared by giver and recipient.

It may even be that disbelief can produce negative results. In one study of touch healing on injured lab mice, those whose cages were periodically held by healers got well faster than those whose cages weren't. But the slowest healers were those whose cages were cradled by skeptical medical students.

you haven't acknowledged to yourself how much you hate it), your energy level evaporates as swiftly as a puddle in the desert; you're depleted before you've begun.

Depression and fatigue are closely linked. Says Dr. Kuhn, "Fatigue can be a form of depression, fatigue can lead to depression or depression can lead to fatigue."

Frequently compounding our misery when we're depressed or fatigued is poor sleep.

If, like millions of other people, you suffer from fatigue, you may not know offhand whether its cause is physical or emotional. If you can be sure the cause is not physical, you can assume that it is probably emotional. To make a clearer distinction between the two, try to answer the following questions.

Is something challenging your peace of mind—a potential conflict, an impending separation, a significant change? Is there a situation that makes you very angry, but which you haven't dealt with yet? Is someone in your family upsetting you? What about work? Are you getting along with your boss and co-workers? Or is there something about the nature of your responsibilities that's getting you down? Are you having trouble making ends meet? Are you suffering from "burnout"?

"You need to examine your life," Dr. Saravay explains, "to find out what it is that's bothering you, what you're dissatisifed with."

In a sense, fatigue isn't an enemy but a friend, pointing out elements in your emotional life that badly need looking after.

## GOOD, SOUND SLEEP

Fatigue should make us want to fall right into bed and slumber away. For good sleepers that means sleeping soundly, then waking up rested and refreshed. That's the way it should be. Good sleep is essential to our physical and mental health. We slow down our body functions (at least during some stages of sleep) and give our organs the rest they need. Deprived of sleep for

about four days, we lose our ability to think clearly.

Since it's so essential to the body and the mind, sleep ought to come as easily as breathing. But sometimes the Sandman goes out on strike. Some 50 million of us regularly have trouble sleeping. We spend millions upon millions of dollars a year on sleeping pills or other aids. There are at least 240 sleep disorder centers around the country, some run by medical centers, that have been established for purposes of research and for treatment of sleep disorders. We may sleep and we may dream, but a lot of us sure don't do it well.

The catch-all term for our troubles is sleep disorders; what it catches is everything from frightening night terrors—high-voltage nightmares of sorts, mercifully forgotten in the morning—to the tossing and turning that characterize garden-variety insomnia. To be sure, not all of those disorders have an emotional basis. Take sleep apnea, for instance, a condition in which sleepers wake up literally hundreds of times a night. You can imagine how they feel in the morning! But with this disorder, the cause is well known and at times can be corrected surgically. People with sleep apnea have obstructed air passages; consequently, they have a lot of trouble breathing and their continuous wake-ups enable them to gulp in mouthfuls of fresh air. Narcolepsy is another physical disorder, though exactly why it occurs isn't known. Narcoleptics can't control their waking state—at any time of the day they suddenly feel on the verge of collapse and actually do drop fast asleep right then and there.

## THE DEPRESSION PATTERN

Most of us, happily, have much more ordinary sleep problems. In a nutshell, we have trouble falling asleep, staying asleep or getting restful sleep. That's insomnia—and, says Thomas D. Borkovec, Ph.D., a psychologist and sleep disorder researcher at Pennsylvania State University, in a large number of cases it occurs because we're anxious or otherwise troubled about something. People who are depressed display an especially distinctive sleep pattern: They wake up in the

## Imaging: Talking to the Pain Creature

Iris thought her arthritis felt like a small, mean monster crawling up her spine, digging its long, horrid claws into the endings of her nerves.

Rather than just endure the agony, Iris mentally pictured the creature and began trying to talk to it, asking what would soothe it, make it stop its awful clawing.

Surprisingly, the creature answered. Its answer was unexpected, too. "Move, walk, stretch," it said. It also wanted more rest, a daily nap. The monster even suggested a position—lying on the floor with her head supported by a couple of pillows and calves comfortably resting on a chair—that Iris has found to be virtually pain free when the attacks get bad and she can't get comfortable in bed.

Iris used a technique called imaging, and she continues to use it. She says that as a result she can move more freely than she's been able to do for years.

She is far from alone in her use of this mental healing technique. A growing number of people with serious diseases use this method—picturing their bodies fighting illness and overcoming pain. And this technique is drawing increasing support from orthodox medical circles. Very simply, imaging seems to work. Here are some examples.

• John, a cancer patient, used imaging to overcome his fear of chemotherapy, and he credits imaging for his total lack of side effects.

Visualizing the chemotherapy as a "healing energy," he says he sees himself operating valves in his brain that regulate the blood flow to the healthy and unhealthy cells. "I never got sick one day. I haven't had any loss of hair," says John.

• Nick is a cancer patient whose tumor has not grown in the years he's been using imaging. "I picture a general feeling of wellness more than anything," says Nick. "I also picture water flushing out the area, a cleansing and a warmth, just feeling it flow through like a warm spring shower. I see an overflowing and all the bad stuff floating away."

• Anne, a woman with a dangerously irregular heartbeat, visualized a little girl on a swing. The little girl swung back and forth rhythmically, just the way Anne wanted her heart to beat. It worked, she says, and her doctor was able to take her off medication.

cold, predawn hours and have a terrible time falling asleep again.

Worry and insomnia go together—so frequently, in fact, that at Penn State, Dr. Borkovec has started doing separate research on the problem of worry itself. Anxious worriers frequently find something to worry about; worrying about sleeping poorly is one of those things. "Obviously, they don't sleep restfully," Dr. Borkovec says, "but they may fall asleep sooner and sleep longer than they think." That's the interesting thing about one class of insomniacs, now called subjective insomniacs. Researchers have discovered that people with this disorder can't really assess their own sleeping pattern very well because they think they sleep more poorly than they actually do. But they aren't good sleepers, either, because in the morning, like other insomniacs, they have to drag themselves out of bed.

What all too many people decide, when faced with yet another endless night, is to get themselves a supply of prescription sleeping pills or over-the-counter sleep preparations. Research has shown that this decision is a very bad one. The drugstore preparations are often nearly worthless. The prescribed drugs—technically called sedative-hypnotics—will help you sleep. But you won't sleep well because these drugs interfere with normal sleep patterns and the stages of sleep we must pass through each night in order to have restful, healthy sleep.

Also, these drugs have potentially serious side effects and can easily become habit forming. Ironically, when used over long periods, they actually produce insomnia. Experts in sleep disorders rarely prescribe them, and then only for a few nights.

## SEVEN STEPS TO BETTER SLEEP

If you have a problem falling asleep or staying asleep, there are drug-free, natural ways you can help yourself get a good night's rest.

1. About an hour before bedtime, do something soothing and pleasant to mellow down. Listen to soothing music, take a warm bath, read a book. Make a conscious effort to put the day's problems on the back burner. Tomorrow there will be time to solve them.

2. Don't go to bed hungry, or your stomach will wake you up. Have a light snack. Warm milk, or milk with cereal, can do wonders to calm some restless sleepers.

3. Try tryptophan, an amino acid found in protein foods. Studies by Ernest Hartmann, M.D., of Tufts University, have shown that tryptophan stimulates the secretion of serotonin, a brain chemical that helps us sleep. According to Dr. Hartmann's research, just 1 gram of tryptophan (two 500-milligram tablets) can help mild insomniacs. However, tryptophan, sold by most suppliers of health foods and supplements, does its chemical job most effectively in the company of high-carbohydrate foods like bread and the aforementioned cereal. Plan your snack plus tryptophan for 45 minutes to an hour before retiring, when Dr. Hartmann says it will work most effectively.

4. Work toward good sleep. Go to bed and get up at the same times each day. Avoid liquor, cigarettes and caffeine shortly before going to bed; these interfere with sound sleep. Regular exercise promotes healthful sleep, but don't go for a jog just before going to bed because it's apt to rev you up instead of relaxing you.

5. Do a relaxation exercise—meditation, biofeedback, progressive relaxation or whatever you discover works best for you. Dr. Borkovec's studies showed that insomniacs experience as much as a 35 to 50 percent reduction in their original poor sleep pattern when they try progressive relaxation (see chapter 4).

6. If you're thrashing about in bed for 10 or 15 minutes, unable to sleep, get up, go to another room, read or watch television until you feel sleepy, then get into bed

again. If after another quarter hour you're still awake, repeat the process. Is it effective? Dr. Borkovec says yes.

7. If your insomnia lasts only a few days, don't worry. But if you're stuck in that pattern of sleeplessness for more than a couple of weeks or so, and you really feel washed out, it's time to take action. Try the techniques recommended here. If necessary, consult a counselor to help you solve that nagging problem or, if your insomnia is severe, consult your local hospital to find the whereabouts of a sleep disorder center.

## IMAGINED ILLNESS

While insomnia is taken seriously by most medical professionals, another disease with an emotional component— hypochondria—is not. Here, for example, is the latest hypochondriac joke making the rounds. A man rushes into his doctor's office, tells him he has just heard about a new disease called Kulla Koema, and insists, "That's my problem, doctor, all the symptoms fit!" The wise doctor calmly replies, "I know all about that disease. People who have it feel no distress. They sleep well, eat well and have loads of energy." More dismayed than ever, the hypochondriac retorts, "I knew it—I have all those symptoms, every one of them!"

Hypochondria is far from a joke, but that little story illustrates the tendency that hypochondriacs show. They inflate real but minor symptoms into catastrophic illnesses; they get a headache and are sure it's a brain tumor, they feel tired or have an ache somewhere and *know* it's cancer. They preoccupy themselves with thoughts of disease. They won't take no for an answer; if a physician says they're fine, they immediately distrust him and go shopping for another who may give them the disastrous news they both hope for and dread. Why should hypochondriacs seek and endure such agony? Because they *do* have a disease. Hypochondria. And its symptoms

# How Placebos Work

Almost everyone has heard of placebos (*plah-SEE-bows*), the so-called dummy pills that produce *real* results. But almost no one knows *why* these sugar pills work. Now a respected group of scientists believes placebos prompt the body to produce its own drugs—endorphins, morphinelike painkillers.

This discovery would explain the astonishing results of one study that showed placebos to be 77 percent as effective as morphine at relieving postsurgical pain. In yet another study, placebos equaled the strength of a recognized and widely used psychiatric medication.

The discoverers of the endorphin-stimulating effects of placebos tested their theory in an ingenious way. Since endorphins lock into the same receptor sites in the brain as narcotics such as heroin and morphine, the researchers used a narcotics-blocker, naloxone, to keep endorphins from entering those sites.

Doctors divided volunteers who had undergone wisdom tooth extraction, an operation usually followed by a lot of pain, into two groups. One received naloxone and a placebo and the other a placebo alone. The researchers' prediction that those receiving naloxone would suffer more pain was confirmed.

While some scientists noted that naloxone itself may enhance perception of pain, Jon D. Levine, M.D., Ph.D., the principal author of the study, says follow-up work has reconfirmed his findings—placebos stimulate the brain to produce its own painkillers.

are something they can't help.

Most of us have a little touch of hypochondria now and then. Our heart skips a beat occasionally (which is perfectly normal) and we interpret it as a sign of heart disease. A friend develops a serious illness and we immediately think we have similar symptoms.

Medical students are warned ahead of time that they're going to think they have each new disease they study. Doctors report filled waiting rooms the morning after a televised drama or documentary dealing with disease, the patients all eager to complain of the symptoms depicted on the show. And, unfortunately, our hypochondriacal tendencies seem to become a little stronger as we grow older.

We worry about illness, but the feelings pass for most of us. For true hypochondriacs, they don't. Every little twinge confirms them in their ill health; as one former hypochondriac puts it, "It's as if you're constantly passing a death sentence on yourself."

## A SELF-FULFILLING PROPHECY

Of course, there are degrees of this bodily preoccupation. The more extreme hypochondriacs live in constant fear and hopelessness — fear that they have that dread disease, a lack of hope that anybody will diagnose it properly. And, as Warren R. Procci, M.D., an associate professor of psychiatry at UCLA, points out, theirs can become a self-fulfilling prophecy. Their hypochondria can make them very sick, often from medications they shouldn't have taken or from surgery they didn't need. Also, like the boy who cried wolf, they may finally find it hard to get anybody to take them seriously when they really are sick. Physicians are often markedly unsympathetic to the hypochondriacs in their practice, and try to shunt them off to other doctors.

As common sense already tells you, people aren't born hypochondriacs. Life circumstances shape them into the role, and it becomes a serious emotional problem. "It often starts in childhood," psychotherapist Ellen Mendel explains, "with a lot of attention being paid to illness." A family member may be seriously ill and require lots of attention, or the child himself may discover that when he's sick his parents focus on his needs more than usual. Or, whenever he's not feeling well, they may become overly anxious. The child, sensing their anxiety, learns that an illness is something *important,* something worthy of worrying about.

Hypochondriacs go through miserable times but, as Ms. Mendel points out, their imaginary illnesses serve some real psychological purpose. In adulthood as in childhood, sickness can be an attention-getting device. It can be used as a way of controlling other people, getting them to do one's bidding, or it can be used to avoid responsibilities the person fears. As Ms. Mendel explains, "If you're sick, not much can be expected of you, and you don't have to face up to your problems." She stresses, however, that the actions of hypochondriacs are not on a conscious level. The people involved really don't know what it is they're doing.

## WHAT CAN BE DONE

Hypochondriacs should get psychological help. Ironically, they often resist the idea because hypochondria is the one health problem they *don't* believe they have.

Family members who maintain a caring attitude and are willing to listen to the person who is hypochondriacal can help a lot, too. Hypochondriacs often have a hard time expressing their innermost feelings and talking about the difficulty they have in coping with life; they need friends and relatives who won't judge them and who are ready to lend a sympathetic ear if they do open up.

Some extreme hypochondriacs have trouble making and keeping friends because they're so obsessed with their health; people simply become tired of listening to them. But milder hypochondriacs often maintain good friends, and generally have satisfactory marriages. They manage to find spouses who get caught up in their eternal quest for health and are willing to take care of them.

All hypochondriacs — whatever the degree of their problem — can help themselves in one specific way. They can make an effort to become more involved in a variety of activities. They can pursue hobbies, sports and other pastimes — and become too busy to worry so much about health. A quickened interest in healthy living — proper exercise, a sound nutritional program and so on—is an excellent prescription when hypochondriacal tendencies surface. It's body involvement, to be sure, but of a positive nature. It's the emotionally healthy way to deal with an anxiety-producing, debilitating emotional problem.

## THE HEALING MIND

**Question:** If what's up there—the mind and its control center, the brain—can make us sick, why can't it channel its enormous powers to make us well?

**Answer:** It can. It does. The mind performs the most wonderful feats of healing, without conscious awareness. Relatively few of us have learned to exploit our healing potential. Moreover, that power is usually pooh-poohed by medical science. Now, however, mind healing is being taken more seriously by a small but growing number of medical scientists. These scientists don't understand everything they see, but from a growing body of laboratory studies, clinical observations and experiments, it's becoming ever clearer that we can be powerful agents in our own healing.

Only recently, for instance, through the development of new biochemical technology, have medical scientists discovered one of the brain's amazing healing abilities. Our bodies actually manufacture pain-relieving medicines called endorphins and enkephalins. These complex chemicals are natural opiates. They go to work when we hurt by raising our threshold of pain.

And that, insofar as our curative powers are concerned, is only the beginning.

Belief, too, is an important element in any kind of healing. A nurse with a healing touch has to believe in the power of that touch; the patient has to believe in it, too. (See "Therapeutic Touch," on page 28.) Faith, belief, optimism, regularly making positive statements (affirmations) silently or aloud—all such elements have a potent healing effect.

Take an imaginary walk through a hospital's coronary care or intensive care unit. You know you're

# Taking Your Mind's Pulse

Keeping a diary can put you in touch with what you really feel, experts say.

The way it works is that a journal both calls up feelings and helps you get perspective on them. Feelings that may be bothering you can become springboards to better self-understanding and to positive changes in your life. But merely writing down your daily doings may not be the most productive way to keep a diary.

Psychologist Ira Progoff, Ph.D., who has written a how-to book called *At a Journal Workshop,* is optimistic that the right kind of diary offers the average person the chance to get "unstuck" when caught in a seeming trap of negative feelings.

One important function of Dr. Progoff's Intensive Journal Method is to provide perspective on where you are in your life *now* by looking at your life as a whole. One innovation is to have the diarist write dialogue, creating the responses of important people or things in his or her life. The intention of this type of journal is to help you see "what your life is trying to become."

Dr. Progoff's journal has 20 sections. Some of the most important are:

**Period Log.** Write "it has been a period in which . . . ," and then finish with your thoughts and feelings about your recent past.

**Twilight Imagery Log.** Close your eyes and let images of the period you have just described flow through your mind. Collect these symbols and impressions. When you feel ready, write them down.

**Stepping Stones.** Write down about a dozen important events in your life having to do with your family, job or physical happenings. The list will give you a picture of your life as a whole.

**Daily Log.** Record the movement of your moods, concerns and feelings over the previous 24-hour period. This is your continuing account of your life as it happens.

**Dream Log.** Yes, it's for your nighttime dreams. Don't worry about analyzing them. They may mean more to you after time has passed.

**Dialogue with Persons.** Choose a person who is or was important to you and write, "As I consider your life, I feel . . . ." When finished, write the person's imagined response and continue the dialogue. This will help clarify the relationship.

**Dialogue with Works.** Choose an activity that matters to you and describe your thoughts and feelings about it. Describe a stepping stone in the life of the work. Talk to it and record its answers.

**Dialogue with the Body.** Record important physical events, sensual experiences, athletic happenings, illnesses, food experiences. Let the list provoke images, and let your body react, too.

**Inner Wisdom Dialogue.** Have a written imaginary conversation with someone you respect about something that concerns you.

**Now: The Open Moment.** Briefly make a statement, prayer or plan for the next moment of your life. This will help you see where you want to go next and where you are right now.

# Seven Ways to Get Happy

Take a look at this list of life's simple pleasures and make sure you're giving yourself enough of the good things. We all need them for physical and mental wholeness.

**Sleep.** Life will lack sparkle if you cheat yourself of this precious gift. If you're tossing, turning and staring at the ceiling, here's what to do: Go to sleep and wake up at the same times each day. Your body functions best on a regular schedule. Avoid strenuous physical exercise before bedtime—it keys you up too much to sleep. Develop a relaxing ritual before retiring—a glass of warm milk, a soothing bath and a good novel do wonders for most people. And be careful to avoid drinks that contain caffeine in the evening hours.

**Nutrition.** Diet can be the make-or-break factor in how we look and feel. For more pep and glow, eat more raw fruits and vegetables, whole grains, lean meats like fish and chicken (but less protein overall) and cut back on fats, sugar, white flour and table salt.

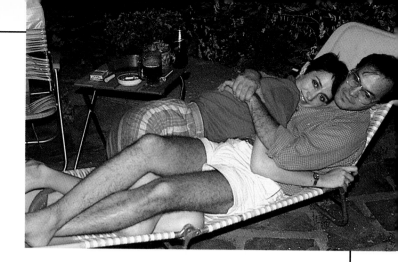

**Play and Relaxation.** These are not maybes, these are musts. It doesn't matter how you play—sewing, singing or parachute-jumping—it matters that you have joyful fun. Doctors and psychologists say play breaks should be at least 30 minutes long and come twice a week or more.

**Affection.** Preoccupation with yourself is the number one warning sign of too little affection. Want to get more? First, learn to recognize and enjoy the signs of caring you're already getting. They *are* there if you look. Second, pay attention to other people. Listen to them and be aware of them. They'll respond affectionately to you.

**Stimuli.** We occasionally need to climb up and peek out of our ruts. Try looking at the world with freshly opened eyes. But if you find yourself desperately short of time and confused by too many choices, it may be that *over*stimulation is your problem.

**Exercise.** To be in great shape both physically and mentally, exercise! At least 30 minutes of aerobics 3 or more times a week for your heart and lungs, stretches for flexibility and some strengthening exercises not only will benefit your body but, studies have shown, will also improve your mood and self-image.

**Satisfaction.** This is a feeling of well-being and a sense that life is worth living. The exact definition of satisfaction, however, has to come from you.

going to encounter some patients who are all fired up about their recovery; their attitude is, "I can't wait to get out of here and get on with my life." Some others have an attitude of hopelessness; they see themselves never really getting well, maybe never even leaving the hospital alive. Which group of patients do you think has the better chance of being restored to health? "The optimists," you'll immediately say, and, of course, you're right. Thomas Hackett, M.D., chief of psychiatry at Massachusetts General Hospital in Boston, studied more than 100 heart attack patients of both sexes. The patients could be divided into two groups in terms of how they felt about their condition—optimists and pessimists. The optimists had a somewhat higher survival rate.

A grim old joke goes, "operation successful, patient died." Unfortunately, that seems to be just what does happen when surgical patients "give up." In a talk to the Society of Surgical Oncology, Theodore Miller, M.D., surgeon emeritus at Memorial Hospital in New York City, told colleagues that when patients think they're going to die, they almost always do—even if the operation itself was technically successful. He urged them not to operate on patients who are convinced they won't survive. The optimists are the survivors.

## THE FABULOUS FAKE

Mostly, placebos are used in new drug tests. One group of patients is given the new drug. Another group with identical symptoms is given the fake pill. If the patients who have taken the new drug get noticeably better in contrast to the placebo group, the pharmaceutical manufacturer considers the drug effective.

Over the years, though, researchers have discovered a funny thing about these worthless placebos. Some people are helped by them; some are *cured* by them. Back in the days of primitive 19th-century medicine, when patients were given "cures" like purging, poisoning, bleeding, leeching and the like, many patients died. But many also became better, much better, even though we now know that none of those treatments had any intrinsic merit and most were, in fact, dangerous. How come they helped? The placebo effect: If the patient *thinks* it's going to work, there's a good chance that it will!

In one celebrated study by Henry K. Beecher, M.D., of Harvard Medical School, patients suffering a great deal of postoperative pain were made subjects of a placebo experiment. One group was given alternating doses of the potent painkiller morphine and a placebo. The other group was started the other way around—first given the placebo, then the morphine. What happened? The first dose of morphine brought pain relief to 52 percent of the patients. The first dose of the placebo—which had no chemical painkilling properties whatever—relieved pain in 40 percent of the patients! In other words, when pain was strongest, the placebo's effectiveness was 77 percent that of morphine—remarkable effectiveness for a "worthless" product. Dr. Beecher also reviewed the existing medical literature on placebos and found that they work roughly one-third of the time—giving satisfactory relief of such symptoms as severe postoperative pain, the pain of angina, headache, cough, anxiety, mood change, seasickness and the common cold.

Some physicians disparage the placebo effect. Others, recognizing the importance of their own role in it, use it deliberately to enhance the effectiveness of all drugs and treatments. It's their way of helping us to mobilize our own internal healing process. As Dr. Dacher puts it, "When I prescribe a pill, I'll tell the patient, 'I'm giving you something that will make you feel better.' So I'm already setting up an expectation, putting my professional magic or power into that pill. But it's really the patient who does the work. I'm convinced we have the power to heal ourselves and placebos demonstrate that. All they do is activate that power."

# The Body's Power over the Mind

## What you eat, where you live, whether you exercise—all affect your mind and mood.

Anger, anxiety, optimism, joy—our moods, emotions, thoughts and expectations all affect our physical health. The mind has a profound influence on the body because it is *part* of the body. We are not made of two separate but equal parts. Rather our beings are a whole, containing both.

Doesn't it make sense then, that if the mind can affect the body, the body also can affect the mind? If this principle seems unlikely, just consider the behavior of infants. Think about how they act when they miss a nap. Or, heaven forbid, a meal. Fatigue makes them cranky and hunger makes them frantic.

Well, what was true for us as infants is still true for us today—the state of the body influences the state of the mind. But because we are adults in a complex world, the cause-and-effect relationship is not as clear-cut as when we were babies.

Surely, when a good friend snaps out with a nasty remark, or when a co-worker behaves irrationally, the first thought that crosses the mind is not, "I wonder what's physically wrong with him." And when we can't shake a case of the blues—maybe for weeks on end—we rarely look to physical causes. But maybe we should.

Scientists know that certain nutrients affect our behavior and mood and that a deficiency can result in mental and emotional problems. That many medicines have side effects that can impact on the mind. That exercise can act as a natural stress releaser and tranquilizer. That our surroundings can influence our moods and mental acuity for better or worse. Science knows all these things and we simply have to apply this knowledge to help us feel happier.

Let's first examine what we know about food. Many people mistakenly assume that the nutrients in our foods are essential only to the maintenance of good *physical* health. The fact is, however, that a number of vitamins, minerals and other nutrients are also vital to emotional health. Deficiencies not only can play havoc with our moods and general outlook on life but also can affect other important brain functions, which, in turn, can trigger severe mental disorders.

If you were stranded on a desert island and needed to survive by your wits alone, you'd want to make sure your food cache was rich in the B

# How to Kick the Caffeine Habit

Do you suffer from headaches, nervousness, irritability, anxiety attacks or insomnia? If so, maybe it's time to cut your intake of coffee, tea, cola and various over-the-counter remedies—all of which contain caffeine, the druglike chemical that can frazzle your nerves.

It won't be easy. But with a little will power and a few basic strategies it can be done.

Begin by gradually cutting down on your coffee consumption. Eliminate a certain amount each day until you reach a level where you feel that you are in control. Then begin working your way down the caffeine chart: Move from coffee to strong tea to weaker tea. Switch from colas and other caffeinated sodas (read the labels; some light-colored sodas—such as Mountain Dew—contain high amounts of caffeine) to fruit juices and water.

Exercise judgment when taking painkillers, cold tablets and other remedies. Read package labels before purchasing so that you know exactly what you are putting into your system.

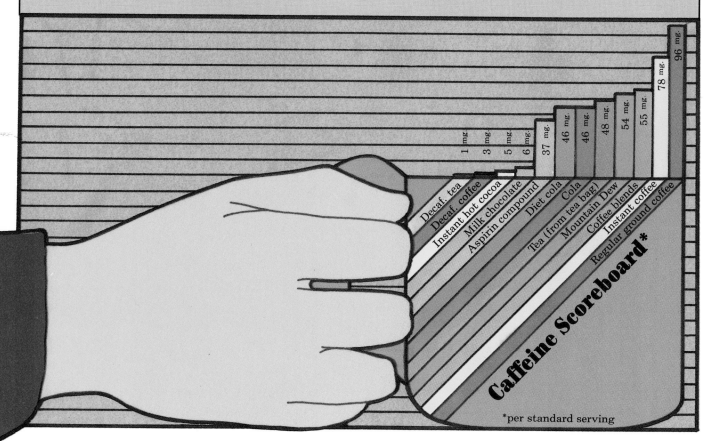

Caffeine Scoreboard*

| Item | Caffeine |
| --- | --- |
| Decaf. tea | 1 mg. |
| Decaf. coffee | 3 mg. |
| Instant hot cocoa | 5 mg. |
| Milk chocolate | 6 mg. |
| Aspirin compound | 37 mg. |
| Diet cola | 46 mg. |
| Cola | 46 mg. |
| Tea (from tea bag) | 48 mg. |
| Mountain Dew | 54 mg. |
| Coffee blends | 55 mg. |
| Instant coffee | 78 mg. |
| Regular ground coffee | 96 mg. |

*per standard serving

# The Anticrime Diet

How do you change a hardened criminal into a useful citizen? Take away his candy bars.

No, it isn't a joke. It's part of a revolutionary change in the diet of our jail and prison populations that's taking place in at least 42 states.

It's the result of a groundbreaking—and ground-shaking—study of what happened when the diet of 276 teenage boys jailed in a Virginia detention center was altered to exclude the huge amounts of white sugar they had been consuming.

After fruit juices replaced colas and carrots replaced cookies, antisocial behavior began to plummet, finally dropping a full 48 percent. Thefts fell 77 percent, and there was an 82 percent drop in assaults. Because the staff members who provided the information did not even know there was a study under way, there's no chance that a desire to see the project work influenced the results.

Can it be that there's a biochemical basis for crime? Mounting evidence suggests a strong link. A study of 318 Ohio convicts found 252 of them suffering from vitamin deficiencies and other signs of poor diet. Those who remained on a new, healthy diet after leaving jail had few problems with the law.

And in Pierce County, Washington, adult offenders fed nutritionally wholesome food as part of an experimental program returned to a life of crime only a third as often as their fellows who'd continued on the standard jailhouse fare.

## How Sugar Was Cut from the Prison Diet

1. All canned fruit packed in syrup was rinsed in water before being served.
2. Fruit juices replaced soft drink mixes and lemonade.
3. Sugar was taken off the table and replaced with honey.
4. Molasses was substituted for sugar in recipes.

5. Candy bars, cakes, pies, cobblers, pudding, etc., yielded to fresh fruit and snacks such as peanuts, cheese, popcorn, and peanut butter and celery.
6. Breakfast cereals with high sugar content were eliminated.
7. Iced tea was served unsweetened.

complex vitamins. The B's will keep your brain functioning at a high level. Let's consider them individually.

**Thiamine (Vitamin $B_1$).** Studies have shown that even a mild deficiency of thiamine can make us irritable and depressed, affect our ability to concentrate, weaken our initiative and affect our memory and sleep.

Whether you're stranded on that island or just leading your day-to-day life, you don't want negative emotions or mental confu-

sion to hamper you. However, it's possible that some people diagnosed as "neurotic"—meaning they have a relatively mild emotional problem may actually be displaying the symptoms of thiamine deficiency. In one study, the average thiamine levels of 65 neurotic patients were compared with those of 49 patients who were not neurotic. The group labeled neurotic had thiamine levels 58 percent lower than those of the other group. Another study examined the thiamine levels of 154 psychiatric patients, including some with severe mental disorders such as schizophrenia. British researchers found that thiamine deficiencies were greater among those who were most seriously disturbed.

**Vitamin B$_6$ (Pyridoxine).** This nutrient plays an important role in brain and central nervous system metabolism. A deficiency can leave us feeling depressed, irritable or otherwise emotionally drained. In a study of seven patients psychiatrically diagnosed as depressed (meaning their depressions were serious emotional disorders, rather than "the blues"), researchers at Virginia Polytechnic Institute and State University found the plasma B$_6$ levels of these patients to be

significantly lower than those of healthy volunteers also tested for B$_6$ deficiency.

**Folate (Folic Acid).** This B vitamin was given a name, not a number. If the intent was to highlight its importance, the decision was a good one. To have healthy red blood cells speeding through your veins, you need folate—and to go through the day feeling happy and cheerful you need folate, too. On the other hand, a deficiency of folate may put a damper on your ability to feel good.

Studies at McGill University in Montreal have shown similar results—people who are very depressed have significantly lower levels of folate in their blood.

None of the researchers is saying *all* depression is caused by a deficiency of folate. But they are suggesting that a particular kind of depression has been found to correlate with low folate levels. And depression—as the McGill researchers describe it—doesn't just mean feeling down in the dumps. It means losing interest in work and other activities. It means feeling full of anxiety. And it means worrying about your health to the point of becoming a hypochondriac.

According to nutritionists who have studied the problem, people most at risk of folate deficiency include pregnant and nursing women; women taking the Pill; people taking certain antibacterial, anti-convulsive or diuretic drugs; adolescents; elderly in low-income groups; and alcoholics. You can add to this list the people who, because of an inadequate diet, don't get enough of it.

**Vitamin B$_{12}$.** Sometimes called the energy vitamin, B$_{12}$ is vital to good mental functioning. Here is one grim but telling case, reported in the journal *Diseases of the Nervous System,* of a man who had a history of mental illness. His problems began after surgery that removed much of his stomach and culminated with an unsuccessful suicide attempt. Doctors suspected he suffered some kind of brain damage. Drugs and shock therapy, however,

---

# The Pill, the Blues, the Cure

Depression may be a serious problem for women taking oral contraceptives. Yet this severe depression can be relieved in an astonishing number of cases by the simple act of taking a B vitamin.

B$_6$—called "the woman's friend"—lifted depression in 76 percent of women on the Pill, one study showed. These women were given 50 milligrams each day, and most of them noticed an upswing in their moods in just one day. Another study showed elevated moods in 56 percent of women given B$_6$ for their Pill-induced blues, but their dose was only 30 milligrams daily.

Also bear in mind that doctors are convinced that the oral contraceptives caused the depletion of B$_6$ to start with—and it is that depletion which is largely responsible for Pill-induced depression. All Pill users and potential users should also note that the artificial hormones in the drug can rob them of riboflavin (vitamin B$_2$), folate, vitamin B$_{12}$, thiamine, zinc and vitamins C and E.

But the good news for the rest of us is that these and other studies indicate that B vitamins may help banish the blues if in fact there is a body deficiency of the vitamin. Moreover, the severity of many of the symptoms linked to monthly hormonal changes may be lessened. But don't take more than 25 to 50 milligrams daily.

did no good. Finally the man's suffering ended when a correct diagnosis—of severe $B_{12}$ deficiency due to malabsorption of the vitamin because of the stomach operation—was made. Hefty shots of $B_{12}$ restored him to health.

**Important Minerals.** Let's move from vitamins to minerals, beginning with one of the most important, iron. While iron deficiency hasn't been directly implicated in mood disorders, studies do suggest that our emotional states are adversely affected. Not getting enough of this mineral leaves us at risk for impaired memory, a worrisome consequence. A deficiency brings on anemia and fatigue, which in turn can open the door to a host of symptoms.

While most of us do not suffer from anemia, the amazing fact is that iron deficiency may be far more widespread in our country than most people think. A deficiency can be found in all age groups, from infants to the aged (women and older persons are among the most vulnerable), and among all economic groups. How come? Poor diet; poor bodily absorption of the iron we do ingest; "iron-fortified" foods that contain a form of iron the body cannot absorb; drinking coffee and tea, which drastically reduce the amount of iron the body can utilize—all are factors.

Beef liver is the best source of iron; 3 ounces provide 7.5 milligrams. Three ounces of roast beef or ground beef offer about 3 milligrams; a tablespoon of blackstrap molasses provides about the same. A half cup of soybeans, lima beans or prunes offers between 2 and 3 milligrams. A tip: When eating iron-rich food, get some vitamin C into your body at the same time. It helps your body absorb more of the iron you eat.

If you're chronically fatigued, also be sure you're getting enough magnesium and potassium in your diet. Magnesium sparks a host of important chemical reactions in the body; soy flour, soybeans, black-eyed peas, wheat germ and almonds are all very good sources. Potassium helps muscles withstand fatigue. Dairy products, meats, fish, poultry,

# Don't Drain Your Brain

Although it's not visible like a bruise, and though even those suffering from it sometimes have difficulty believing in it, brain fatigue does exist, doctors say. There's even a nickname for it—brain fag.

In fact, it's a common condition that most of us experience in a mild form daily. But when we change what we're doing—putting down a book to go for a walk or have dinner—the switch allows the mind to rest. In addition, we get enough sleep. The next day, we're ready to go to work again.

But for some people—most often workaholics who compulsively fill their time with labor—brain fatigue can be too serious to be cured simply with a change of pace and a good night's sleep. In fact, one of the unfortunate symptoms may be difficulty in falling asleep and staying asleep.

You can suspect brain fatigue if you know you've been driving yourself hard, if you find it hard to concentrate and if you have trouble putting your thoughts together. Minor problems irritate you out of proportion to their consequence. You're jumpy and nervous. Your brain, which scientists say operates through a process of excitation and inhibition, has gotten these functions confused, and your reactions are unreliable.

The cure is simple—but not easy for the workaholic. It's this: good food, good sleep and exercise. Plus, the gift to yourself of some truly free time, unconnected with any obligation. Loosen up and try to think of something to do that's *not* constructive, *not* structured, *not* purposeful. In other words, relax!

vegetables (especially potatoes) and many fruits (avocados and raisins, in particular) are all excellent potassium sources. Both minerals are also available as supplements.

## NUTRIENTS AS HEAVY HITTERS

As all this suggests, our bodies have an exceedingly complicated relationship with the nutrients we ingest. A missing element here inhibits the production of a chemical there, which prevents a connection from being made farther down the physiological line, which in turn triggers the emotional reactions that puzzle, exasperate and torment us.

Recognizing the powerful role of nutrients in brain chemistry, psychiatrists belonging to a subspecialty of psychiatry—generally known as orthomolecular psychiatry— try to restore body and mind to a balanced state via the use of specific vitamins, minerals and amino acids like tryptophan, the one that's useful in helping us sleep.

Tryptophan has a calming, relaxing effect in general. At McGill University, in fact, A. Missagh Ghadirian, M.D., is treating a group of manic-depressive patients with a combination of lithium (an antidepressant agent that can produce serious toxic side effects, including kidney damage) and tryptophan. The hope is that the amino acid will potentiate (greatly heighten) the effects of lithium, so that less of the drug need be used.

Another nutrient being tested for its therapeutic effect on the mind is choline, a vitaminlike substance found in soybean lecithin, beef liver, eggs and fish. There's lots of excitement in the scientific community about using choline to improve memory.

Doctors became interested in testing choline because it is a forerunner of acetylcholine, a brain compound essential for the smooth flow of nerve impulses. Studies have shown that extra choline in the diet increases levels of acetylcholine in the brain, and may therefore aid memory. It also is being used experimentally in the treatment of Alzheimer's disease, a degenerative brain disease that causes severe memory loss. It's known that people with Alzheimer's disease have a deficiency of the enzyme that produces acetylcholine. Fortunately, the body can synthesize acetylcholine from lecithin, which contains choline.

Niacin therapy is being used in the treatment of schizophrenia and other severe mental disorders. Moke Williams, M.D., medical director of the Coral Ridge Bio-Psychiatric Hospital and Institute in Fort Lauderdale, Florida, treats schizo-phrenic patients with a combination of psychotherapy and a strong nutritional approach involving the use of vitamin therapy. How are these patients faring? "They're able to be self-sufficient, to earn a living and to exericise good judgment," Dr. Williams says.

Schizophrenia, manic-depression—such torturous mental disorders and their treatment are not, fortunately, of very personal concern to most of us. But the fact that nutrient deficiency may well be a causative factor and nutrient therapy a promising treatment in these and other mental disorders is of far more than academic interest. To a greater or lesser degree, nutrition affects everybody's mental and emotional states.

## THE DRUG TRAP

When a physician writes out a prescription, most of us never ask the doctor what the side effects may be. We don't read the package insert if there is one, although usually there's not. We don't ask the pharmacist to give us some information on this particular product. We passively accept what we've been given.

All of this is too bad, because every pharmaceutical ever made has some possible side effects, some possible adverse effects, some cautions. Many of these unwanted effects are physical—stomach upset, blurred vision, dizziness and the like—but quite a few of the medicines we swallow so easily also affect our moods. And some pills we deliberately take to improve our moods can do far more harm than good.

Over 100 million prescriptions for mood-changing drugs are written every year. We can be more specific. Valium—and Librium and Dalmane, a popular sleeping pill—belong to a class of drugs known as the benzodiazepines. Though unfavorable publicity has lessened their popularity, 57.6 million prescriptions for the benzodiazepines were written in 1983, the last year for which the U. S. Food and Drug Administration (FDA) has figures.

# Food Sources of Choline from Lecithin

| Food (100 g.; 3½ oz.) | Lecithin (mg.) | Food (100 g.; 3½ oz.) | Lecithin (mg.) |
|---|---|---|---|
| Wheat germ | 2,820 | Red snapper | 560 |
| Soybeans | 1,480 | Beef (round) | 453 |
| Peanuts | 1,113 | Egg | 394 |
| Peanut butter | 966 | Pecans | 333 |
| Wheat bran | 953 | Cornmeal | 280 |
| Veal roast (leg) | 880 | Butter | 150 |
| Calves' liver | 850 | Cheese | 50-100 |
| Ham | 800 | Spinach | 6-14 |
| Lamb chop | 753 | Milk | 6-10 |
| Oatmeal | 650 | Carrots | 5-8 |
| Veal chop | 646 | Celery | 5-8 |
| Wheat | 613 | Leeks | 3 |
| Polished rice | 586 | Brussels sprouts | 2 |
| Trout | 580 | Cauliflower | 2 |
| Lamb (leg) | 560 | Potato (white) | 1 |

Such widespread use is a telling comment about our society's mental health. We are stressed. And, when stressed, we seek instant, chemical relief. Observes U.S. Navy captain Joseph A. Prusch, M.D., who helped former First Lady Betty Ford overcome her pill/alcohol addiction, this approach dooms us to disappointment and diminishes our humanness.

All drugs are chemicals; all chemicals have their reactions, some wanted, some not. Moreover, almost all drugs have side effects we can well do without—both emotionally and physically. The benzodiazepines are a case in point. The FDA considers them safe when properly prescribed, used and monitored. In fact, they're often improperly prescribed, improperly used and improperly monitored. According to Nelson Hendler, M.D., an assistant professor of psychiatry at Johns Hopkins Hospital, they're appropriate as a muscle relaxant and for relief of tension. But they're often *in*appropriately prescribed for premenstrual tension, as a sleeping aid (they interfere with natural sleep), for depression, for the anxiety that's often associated with depression (they block the action of brain chemicals that relieve depression), for panic attacks and for everyday stress.

Worst of all, the benzodiazepines suck us in: The more we take, the more we want. Psychological dependence comes easily and there's also a serious risk of physical dependence. These drugs are similar to alcohol, Dr. Hendler points out, in that over time a larger and larger quantity may be needed to produce the same result because the body builds up a tolerance to them. Long-term users find stopping very rough; without realizing it, they've become addicted. Withdrawal symptoms—particularly for people who try to stop cold turkey—can be as agonizing as withdrawal from heroin addiction.

Given the benzodiazepines' problems, Dr. Hendler advises cautious and short-term use only—two to four weeks *at most*.

## SIDE EFFECTS, ADVERSE REACTIONS

Beware, too, of painkillers. Quite a few—for example, Darvon, Demerol and Percodan—are narcotics and thus are highly addictive. These narcotics are especially insidious because they produce what users describe as an "everything's-okay-with-the-world" kind of feeling. Very seductive.

Of course, we don't all react to the same drugs in the same way. Drugs impact on some people more

Choline—which researchers have used to improve memory in people with senility—is a component of lecithin (like hydrogen is a component of water). Lecithin is abundant in so many common foods that even persons who must observe dietary restrictions can get a good supply.

# How Herbs Affect Your Mood

What do hops, catnip, lady's slippers and marijuana have in common? If you answered that they're all herbs, give yourself an A. And if you added that they all have the ability to affect the mind and emotions, give yourself an A+.

Herbs were the very basis of medieval medicine, and even today they are used by

An infusion of the flowers is reported to chase away nightmares; today it is also used to soothe the nerves.

The root of this costly herb, which was discovered in China 5,000 years ago, was believed to have aphrodisiacal powers.

The dried roots of this plant have been taken to reduce excitability. They also have been used as a sedative.

It is said that one could cure himself of epilepsy just by sitting under this tree. The tea is also considered useful for hysteria.

strongly than on others. Often the people involved have had no warning that the medication prescribed for them can have these effects. They may think there's something terribly wrong with *them*, when in fact it's the pharmaceutical product that's creating behavior changes. Some women who take oral contraceptives, for example, become quite depressed; some others become very nervous. A number of drugs being prescribed for the reduction of high blood pressure can play havoc with the emotions, causing feelings of depression, nervousness and restlessness, and producing nightmares. (See the table "Mental-Health Side Effects of Drugs," on pages 50-52.)

Always ask your physician if a prescription is absolutely necessary. Find out from the doctor or pharmacist what the possible emotional and physical side effects are.

Never mix drugs with alcohol; doing so can easily create a synergistic effect, in which the power of the drug increases tremendously.

People who have become dependent on pills (or a combination of pills and alcohol) usually need outside help to break the addiction. Some useful contacts in this respect: physicians, clergymen, colleges and universities (especially those with student health departments), community mental-health centers, family service agencies and substance many who've had family remedies passed along to them. Some of these folk remedies are absolutely charming—but may or may not really work. Nevertheless, they've been used safely for years—centuries, in fact. So if you feel so inclined, try Granny's herbal potion for jumpy nerves. It might work!

This herb is famous for its use in brewing beer. However, it's been said that if you fill a pillow with it, you'll slip serenely into dreamland.

It is said that the dried leaves of this herb are a great source of emotional courage and a cure for the blues.

Although this herb is best known for turning the fiercest cat into a silly kitty, it also can affect people. Catnip tea is said to calm the nervous and restless.

A syrup made from an infusion of this plant was used as a sedative; today this syrup is recognized as an expectorant and is helpful in treating a cough.

abuse agencies in state departments of health or mental health.

## THE NO-DRUG DRUGS

Are alcohol, nicotine and caffeine drugs? Many people would deny it. We don't need a prescription to buy them, and they're supposed to be available for our pleasure.

Let's start with alcohol. Social drinking isn't too social if one winds up with impaired brain function and other serious mental and emotional problems. If the government required every bottle of beer, wine and liquor to have "truth-in-drinking" label information, that label would read: "In quantity depletes the body of nutrients and causes malabsorption of nutrients; damages nerves in the brain cells; impairs memory; triggers violent reactions and other unpredictable mood changes; disturbs normal sleeping patterns; creates or increases accident-proneness; is addictive."

As a mood changer, alcohol is insidious. Most people drink to relax and be sociable, but what form that sociability takes depends on who's doing the drinking. As almost any party-goer can verify, a drink or two may make the phlegmatic person more lively, the normally livelier person may become the life of the party, the life-of-the-party type may become a nuisance.

Another "social" phenomenon is smoking. We all know the physical impact of cigarette smoking—lung cancer, emphysema, heart disease and much, much more. Even smokers know of these dangers, yet they continue to light up. Certainly cigarette smoking could properly be called nicotine addiction.

Its effect on a smoker's emotions becomes clearly apparent when he or she runs out of cigarettes. Too many of us have seen (or experienced) a "nicotine fit." And no wonder. Most of the nicotine sucked into the lungs goes straight to the brain, binding to specific sites.

What's the effect on the smoker? According to Ellen R. Gritz, Ph.D., research psychologist at the Jonsson Comprehensive Cancer Center at UCLA, agitated people calm down and tired people perk up. But another, less obvious effect is memory loss.

In one experiment, researchers from the University of California at Los Angeles divided 23 habitual smokers into two groups. One group was asked to smoke a non-nicotine cigarette and the other a cigarette containing nicotine. Both groups were then tested by recalling a series of 75-item lists containing names, professions, animals, vegetables and minerals. After three trials, the non-nicotine group recalled an average of 24 percent more of the words than the nicotine group.

## PERKING UP A CASE OF NERVES

As you're reading this, you might be relaxing in your easy chair, a cup of coffee close at hand. What you really have at hand is a fairly strong drug—the stimulant caffeine. It's present not only in coffee and tea but also in cola, cocoa and certain common medications such as Anacin. In pure form caffeine is a bitter-tasting white crystal called trimethylxanthine—and, pure or not, it has a definite effect on the central nervous system, just as amphetamines and cocaine do. It sharpens our thinking processes, dispels fatigue, heightens the senses and gives us a lift. But for all its seeming desirable effects, this mind-bender is a real mental-health hazard.

You've heard of "coffee nerves"? Some people get them after just one cup of coffee (about 50 to 100 milligrams of caffeine); with others it may take seven or eight cups or more, but the symptoms of caffeine overload are the same: shaky hands, trembling muscles, a jittery feeling, nervousness, restlessness, headache. People who regularly take into their bodies 500 milligrams of caffeine a day—nearly five cups of regular ground coffee, for example—are subject to a syndrome known clinically as "caffeinism." It looks and feels very much like anxiety neurosis; the people who have it suffer from nervousness, irritability, agitation, headache, twitching muscles and rapid heartbeat.

In a case reported in the *American Journal of Psychiatry,* an Army nurse suffering from some of

## Moderate Your Sugar to Moderate Your Moods

Feeling down in the dumps? Before you head for the doctor, head for the kitchen. Maybe that cabinet full of cookies, candy and cola is what's fueling your bad mood.

Lester I. Tavel, M.D., D.O., Dr. P.H. (doctor of public health) believes that large amounts of sugar in the diet can be an emotional downer.

"Too much sugar causes an increase in the insulin in the body, and the result is low sugar," he says, adding that this may lead to such symptoms as depression, nervousness and weakness.

He suggests that a modified diet can stop these symptoms. "I recommend that the patient moderate his sugar intake, perhaps drastically, depending on the patient."

Dr. Tavel adds that further dietary changes also may help to improve mood. He recommends increasing the amount of complex carbohydrates you eat, as well as increasing protein consumption.

While changes like these may seem drastic, the benefits far outweigh the adjustment required—benefits that include not only greater emotional stability but also possible weight loss.

## Shake Those Monthly Blues Away

It is possible to prevent some uncomfortable premenstrual symptoms from occurring each month. In fact, it's not even difficult. By limiting the amount of sodium in your diet the week before the menstrual cycle begins, you can ward off the discomfort of bloating and swelling.

Both the sodium and water levels in your body are regulated by the kidneys. Moreover, the sodium level influences the water level, so that if the sodium level is high, the water level will be high, too. And if sodium is reduced, then water also will be reduced.

During the 2 weeks before menstruation, the progesterone in a woman's body may be relatively low, causing retention of sodium and water, thus leading to discomfort.

To help maintain a normal level of sodium in the body, it is necessary to reduce the intake of foods cooked or processed with salt. There are several easy ways to accomplish this. First, steer clear of salted snacks such as potato chips and pretzels; load up on

fresh fruit instead. Second, don't use salt when cooking. Third, avoid processed foods whenever possible; make use of fresh, natural foods instead.

these and other symptoms was referred to a psychiatric clinic with the diagnosis of "anxiety reaction." The doctors figured it resulted from the fear that her husband would be transferred to Vietnam. But the nurse herself finally got to the bottom of the problem—she'd been drinking 10 to 12 cups of coffee a day, and when she tapered off the symptoms disappeared. Many other cases of a similar nature have been reported in psychiatric journals.

Is caffeine addictive? We all know someone who can't face the day without having a mug of it first, who has to have a "fix" with periodic coffee breaks throughout the day.

Those people are hardly take-it-or-leave-it coffee drinkers. Whether heavy coffee drinking is clinically addictive is a matter of some debate, but we don't have to get technical.

Can't get along without it? You're caffeine dependent. And there's little dispute that stopping cold turkey leads to withdrawal symptoms. it definitely does. Headache is the biggie—in fact, your brain feels too big for your head and goes on to a throbbing headache that could last a day or so. Other common symptoms are irritability, nervousness, anxiety and lethargy.

### JUMPING FOR JOY

Ask Jayne Mangino, a 34-year-old publicist, what *emotional* benefits exercise gives her, and she waxes rhapsodic. A strong swimmer, Jayne says, "When I swim regularly I'm happier. My body looks and feels better, which heightens my already good feelings. I have a lot more

*(continued on page 52)*

# The Mental-Health Side Effects of Drugs

**"T**he cure is worse than the disease." That cliché unfortunately rings all too true for some of us who, seeking relief, find further suffering in the medicine we hope will relieve our pain. In some cases, what is toxic to microbes, viruses, fungi and wayward cells is also somewhat toxic to us and can negatively alter our emotional state. With some drugs we have the liberty of choice—to ask ourselves, "Is it worth it to me to trade a stuffed nose for a woozy head?" Other times, seriously afflicted and convinced it is our best choice, we are well advised, as the doctor suggests, to take our medicine. A positive attitude—that the drug is helping us—can help control side effects, experts say.

| Drug Category | Use | Possible Side Effects |
|---|---|---|
| **Analgesics** | relief of pain | confusion, euphoria, sedation, restlessness, disorientation, hallucinations, agitation |
| **Anorexics** | control of obesity due to overeating | overstimulation, euphoria, restlessness, anxiety, change in libido, psychotic episodes at high doses |
| **Antianginals** | relief of angina pectoris | restlessness, confusion, depression |
| **Antiarrhythmials** | control of arrhythmias such as tachycardia, fibrillation or premature contractions | depression, confusion, excitability, insomnia, delirium, hallucinations |
| **Antiarthritics and antigout medications** | relief of pain due to arthritis, bursitis or gout | confusion, nervousness, anxiety, agitation, depression, psychotic episodes |
| **Anticonvulsants** | prevention and treatment of seizures | confusion, nervousness, depression, irritability, emotional disturbance |
| **Antidepressants** | treatment of depression and anxiety | anxiety, disorientation, confusion, insomnia, nightmares, changes in libido, delusions, euphoria, poor concentration, hallucinations |
| **Antidiarrheals** | relief of diarrhea | normally none, though a few drugs may cause depression or euphoria |
| **Antihistamines** | relief of cold or allergy symptoms | nervousness, confusion, hysteria, euphoria, insomnia, irritability or excitability, especially in children |
| **Anti-hypertensives** | treatment of hypertension | nervousness, restlessness, insomnia, depression, mental confusion, change in libido, impotence |
| **Anti-inflammatory agents** | relief of pain due to arthritis, dysmenorrhea or ulcerative colitis | confusion, lethargy, agitation, insomnia, nervousness, depression, hallucinations |
| **Antimigraines** | relief of migraine and cluster headaches | insomnia, disorientation, euphoria, depression |

| Drug Category | Use | Possible Side Effects |
|---|---|---|
| **Antinauseants** | relief of nausea and vomiting due to motion sickness, vertigo, anxiety or anesthesia during surgery | insomnia, nervousness, restlessness, disorientation, nightmares, psychotic symptoms, catatonic state, changes in libido |
| **Antineoplastics** | treatment of cancer | lethargy, disorientation, depression, premenstrual-like symptoms, changes in libido |
| **Antipruritics (Most antipruritics are creams; these effects are for ingestable products only.)** | relief of itching due to allergy | nervousness, excitability, hysteria, euphoria, weariness, insomnia, catatonic-like states |
| **Antispasmodics (gastrointestinal)** | relief of spasms associated with ulcer or irritable bowel syndrome | nervousness, insomnia, impotence, confusion and excitability, especially in the elderly |
| **Antispasmodics (urinary)** | relief of urinary tract spasms | nervousness, insomnia |
| **Bronchodilators (includes antihistamines)** | relief of bronchospasms due to bronchial asthma, bronchitis or emphysema | nervousness, insomnia, irritability, restlessness |
| **Cholesterol reducers** | treatment of elevated cholesterol and triglycerides | nervousness, anxiety, insomnia, changes in libido |
| **Cold and cough medications** | treatment of colds, coughs, hay fever, sinusitis or upper respiratory infection | excitability or irritability, especially in children, weariness, giddiness, confusion, restlessness, insomnia, nervousness, hallucinations, euphoria, anxiety, changes in libido |
| **Cortisonelike drugs (steroids)** | treatment of hormonal disorders, arthritic diseases, collagen diseases, allergic states, dermatological diseases, ophthalmic diseases or ulcerative colitis | confusion, euphoria |
| **Decongestants** | relief of congestion associated with colds or allergy | nervousness, restlessness, excitability, confusion, euphoria, anxiety, insomnia, irritability, hallucinations |
| **Diuretics** | treatment of edema and hypertension | confusion, nervousness, restlessness, depression, changes in libido, impotence |
| **Fertility drugs** | treatment of infertility | depression, restlessness, nervousness |

*(continued)*

## MENTAL-HEALTH SIDE EFFECTS OF DRUGS—*Continued*

| Drug Category | Use | Possible Side Effects |
|---|---|---|
| **Hormones (androgens)** | treatment of anemia, post-partum breast pain, mammary tumors or eunuchism | changes in libido, impotence, excitability, insomnia |
| **Hormones (estrogens)** | relief of atrophic vaginitis, ovarian failure, some cancers or vasomotor symptoms associated with menopause | depression, premenstrual-like symptoms, changes in libido |
| **Muscle relaxants** | relief of painful musculo-skeletal conditions | anxiety, agitation, excitability, confusion, insomnia, depression, changes in libido |
| **Oral contraceptives** | birth control | depression, nervousness, premenstrual-like symptoms, changes in libido |
| **Sedatives** | relief of insomnia, anxiety and tension, or as an anesthetic | nervousness, agitation, confusion, anxiety, insomnia, nightmares, disorientation, depression, hallucinations, "hangover effect" |
| **Thyroid preparations** | treatment of absent or decreased thyroid function | nervousness, insomnia |
| **Tranquilizers** | treatment of anxiety, manic-depression and other psychotic disorders | depression, disorientation, confusion, anxiety, restlessness, hyperactivity, giddiness, lethargy, euphoria, nervousness, excitability, nightmares, aggravation of psychosis, changes in libido, impotence, hallucinations |
| **Vasodilators** | treatment of bronchospasms, angina pectoris and cerebral, peripheral and myocardial ischemia (deficiency of blood supply) | restlessness, nervousness |

energy, I'm a lot more alert. Exercising gives me a kind of joy."

As Jayne goes, so goes the nation. From all over the country men and women expound on the good feelings that good workouts bring them.

"Exercise is emotional aerobics," says Bob Conroy, M.D., a psychiatrist at the Menninger Clinic in Topeka, Kansas, who organized a cardiovascular fitness program there. "We've found that running can literally cure some moderate depression," notes John H. Greist, M.D., an associate professor of psychiatry at the University of Wisconsin. He adds, "We believe that many physical activities such as swimming, cycling, rowing, fast walking and dancing, which involve the rhythmic movement of the large muscle masses, will produce similar mood effects."

Unfortunately, when most people feel depressed, they're more inclined to mope than move. Knowing that they can shake their bleak mood, however, may serve as a motivation. Remember that exercise changes brain chemistry, producing endorphins and other brain chemicals that dispel the blues and lift the spirits. Exactly *how* these biochemical changes work remains a matter of scientific speculation, but work they do!

If exercise can chase the blues, is it also effective for worries and jitters? Happily, the answer is yes. This good news comes from Herbert A. deVries, Ph.D., former director of the exercise physiology lab at Andrus Gerontology Center of the University of Southern California, Los Angeles. Based on a study of research papers on the subject and on his own experiments at USC, Dr. deVries concludes that appropriate exercise has a definite tranquilizing effect on people of all age groups. Most effective, he found, is rhythmic exercise like walking, jogging, cycling and bench stepping, working for 5 to 30 minutes and at 30 to 60 percent maximum intensity.

When you're frantic because you're planning a barbeque and the weatherman says "rain"—that's the time to pump the exercycle. Hard. After 15 or 20 minutes you'll feel calmer.

## STORMY FEELINGS

You're running home under darkened skies, hoping to avoid an impending storm. You turn on the light—even though it's still early afternoon— just as the first peal of thunder reverberates. You feel tremendously invigorated. Why? The light? The weather? The noise? Actually, any of these environmental factors might be responsible. Light, weather or noise can impact on our emotions in the most astonishing and little-understood ways.

You don't need a battery of expensive scientific studies to tell you how good you feel when you're outside on a bright, sunny day. Or how glum you feel after a few days of leaden skies.

Lately, however, photobiologists— researchers who study the effects of light on animals and plants—have made some exciting new discoveries. They, as well as social scientists working in related fields, are becoming more and more persuaded that light affects every aspect of our emotional, as well as physical, health.

Seasonal mood changes are an example of the way sunlight affects us. Some people feel severely depressed in winter's drab light— and slightly manic in summer's golden sun. In a case reported by Norman Rosenthal, M.D., of the Clinical Psychobiology Branch, National Institute of Mental Health, a woman who had moved to Connecticut from Florida solved the problem of her devastating winter depressions by sitting under plant "grow lights" for a few hours a day!

She may just have stumbled onto something. Dr. Rosenthal and a number of colleagues have given supervised, experimental, bright white light treatments to a number of patients with seasonal depressions—and found that in every case the patient's depressions lifted after a few days' exposure.

Sunlight, or a substitute for it—full-spectrum fluorescent light—is obviously good for our emotional well-being. Can the same be said for ordinary fluorescent lighting used in offices, shops and schools? According to light expert John Ott, author of *Light, Radiation, and You,* the answer is a resounding no. Both the light itself and the radiation that emanates from it have negative effects, he says.

## SUNNY BEHAVIOR

In one striking experiment, Dr. Ott fitted two elementary school classrooms in Sarasota, Florida, with shielded full-spectrum fluorescent tubes—those most similar to sunlight— and two with ordinary fluorescent tubes. Several hyperactive children who were to be transferred to a special school were in each of those classrooms. For 90 days the children were observed with hidden time-lapse cameras. What happened? The children in the full-spectrum classrooms quieted down to the point where they were no longer subject to transfer; the children in the other classrooms showed no improvement.

Observations in prisons show that inmates exposed to full-spectrum light—sunlight, specifically—for a few hours a day were less violent in their behavior.

Like so much environmental research, photobiology is in its infancy. Researchers talk, however, of one day using light to cure sleep disorders, depression and other mood-related disorders. There's more to light than meets the eye.

## UNDER THE WEATHER

If light can affect the mind and body, what about clouds and storms and winds and shifting barometric pressure and other weather phenomena? Well, whoever coined the phrase, "I'm feeling under the weather," caught on to one of nature's most amazing truths.

Scientists specializing in the relatively new science of bio-meteorology, which deals specifically with the effects of weather on mind and body, have been accumulating evidence showing that, in a sense, we're all under the weather all of the time. Certain people—called weather-sensitive—are the most reactive.

Here's Stella, playing Lady Butterfingers again. While making an omelet for breakfast, she drops an egg on the floor. Dressing, she snags her stockings on a fingernail. In the supermarket she knocks a half-gallon of apple juice from the shelf in an explosion of glass shards. She's clumsy, but only *sometimes*. Stella is weather-reactive.

Falling barometric pressure and related temperature changes can produce all kinds of problems when we're weather-reactive—for example, poorer coordination, failing concentration and forgetfulness. Stephen Rosen, Ph.D., a scientist and the author of a book about the effects of the atmosphere on moods and health, discovered that people who are weather-reactive have special problems. They say they tire easily; become irritable and restless; have trouble concentrating; suffer headaches, nervousness, depression; they make mistakes and are increasingly forgetful. In one of the early books about medical climatology, author Clarence A. Mills, M.D., Ph.D., reported that on low-pressure days more packages and umbrellas are left on buses.

## THE BAROMETER MADE ME DO IT

Children seem especially restless and nervous when the barometric pressure falls. A number of researchers have noticed a distinct correlation between falling pressure and student mischief. Earl A. Sargent, Ph.D., professor emeritus of meteorology at the University of Tulsa, recalls what happened when a very potent cold front with falling pressure moved into Tulsa a few years ago. He predicted that students in school would misbehave, and he couldn't have been more correct. When he called school principals around town late in the day to find out how they fared, he heard remarks like, "It's the worst day I've ever had!"

People are more prone to illness, too, Dr. Sargent points out, when barometric pressure falls. Arthritis, asthma, migraine headaches, rheumatism—all such conditions come on or get worse. Both physically and emotionally the worst time, he says, is just when a fast-moving cold front arrives, with the pressure lowering rapidly and relative humidity very high.

The high humidity Dr. Sargent mentions is itself an important mood changer. James Rotton, Ph.D., of Florida International University of North Miami, points out that there's a definite relationship between humidity and depression. Dr. Rotton, who conducts research on how the weather affects us, says studies show more depressed people are admitted to mental hospitals on humid days than when the air isn't loaded with moisture.

## A HOT TEMPER

Let's not leave out heat. "Long hot summers" have been with us forever, it seems. At the turn of the century, a famous Italian criminologist named Enrico Ferri calculated that everywhere in the world more crimes are committed in hot months than in cool ones. Heat is an important factor in bringing out our aggressive tendencies, Dr. Rotton agrees, pointing to such studies as those done in Indianapolis and the Dallas-Fort Worth area, which showed that higher rates of assault are recorded on police blotters in the summer.

Things are worst for us—as everybody knows—when temperature *and* humidity reach a certain level. That's when we reach what Dr. Rotton calls an "aversive state," when more than a few people really go to extremes emotionally. "Some researchers have suggested that if you're under stress to begin with—if you're trying to deal with a family that's falling apart, or coping with an impossible boss—this double-whammy of heat and humidity could be the straw that breaks the camel's back," Dr. Rotton says.

Of course, some people are far more sensitive to the weather than others. Helmut E. Landsberg, Ph.D., a prominent biometeorological researcher and past president of the American Institute of Medical Climatology, estimates that a third of the population is very susceptible to weather's effects, a third moderately so, a third not at all. A number of persons are so weather-sensitive, he claims, that they are affected by the electromagnetic waves emanating from a thunderstorm when it's still quite far away. They become drowsy, anxious, "hyper" or depressed.

On the other hand, Dr. Rotton says, there are people who become exhilarated and exuberant—charged up—just before a storm. It's the charged particles in the air—ions—that do it. Many laboratory studies in the United States and elsewhere in the world show that negative ions (which lightning increases) improve mental functioning and promote a sense of well-being; positive ions do just the opposite.

Because weather phenomena are so complicated, there's a lot of controversy about how weather/body interactions actually occur. There's no question, however, about the fact that they *do* occur.

As the old saying goes, "Everybody talks about the weather but nobody does anything about it." Well, here's what you can do. To see how weather-sensitive you are, use your calendar. Simply jot down daily weather conditions and how you feel both emotionally and physically. Do this for two or three months to get a sense of your pattern. If falling barometric pressure disturbs you, be especially careful when driving and crossing streets on those days. Make an effort to keep your temper in check. Try to postpone commitments and engagements. And don't stress your system by exposing it to drastic environmental changes, as from a frigid, air-conditioned room to the hot, moist outdoors.

And remember: As the storm fades, the pressure rises, it becomes clear and cool outside, aches and pains fade, the mind sharpens—you suddenly feel wonderful again!

## NOISE POLLUTION HURTS

We've become so inured to the loud sounds of daily life that we take them as much for granted as we do weather's vagaries. Yet they, too, have their subtle, insidious effect on our emotional health. And we don't have to live next door to a big-city airport to be the targets of those effects.

The Environmental Protection Agency (EPA) estimates that over 70 million of us live in neighborhoods too noisy to be comfortable for human ears and human sensibilities. And, the EPA says, over 20 million of us are daily exposed to a din loud enough to cause permanent damage to our hearing.

Sustained loud noise not only can cause deafness, it also can elevate blood pressure, speed up the heart and respiratory rates and in a variety of other ways prompt our bodies to act as if we were stressed. When we're subject to chronic noise pollution, we are subject to chronic stress. As a result, we're much more likely to become victims of emotion-linked diseases like headaches, ulcers, asthma and colitis.

The fact that sustained loud noises can affect our concentration, our ability to think and learn, is something scientists have known for many decades. As far back as the early 1900s, "quiet zones" were

## The Allergic Brain

Milk may provoke melancholy, doughnuts can cause depression and corn can create temporary mania. They can, that is, in those whose brains are allergic to them.

When allergies target the brain, the effect is much like that of pollen on the allergic nose. But in the brain, swelling can affect feelings and thoughts. Shifts in mood and behavior may be sudden and bizarre.

Some doctors estimate that brain allergies, still poorly understood by most of the medical profession, may be a significant factor in up to 15 percent of schizophrenics. Milder manifestations may be much more common. At least one doctor thinks almost 70 percent of ordinary headaches come from brain allergies.

Extreme, frequent and hard-to-understand mood swings can be symptomatic of brain allergy, particularly if other allergic reactions also are present. Surprisingly, cravings can also signal a possible food allergy, particularly if a short-lived "high" from a food is followed by headache, irritability and other withdrawal symptoms.

What are the most common brain allergens? Not exotic edibles, but the most familiar of foods—milk, wheat, eggs, sugar, corn (including corn syrup and corn oil) and citrus fruits.

If you suspect an allergy, try eliminating the substance from your diet for at least 2 weeks to see how you feel.

established around many of the nation's schools to increase educational efficiency. It's obvious that against a noisy background children will have trouble "hearing themselves think."

And while children may be the most vulnerable, adults aren't much better off. See if you can read something—even the most engrossing novel—while your kids have the stereo blasting. After a couple of futile tries you'll probably become so annoyed you'll yell at them to turn the darn thing off.

## DANGER IN DECIBELS

Annoyance, irritation, impatience, inability to concentrate, anger, frustration—all are noise-triggered reactions. A University of Wisconsin study showed that the "ordinary" household noises—quarreling, shouting, the hum of vent fans, the whine of electric mixers, the whir of garbage disposals—take an emotional as well as a physical toll. They produce heightened body arousal and nervous tension.

It's no easier at work. Studies also have shown that industrial noise increases tensions between employers and employees, and what may begin as annoyance can become a loss of control that can end in a simple temper tantrum, or outright violence. The EPA reports that a night clerical worker, "upset about noise outside his apartment, shot one of the boys causing the disturbance after he had shouted at them, to no avail, 'Stop that noise!'" In other cases fierce anger about noise has triggered threats, assaults and attempted shootings. "Antisocial behavior caused by noise may be more prevalent than is realized," the EPA report states.

Until now you probably never thought about noise in connection with your moods. But now that you know the impact noise can have, it's important to protect yourself as much as possible. Most important: Try to wear earplugs anytime you're exposed to loud noises. You may not fancy the Walkman-type headphone stereos, but if you do, Mark N. Goldstein, M.D., attending physician at the Long Island Jewish-Hillside Medical Center, urges you not to play it above level 4. Don't hesitate to see your physician if you begin to have a hearing problem— anything from an earache to ringing in the ears. You may not be able to quiet the noisy environment all around you, but you can do things to make life calmer, quieter and saner for yourself.

# Young at Heart, Young at Mind

Exercise can give you ideas—literally. It can make you more creative, improve your memory and actually raise your intelligence.

Those are the results of before-and-after studies of people who went from a sedentary lifestyle into a progressive program of aerobic exercise. In fact, intelligence and memory tests showed significant changes even among hospital-ized elderly patients who entered physical training programs.

Scientists tell us, too, that they've found that aerobic exercise optimizes the level of the quality they call arousal, which is related to wakefulness or alertness. Too little arousal means you feel bored, depressed. Too much makes for anxiety and restlessness.

And our old friend, regular vigorous, physical exercise, generates levels of arousal most compatible with acquiring new skills and information.

In addition, rhythmic aerobic exercise—running at a steady pace, for instance—also makes the mind more playful and creative. Scans of the brains of people while exercising show increased blood flow to the right, so-called female side of the brain—the part thought to be the site of much of our intuition and imagination. Postexercise tests of other subjects confirmed these findings. Exercise caused imaginativeness scores to jump markedly.

There's more. Aerobic workouts also improve reaction time, the time it takes your brain to tell your muscles to get to it, and thus your ability to react quickly, a hallmark of the young mind.

**4**

# People Need People

Human relationships are essential to emotional health. Closeness to others brings happiness.

Short of the death penalty, the worst punishment that can be inflicted upon a prisoner is solitary confinement. A deprivation of human contact—a deprivation almost as severe as lack of food or shelter from the elements. Contact with fellow human beings—with "our gang"— is a deep and lasting need, and the nature of that contact profoundly affects our emotional well-being. A number of social scientists are convinced that the need for human connectedness is actually implanted in our genes—that, as the German scientist Irenaus Eibl-Eibsesfeldt has put it, we're "programmed" to reach out to others. It is, he says, a matter of basic survival.

In the typical way of humans, however, our deepest relationships are also sometimes the most confusing and troubling. Did your parents love you? Enough? Are your children grateful? Enough? Is your marriage happy? Enough? These key relationships bring us joy—and can bring us anguish, as well. It's as though the people at the center of our lives—those whom psychologists call significant others—are sometimes so significant we don't always quite know how to make a smooth emotional fit with them. The result: At times hurt and anger are triggered when none of us really wants that to happen.

On another level, we may find great satisfaction in being praised by someone who is a relative stranger—say, the boss—and comfort in the support and team spirit of co-workers.

Relationships—intimate and casual—affect the way we feel about ourselves and others. Because they are so crucial, it is important to know how to have the "healthiest" relationships with those near and dear, and what to do when you're feeling squeezed by the conflicting needs of those you care so much about.

## HUMAN CONTACT

People are good for our health—our emotional *and* physical health. Proof of this comes right at the beginning of life. We know what happens when a child is somehow raised with the barest, most minimal of human contact. A number of years ago, for instance, there was the famous case of Anna, an illegitimate child whose mother literally hid her away because of the shame involved. Except for being fed and given minimal care, she was left completely alone; when she was discovered, she couldn't walk, couldn't talk, couldn't do anything that showed intelligence.

Social scientists don't deliberately isolate children to see how they fare, of course, but a husband-and-wife team of researchers, Harry F. and Margaret K. Harlow, did the next best (or worst) thing; at their Primate Laboratory of the University of Wisconsin they reared rhesus monkeys in total isolation for the first two years of their lives. The monkeys were in excellent physical health, adequately fed by remote control and observed through one-way mirrors. What happened? At the end of those two years they were seriously deficient psychologically, socially and sexually. They didn't play. They didn't defend themselves when attacked. They didn't try to have contact with other monkeys. Though sexually mature, they made no attempt to mate.

What such studies show is that normal adult behavior develops only through contact with others. In other words, human beings *teach* us to be human.

What happens to adults who are deprived of all human contact? We don't fare so well, either. Some political prisoners and prisoners of war kept totally isolated for long periods have written accounts of their ordeals. In large measure they wrote about their efforts to keep from going mad. A man kept in solitary for a long time by the Germans in World War II, for instance, said afterward that one day he discovered a snail in the yard; it became his "companion" and kept him sane.

In a controlled experiment at McGill University in Montreal, Canada, student volunteers took part in an isolation experiment. Within a few days many lost the ability to concentrate. They became irritable, restless and confused. They began to hallucinate. In effect, they began to become abnormal.

## PEOPLE WHO NEED PEOPLE

What makes companionship so important to our emotional health? In *Liking and Loving,* a book-length survey of interpersonal relationships, social psychologist Zick Rubin, Ph.D., cites one important factor. We need other people, Dr. Rubin says, to affirm our perceptions, our impressions, our very identities. When other people talk to us—and talk about us—we're "real" in a way we wouldn't be if we didn't have this human contact. It's no coincidence that three severe mental illnesses—autism in children, schizophrenia in children and adults and very severe emotional depression—are all characterized by an extreme withdrawal from others. You might say that people suffering from those mental illnesses are less "real" in relation to normal society.

In a sense, the people around us, the people we're closest to, are the "vitamins and minerals" of the psyche, keeping us mentally whole and healthy. Consider two British studies. The English sociologist George W. Brown studied a group of women who were undergoing serious emotional upheavals, such as the threat of separation or divorce, the illness of a loved one, loss of employment, the threat of eviction. You'd expect people in the midst of such life stresses to be more depressed than those traveling a smoother path. But Dr. Brown found just the contrary; women who had an intimate and confiding relationship with a husband or boyfriend seemed to be protected against severe depressive symptoms.

In this one study, less intimate friendships didn't seem to protect against depression, but a large-scale study of both women and men in Edinburgh, Scotland, showed that

# Have Faith in Your Health

Regular church attendance provides a sense of community, long-term friendships and a feeling of security in the rapidly changing and fast-paced world. It can even lower blood pressure!

According to Gene Stainbrook, Ph.D., M.P.H., from the Center for Health Promotion, Research and Development at the University of Texas, regular attendance at a church, synogogue or other place of worship has many physical and emotional benefits. "Regular attendance gives people social support, a sense of fellowship and common goals," says Dr. Stainbrook.

He also suggests that church gives people a moral and ethical framework which helps them handle everyday stress. And attending church provides many community service opportunities. "There are indications that helping others makes you happier and healthier," reports Dr. Stainbrook.

A study done at Bowling Green State University in Ohio supports these theories. Researchers studied what is perhaps life's most stressful situation—the "twin processes" of immigration and assimilation into a new culture. They found that new citizens who had a religious association experienced a fuller sense of community *and* had lower blood pressure than did their nonattending counterparts. And church-going newcomers were also more likely to become U.S. citizens.

The ritual itself is another important aspect of any religious service. Both passive and active types of rituals have organizing and calming effects on church-goers. "Some people want a lot of active involvement in their religious service, others want quiet and meditation— both are beneficial," says Dr. Stainbrook. "What you choose just depends on which you prefer."

having any kind of confidant did help.

What the researchers did was to question 337 patients about certain physical and emotional symptoms—tiredness, anxiety, depression, backaches, headaches, breathlessness and the like—as well as about their friendship patterns. Here's what they found: Those women who had neighborhood friends, and trusting friends with whom they could discuss personal matters, had significantly fewer symptoms than

the others. This pattern seemed to hold true for the men in the study, too.

Yet another study, this one centered upon nearly 7,000 residents of Alameda, California, gives the clearest picture of the extent to which close human ties protect us from the ravages of life's stresses. The researchers, Lisa Berkman, Ph.D., and S. Leonard Syme, Ph.D., found an amazing relationship between long life and social networks.

# Birth Order and Personality

Your position as the only, oldest, middle or youngest child in the family can factor into what kind of person you become, according to Robert L. Powers, president of the Americas Institute of Adlerian Studies, Chicago.

"Only children are independent," Powers says. "Because they grow up with no other siblings they are not trained for give and take. But they are high achievers in areas where they can solve problems on their own.

"Oldest children were only children at one time, but when they were 'dethroned' they reacted by striving toward maturity. They are achievement oriented and like to stay ahead.

"Middle children are less rule-bound than first-borns," he continues. "Because of their position they are also more sensitive to unfairness and injustice.

"Finally, youngest children are ambitious—they want to catch up to the others. They are usually creative because they have a variety of examples of problem-solving behavior available to them in their older brothers and sisters.

"However, it's not only the situation that you're born into," Powers stresses, "but also what you make of it."

Married people in this large-scale study lived longer than single people. People who had close contact with friends and relatives lived longer than those who didn't have such contacts. (Complete details of this study can be found in the box, "Siblings: Early Enemies—Future Friends.")

When we talk about social networks today, it's usually business and professional networking—to get ahead, to be more successful—that people refer to. But the most old-fashioned network of all—a circle of close, loving family and friends—is really the one that does the most for us. Go ahead and hug your spouse, play with your children, visit or call your parents, laugh with your friends, exchange some friendly words with a stranger, join a club, go to a church or synagogue—you'll be practicing the best of emotional and physical health.

## MOTHER AND FATHER

Our first human contact was, of course, with our parents. They supplied all our needs; they taught us many things about the world and how to get along in it. Our first intimate relationship was with them, and the "roles" we each played were clearly defined. But what about now? How do you define a "healthy" relationship between grown children and their parents?

"Ideally," says Edith Szold of Westchester Jewish Community Services in New York, "there's a very special, tender bond. An enjoyment of each other. A sharing, based on a long history of caring. A recognition of the fact that you're all adults—which means a respect for each other's differences and each other's privacy."

At their best, adult child/parent relationships can be like deep, loving friendships. At the same time, though, in emotional terms child-parent relationships are extremely complex. Sometimes it takes lots of time, and some careful rethinking, before that friendship can be achieved. In even the most loving of relationships, problems either occur or simply remain, left over from childhood.

That problems exist is a fact of life; their presence does not have to mar the love and pleasure inherent in the relationship. When Elizabeth S. Johnson, Ph.D., and Barbara J. Bursk, of the Boston University School of Social Work, conducted a study on how adult children and their parents get along, they found that when values were similar and there was mutual respect, both parents and children rated their relationship as high. Yet the interviews showed that even in these happy families, some problems still exist.

These problems, however, are ordinary ones, the kind most families have. For example, mothers and fathers who have trouble letting go, or who continue patterns of behavior that have always upset their children. And children who, unrealistically, keep expecting their

## Siblings: Early Enemies— Future Friends

Remember your brother who locked you in the closet or your sister who *always* tattled on you? You swore you'd be enemies for life. But as you grew older, you also grew together, becoming friends. Why?

Two researchers at the University of Cincinnati who study adult sibling relationships found that brothers and sisters often become friends for two simple reasons.

First, the causes of sibling conflicts diminish with age, explains Joel Milgram, Ph.D. "Competition and favoritism disappear as children develop their own identities and greater self-confidence," he says. "Even the dreaded idea of being someone's kid sister can be funny when you're 60."

Second, Dr. Milgram explains, "With age, one realizes that a sibling relationship lasts longer than any other. People learn that their siblings are the only validation of their personal history—a witness to something they don't want to forget."

## All You Need Is Love

Recipe for a happy, healthy baby: Feed when hungry. Change when wet. Shower with hugs and kisses.

The last instruction is important because babies who are not fondled may grow up to be very unhappy people. In fact, with severe deprivation, babies can fail to thrive. They are listless, weak, unable to walk and often lose their appetites. The mortality rate among such infants is high. They are, quite literally, starved for affection.

Fortunately, this unhappy condition is less common today than in past years. Enrichment programs and foster homes are available to give once-neglected children their daily ration of TLC.

parents to change in certain ways.

Overprotectiveness is an example. Parents, of course, are protective of their children. However, some parents carry that protectiveness too far and continue it too long, treating adult children like irresponsible kids, no matter how old and well-established those grown children are.

Intrusiveness is another example. Some parents find it hard not to be intrusive or bossy—like the mother who keeps telling her son (and her daughter-in-law) how to raise their children.

Some parents carry on a well-established pattern of favoritism, although they may sincerely deny having a favorite child. Phil, a lawyer in his late forties with a family of his own, admits it still hurts when he and his brother are together with their parents and, as always, they dote on his brother. "It's crazy. When we're all together like that I still feel like the little kid who's always left out," Phil says.

### GROWING UP

Such situations become easier to accept and to deal with when the adult children involved can review their family relationship through mature eyes. "When we were young and helpless, we saw our parents as perfect beings, all-giving and all-knowing," explains New Jersey-

based psychotherapist Muriel Reid, who has counseled many adult children. "As we grow up we learn differently, but those early feelings and expectations are hard to shake off altogether." Adult children who keep expecting their parents to behave "perfectly" keep on being disappointed.

Another important factor: When we were very young we were totally dependent on our mothers and fathers, and thus terrified of losing them. We were bonded to them as a unit. In his book, *Cutting Loose: An Adult Guide to Coming to Terms with Your Parents,* psychologist Howard M. Halpern writes eloquently of the "family's compelling pull" and its hold on us no matter how old we are. This universal phenomenon is called emotional fusion.

Both emotional fusion and the wish for the perfect parent sometimes make it hard for adult children to say no to parents, to make decisions that might displease them and to get rid of hurts (such as Phil's) that began in childhood. But there are ways of "rewriting the script," as psychologists sometimes like to put it, so as to establish a more mature and satisfying adult child/older parent relationship. Here are the experts' suggestions.

- Accept the fact that your parents are people—with weaknesses as well as strengths, faults as well as virtues. "Whatever their shortcomings," Ms. Reid says, "they've done the best they can."
- Give yourself "permission" to preserve your privacy and your independence. If your parents are intrusive or interfering, you have every right to set limits.
- Avoid clashes. Not every minor disagreement has to become an angry confrontation or power struggle. Estelle Rosen, of New York City's Jewish Board of Family and Children's Services, says, "You can listen to parents' views, consider their advice, then decide how you want to do things. At some point, though, you may have to say, 'This is how I prefer it.'"
- Avoid anger and accusations. If you're having differences with a parent, don't "lay down the law." Keep things calm and light. Ms. Rosen advises that "humor always helps."
- Let go of the hurts. Concentrating on your parents' shortcomings only rubs more salt into wounds. Ms. Reid's advice: "Forget what they didn't give you and you'll be surprised at how much they did give, and continue to give, to you."

Once grown children shed unrealistic expectations, she says, they discover the fun to be had together, the wisdom to be exchanged, the parents' experience in living from which the child can profit, the child's freshness of view from which the parent can derive pleasure, and the joy of shared memories.

Family hassles are hard sometimes, but the inevitable reality of life—that at some point a parent may need physical, financial or emotional help—can be harder and more painful still.

## ROLE REVERSAL

Actually, over the years a gradual change takes place in our relation-

## Shakes, Pats, Pinches and Hugs —The Language of Touch

Sometimes we forget that touching is one of our five senses—right up there with hearing, seeing, smelling and tasting. Touching is vitally important to our emotional well-being. In children, for example, a substantial amount of touching has the power to foster intellectual, social and emotional growth. In adults it can even improve conversational abilities and lead to more positive attitudes.

And touching can change the way we perceive the world around us. For example, in a study completed at Purdue University in Lafayette, Indiana, library clerks either touched (as if by accident) or avoided touching students when returning their library cards. After leaving the library, the students were interviewed. Those who had been touched felt more upbeat and positive—not only toward the librarian, but toward the world at large.

No longer governed by the confining rules of etiquette, the popularity of touching in the U.S. has been increasing, especially among adults. In a 1976 study, both men and women were observed touching friends of the opposite sex more frequently than they had 10 years earlier.

It's also important to realize that touch has a language of its own—conveying feelings of intimacy, intensity or any other conceivable emotion. Few other means of expression are as effective.

So the next time you're thinking about shaking someone's hand or giving them a pat on the back, go ahead. It'll do you good to keep in touch.

ship with our parents. In large ways and small, we find ourselves becoming parents to our parents. It's a kind of role reversal. For instance, you may become more protective—more prone to withhold bad news from them. You may find yourself suggesting ways to ease their lives and secure their welfare. You may find them turning more to you for help.

"You become aware of when they need coddling," Mrs. Szold says. "When my father was ill, my mother said to me, 'You're the only person I know I can cry with.' She was turning to me the way I had turned to her years ago."

However, the parenting of a parent can go too far. *Never,* the experts caution, treat aging parents as children—it robs them of their dignity and only serves to make them more dependent. *Always* listen to what they want and, as long as they're of sound mind and it's possible, respect their wishes. They're still in control of their lives.

In its own way this new aspect of the relationship can be deeply satisfying to a child. Given such a lot of care from a parent, it is wonderful to be able to give some care in return.

A very difficult situation occurs when a parent suddenly becomes ill or widowed, or needs urgent help and attention. "It's especially hard on an adult child when an aging parent has this need and his own children have their own important needs at the very same time," Ms. Reid says. Helping the parent may mean giving short shrift— temporarily—to other members of the family. For instance, if there's just enough money available for a child's college education or a parent's urgent medical needs, college may have to wait.

"The choices can be heart-breaking, but the important thing is to be honest with the family members concerned, to talk with them, to explain," Mrs. Szold counsels. A lot of anger and resentment may come to the fore, but at least the feelings are being dealt with.

A final cautionary note from Ms. Reid: Don't neglect your own needs. You can't be all things to everybody. When a crisis involving a parent occurs, assess what you can do; set limits for yourself. Enlist the aid of other family members. Take time out to do things for yourself—a shopping trip, an evening out, a few days in the country. Only by nurturing yourself will you retain the strength to nurture your aging parent and the others in your family.

## BEING A BETTER PARENT

When our children are small, defining the relationship isn't the problem it is with our parents. If there is a problem—and often enough there is—it's in going around and around in irritating hassles with them. Consider a couple of scenes familiar to most mothers and fathers:

PARENT: No, you can't.
SMALL CHILD (shrieking): Yes, I can!

PARENT: Be sure you're home before midnight.
TEENAGER: (shrieking): Mother, be reasonable!

We love our children, but sometimes it's love in a combat zone. Sometimes we find them—and they us—exasperating, argumentative, intransigent. Sometimes we find parenthood very difficult.

"Parenting is a confusing experience for a lot of mothers and fathers," agrees Nancy Samalin, director of New York City's Parent Guidance Workshops. "Almost all parents love their kids, they want to do a good job, they work very hard for their kids." There's a *but* behind her words, and it's that parents have very good intentions *but* often lack the skills with which to do a very effective job. "Even if you are hired for a very simple job, you have to learn some skills to do it, and raising a child is, I think, the most difficult job in the world," adds Ms. Samalin, who also teaches parenting at the New School for Social Research and was trained in the child-rearing methods of the late child psychologist Haim Ginott, Ph.D.

Numerous studies show that, unwittingly, parents tend to raise their children the way they were raised. That's so, Ms. Samalin agrees, but "if you're just going to do what comes naturally, or do what your parents did, you may not be taking advantage of all the possibilities open to you."

Possibilities for an effective parent-child relationship are always limited when mothers or fathers take rather extreme positions. Diana Baumrind, Ph.D., of the Institute of Human Development, University of California at Berkeley, has done extensive research into how various parenting approaches affect children's behavior. She has found three types of parents: authoritarian, permissive and authoritative.

**Authoritarian.** These are parents who value obedience as a virtue. They're very traditional, telling the child what to do and expecting obedience—no discussions, no talking back.

**Permissive.** These parents set very few limits. They give their children a great deal of freedom. As Dr. Baumrind puts it, "Freedom to the permissive parent means absence of restraint."

**Authoritative.** These parents, on the other hand, "attempt to direct the child's activities in a rational, issue-oriented manner." They value discipline *and* independence; they set standards and enforce them firmly, but also listen to their children; they use reason, power and rewards for good behavior.

Dr. Baumrind's research shows that both of the more extreme positions create problems. Neither the authoritarian nor the permissive parents in her study were really confident in their child-rearing practices. They didn't do as good a job of enriching their children's environment. What's more, they lacked a balance between the support they gave their children and what they expected in return.

Many parents find the job of effectively setting limits and disciplining an extremely hard one to do. "One reason parents find it hard to set limits is because they feel they have to make their children happy, and they feel like bad parents when their children become upset with them for saying no," Ms. Samalin explains. As for discipline, she says, children and parents are naturally at odds about it. "They have conflicting needs. Children have a need to dawdle, to make a mess, to play all day long; parents have a need for speed, neatness, cleanliness, getting things done."

## MUTUAL RESPECT

Good communication is at the heart of success in setting limits, in disciplining and in being an effective

## Working Moms Are Good for Kids

Your child is standing at the window, tears streaming down her tiny face, as you leave for work. You feel guilty, and you wonder whether you're turning her into a juvenile delinquent or a school dropout.

But you needn't feel guilt, fear or heartbreak, says modern child expert Mary Howell, M.D., Ph.D., a consulting pediatrician with a degree in development psychology, who is the mother of six.

When Mom works, she points out, children have more opportunity to form emotional attachments to people other than their mother, have a greater chance to develop self-reliance and enjoy a more valuable role in the family because the chores they do are really needed. Moreover, working moms may provide a better role model for their daughters.

All children have separation fears and must work through them, she adds. When mother has a paid job, the children simply go through these fears at an earlier age. "They learn that mother does go away," says Dr. Howell, "but that she also comes back."

parent generally. Good communication requires empathy and respect. Being empathic and respectful is as important in talking to children as it is in talking to adults— something parents often don't realize. "We say things to kids we wouldn't say to people we care about who are adults—'watch what you're doing'; 'leave it alone'; 'eat your vegetables or you'll get no dessert'; 'you're always bugging me . . .' " Ms. Samalin points out. "We wouldn't say to an adult, to a guest, 'Look, I slaved over a hot stove, I made you my special dish and you're not even tasting it, what's the matter with you?' But that's the way we talk to children. We do it automatically— say things that are critical and disrespectful, probably because it's familiar, that's how we were talked to."

This approach backfires because disrespect breeds disrespect—and resistance. Since it's an easy pattern to slip into, how can we stop it? Awareness is one way—by becoming more consciously aware of how we talk to our children. Making "I"

statements to express our feelings instead of being accusatory also helps. Not, "Don't be a pest," but, "I don't like being pushed."

Children don't learn by being told what's wrong with them; they learn by being told what's right with them. As Ms. Samalin says, "Then they have a positive model and see themselves as okay people." It also lessens the chance of getting into a power struggle.

## PROBLEMS WITH POWER GAMES

Power struggles are an unfortunate fact of life in parent-child relationships. They're easy to get into, hard to get out of and very undermining of discipline. Power struggles are clashes of wills. Orders and threats easily bring them on. You can say, "Hang up your clothes or there's no television for you tonight," which immediately breeds resistance. Or you can say, "I'd really appreciate it if. . . ." Or, "You

# Surviving the Terrible Teens

If your sweet baby—at the age of 13 or 14—has become irresponsible, disrespectful and somewhat sullen, there is good news and bad news for you. The good news is: This behavior is part of a perfectly normal phase that almost every teenager goes through. The bad news is: It's going to last for years.

In his book, *Between Parent and Teenager*, the late Haim G. Ginott, Ph.D., explained that your child is going through a change in life from a stage of organization (childhood) to disorganization (adolescence) to reorganization (adulthood).

can hang them up now or before you go to bed, but I do expect it to be done." This latter approach offers firmness and leeway, and avoids a flat-out order.

"I think kids are allergic to orders," Ms. Samalin says. "Even when you win, you lose. You may make Johnny eat his spinach even if it takes 2 hours, because you have the power. But now you've made him feel helpless, so now he's going to provoke another incident—scream or spit it out—to prove he's not powerless."

With older children, power struggles take on a different quality. Teenagers generally get a far worse press than they deserve. A study of normal teenage boys by Daniel Offer, M.D., of the Michael Reese Hospital and Medical Center in Chicago, showed that these teenagers were somewhat rebellious, especially in their early teenage years, but by and large shared their parents' values. Other studies of teenagers have come up with similar findings. Yet life with a teenager can be *very* rough, because they're so moody, so up, so down, so passionate about everything. And because of their size and weight they have a lot more physical power than younger children. You can't simply carry them off to their room to quell a tantrum.

Realistically, Ms. Samalin says, parents of teenagers don't have that much influence or control—unless the teens care how their parents feel. Teenagers may be rebellious, but they are much more cooperative if they're listened to, treated with respect—and if they feel the rules make sense. For instance, you might say, "I want you home by midnight." The teenager might angrily respond, "You treat me like a baby!" to which you could reply, "I know how you feel, but if you stay out till two, having fun, I'll be staying up, worrying." That makes some sense. When Ms. Samalin and her husband wanted their own teenagers home from a party by midnight for safety's sake, the children pointed

*(continued on page 72)*

During this period of transition, a teenager is striving to find his own separate identity. To reach this goal, childhood ties must be broken—even ties to you, the loving parents. While your teenager experiments with disobeying house rules and while he withdraws his thoughts and feelings, you, too, will enter a stage of transition. You will have to learn to cope with, and continue to love, this emerging adult.

Dr. Ginott explains that your continued support will come more easily if you understand what a teenager is experiencing. Moreover, he suggests several ways you can make this difficult phase a little easier to endure.

• Communicate with your teenager—talk and listen. Avoid lecturing.

• Accept the child's need to break free but don't be overly accepting. If you appear to approve of a teenager's rebellion, he'll be forced to push even harder to break the parental ties.

• Above all, relate to your teenager as a young adult, not as a young child—employ consideration and thoughtfulness.

# Living with Your Children... Again

*F*rom this date henceforward, the party of the first part and the party of the second part, for the purposes of binding, securing and ensuring the domestic tranquility...

If this legal mumbo jumbo seems quite beside the point to you as your grown child moves back into the family nest after having lived independently for a while, think again, say those who've tried it. Conflict is built into this living arrangement. One practical approach to keeping it at a minimum is to write up a contract. Here are some things you'll at least want to talk over.

## Privacy

This is the most frequently mentioned area of conflict. You'll each want to know what the others consider an intrusion in terms of time alone, untrammeled space and quiet. If you don't want Mom poking about your bedroom—ever—say so. If you don't want Son sprawled across your king-size mattress, monopolizing your bedroom TV, spell it out. Loud music can be invasive, too.

## Housework

Sure, Daughter cleans her own room. Should she also take a turn at cleaning the other rooms she uses—the kitchen, the bathroom, the living room? If so, how often? Agree on how the housework should be shared, and put it in writing.

## Phone

"Brrrng, brrrng," it's 2 A.M. Who pays for the phone isn't the only issue. How late and early are calls acceptable? How much use is too much?

## Duration of Stay

It's important for all of you to know if this is a limited engagement or open ended. And if you hadn't thought about it, do.

## Guests

Humans are social creatures and it's only natural for a grown child to want guests from time to time. Agree on whether you require advance notice—perhaps so you can make plans for an evening out. Agree on the number of guests —a dinner party for 8 is quite different from a beer bash for 50. Take pains to clarify the rules.

Grown children may be used to having overnight guests of the opposite sex, and this is sometimes a touchy subject. Can you live with it? Can they live without it?

## Expenses

How is the rent or mortgage to be split, the food costs, gas, utilities and phone bill? Money is a sensitive subject for everyone, but most grown children will (or should) want to pay, with either money or work, for their food and lodging.

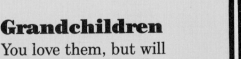

## Grandchildren

You love them, but will you be taking on full-time babysitting/ day care chores? Better work it out beforehand.

out that this request didn't make any sense—they'd have to walk the streets by themselves instead of with a group. So she and her husband revised the curfew—within limits.

## SENSIBLE RULES

To keep power fights with teenagers at a minimum, keep rules at a minimum, experts urge. In theory, you could spend five years trying to get a teenager to help wash the dishes or dress the way you'd like. But you'd have five years spent in a tug of war. Instead, limit requests to the things that matter very much to you—and enforce them firmly.

To keep confusion and anger at a minimum, be consistent. Don't set down edicts you strictly enforce one week and ignore the next. On the other hand, consistency can be carried too far. If the rule for younger children is no television after 10 P.M. on weekdays, but one weekday evening there's a marvelous documentary on dolphins that you think is important educationally and that you know your children would like to see, it's fine to let them see it. Make it clear that this is an exception. "Parents are terrified to do this; they think their children will be after them the next night, too," Ms. Samalin says. "You *can* enforce the rule again."

The best parent in the world is not always going to be perfect. There *will* be times when you're tired or cross or upset—times you'll be short-tempered with your children, or yell at them or say something insulting that you'll later regret. Feeling guilty about it is less helpful than having a talk about what happened with the child involved. Elicit your child's feelings about the incident. Admit you blew your cool and you wish you hadn't said those things. "Children are amazingly forgiving because they need your good will," Ms. Samalin points out.

The essence of a good parent-child relationship, she says, "is a caring relationship where each is concerned about the other's feelings. Help your children feel you understand them and care about their feelings. You may not always agree, but you understand. It's important for them to feel that we truly *like* them—loving a child who gets an F in math isn't as easy as loving a child who gets an A in math, but the child with the F needs it more."

## THE ETIQUETTE OF PARENTING

Once they were toddlers, and you were learning the skills needed to be a good parent. Now they tower over you, maybe with toddlers of their own in tow. Things are different now that they're adults in their own right. Old habits die hard, they say, and sometimes parents fall back into the comfortable old pattern of treating their kids like . . . well, kids. The result is usually unpleasant.

The unfortunate fact of the matter is that parents of adult children must learn new patterns of behavior. But that's no problem. Wherever we are in life, there's an "etiquette" to be observed in relating to one's grown children.

A good relationship—a healthy relationship—between you and your grown-up children embodies the same characteristics as a good, healthy relationship between you and your parents. Respect for each other's privacy and individuality, as well as a live-and-let-live attitude, figure prominently.

Many parents, even those whose relationship with their children was quite troubling during their adolescence, make a joyous discovery. As the years pass, the parent/adult child tie becomes richer. Closer. This usually begins when the children are in their early or middle twenties. They listen to their parents in a way they perhaps hadn't for some time. They show more concern for their parents' lives and problems. They begin to see past conflicts or episodes in a different light.

You can't hurry up the new warmth, closeness and understanding, however. It has to come in its own time. It comes, Ms. Reid explains, when your children have "separated" from you emotionally enough to be at least somewhat self-sufficient. In other words, once they no longer feel they need you in the old, dependent, childlike ways, they can respond much more positively to you—adult to adult. Having studied parent-child patterns for decades, Ms. Reid says, she has seen this pattern occurring repeatedly.

"No matter how stormy children's adolescence may have been, in young adulthood they usually come back when they've got the self-confidence to feel they can stand on their own," Ms. Reid says. "Then they recognize that, even though you may have seemed unreasonable to them when they were younger, you were a caring parent."

## A NEW EQUITY

Of course, at least minor conflicts are still bound to happen from time to time. Leftover resentments burst forth. Generational differences create clashes. There may be a pull on the children's part to be taken care of as they were years ago—a pull they have to struggle against. This theory helps to explain why some adult children react angrily when their parents tell them to take a raincoat or put on a sweater. They still feel too vulnerable—too much the "child"—to deal with this kind of habitual protectiveness with a shrug and a smile. Sometimes their struggle between independence and dependence continues for many years, even into their forties and fifties.

Parents always have to be on guard, in a way, not to "take over" their children's lives. The parent who quietly points out the dangers of a questionable neighborhood where a grown child thinks of living is being helpful; the parent who says, "Promise me you won't live there," is taking over.

## LETTING GO

Sometimes parents, without meaning to, do things to hinder their child's growth and maturity. If a child in his twenties, say, moves into his own apartment a few miles from his parents' home, but his mother

# Behind Every Successful Woman Is... Her Father

The relationship a girl has with her father, even more than the one she maintains with her mother, can be the key to turning Daddy's little girl into the successful career woman of the future.

According to a study conducted at the Wright Institute of the University of California, Berkeley, college-age women who were encouraged by their fathers to be competent, to value their accomplishments and to explore the world outside the home are likely to have high levels of self-esteem and independence. The study also shows that to achieve a high degree of self-confidence, a woman should identify not only with the traditional female role in our society, but also with the male role.

Some would expect that encouragement of this sort would draw a daughter away from her mother. However, the study found that women who were given such stimulating treatment were close not only to their fathers, but to their mothers as well.

still does his laundry regularly—or if his parents call every day "to make sure everything is okay"—then it's a geographical but not a psychological move. "It's more as if he'd just moved his bedroom a few miles down the road," as one psychotherapist puts it. This is not helping the young adult to learn to stand on his own.

If an adult child still lives with his parents or has come back to live there for financial or other reasons, it's harder for everybody concerned. In a way it seems like old times. With that child in his old room again, it becomes very easy to forget he's in his twenties or thirties now—very easy to relate to him as if he were still a youngster. When adult children live at home, counselors say, parents must make a special effort to relate to their children as the adults they really are.

Lots of tender loving tact is needed, too, with married children. According to Estelle Rosen, the early years of a marriage are especially sensitive. It takes a while for a couple to become a "marital unit"—fully committed as husband and wife. Until they do, they're apt to have one foot in the marriage and one foot still back home. If they're having fights, your child might want to involve you. Stay out of the situation, Ms. Rosen advises; they need to work things out by themselves.

Another caution: Your child might want to have a special relationship with you—share secrets the other partner isn't privy to, and so on. Avoid such an involvement because it will only create resentment on the part of the left-out spouse.

Whether the marriage is young or old, you want to give husband and wife all the privacy and autonomy they need. The less advice you volunteer, the better. If they ask for it, that's a different story, of course, though they should still be free to accept or reject the advice you offer.

Some parents experience a lingering sense of loss once their children are married; theirs is now a secondary role in their children's lives. The feelings of displacement are natural, as is the shift itself; it happens from generation to

## Juggling Marriage and Career

Stop trying to be Superwoman. That's the message from health professionals to women attempting to balance careers and families. It is wives, say the experts, who need the help in a two-career marriage, because their husbands, the rest of society and even the wives themselves still expect "the weaker sex" to carry the heavier load of housework and child care.

"The father may take the kids to the zoo or the ballpark once in a while, but he won't take on the drudgy chores like scrubbing floors," says one doctor.

And today's woman expects more of herself than just a clean house. She attempts to be a gourmet cook, a confident executive, a sexy siren, the perfect housekeeper, hostess, mother and teacher, generation. But while things are different, married children don't stop loving their parents. On the contrary, parents keep discovering how much richer and deeper their parent-child relationship becomes once they join together as adults.

Ideally, marriages, too, become richer, deeper, more intimate as the years go by. But it's a funny thing about marital intimacy: Almost everybody wants it, but a lot of people don't know how to get it. Often the marital partners involved truly love each other. They *want* to be emotionally intimate with each other, but something seems to get in the way. Frequently that "something" is their misconceptions and confusions about the nature of intimacy.

## THE MARRIAGE OF TWO MINDS

Pretend you're looking at a set of pictures, each depicting a married couple engaged in some activity. Here's one couple engaged in a passionate embrace. Here's a second couple on the bank of a river; they're fishing. Here's a third weeding their garden. Here's a fourth strolling in the park, holding hands. Here's a fifth, obviously engaged in an intense, serious discussion. Which of these couples is engaged in "marital intimacy"?

You might pick the passionate couple, or maybe the one walking hand-in-hand. If you did so, and excluded the others, you'd be wrong. In fact, each of those couples *could* be engaged in marital intimacy. It's not the act that counts most, it's the feeling husband and wife bring to the activity. Even sex doesn't have to be "intimate" except for the loving we bring to it.

By its very definition, an intimate relationship is deep, emotionally intense and open. We reveal more of ourselves—the warts as well as the exquisite parts of ourselves—and expect to be accepted. In an intimate relationship we can afford to be a little childish or needy or irrationally angry every once in a while—again, trusting that our partners aren't going to throw up their hands and walk out on us.

Intimate behavior can vary considerably from couple to couple and encompasses more than sex. As

the smartest shopper and the most brilliant decorator. As a result she is nothing but exhausted, vulnerable to illness and guilty for failing, say the experts. Women need to learn how to handle the pressures both at work and at home.

Rather than try to satisfy all these demands, women must learn to limit them, instead. At work, women need to be able to demand help and to set limits. At home, they also need to learn to delegate chores to the family, to a cleaning person, to a laundry or dry cleaner.

Husbands must learn to appreciate the amount of energy a working wife puts forth each day, and learn not to resent some inevitable lapses of loving attention.

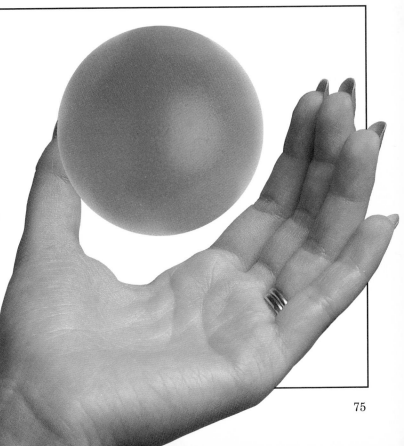

Susan Hartman of the Family and Children's Service, a broad-based counseling service in Minneapolis, Minnesota, explains, "There are many different kinds of intimacy, such as sexual, emotional, social, recreational. There's no one 'right' way to achieve intimacy. Realizing that people show intimacy in many different ways can help them to appreciate their partners more."

Carl and Mae, a St. Paul couple, are one example. Carl loves to take his wife on weekend camping trips in the lake country an hour or two away. An avid amateur naturalist,

he tells his wife about the different birds and plant life they encounter. Mae could say, "Ho-hum." She could refuse to go. In truth, her interest isn't as intense as Carl's, but she's fully aware that in sharing these trips with her he's giving himself in a special way. He's saying, "I love you."

## SHARING ACTIVITIES

A study of happy and unhappy marriages by Gary R. Birchler, Ph.D., of the University of California School of Medicine and the

---

# How to Make Friends

SOFTEN. This word can help you make friends. An acronym (each letter stands for something) created by psychologist Arthur C. Wassmer, Ph.D., author of *Making Contact,* SOFTEN will remind you to:

**Smile.** "Smiling says I enjoy being with you," says Dr. Wassmer. "It's a voluntary act. Anyone can do it."

**Open Posture.** Let your body say you want to be friends. Uncross your arms and legs. The more open your posture, the more welcoming.

**Forward Lean.** If you lean toward people, they get the message that you're interested in them and they'll like you for it.

**Touch.** Touch is one of the most powerful nonverbal ways of communicating. Try

shaking hands with two hands. Or, pat your friend on the back.

**Eye Contact.** Another potent way to express interest, attention and respect.

**Nod.** People love it when you nod when they're talking. It doesn't mean you agree, just that you're attentive.

If you're shy, practicing these behaviors will eventually change how you feel, says Dr. Wassmer. And if you find it hard to make friends, he suggests that you try thinking of other people not as demanding, but as needy.

"People want just what you want," says Dr. Wassmer; "a little love, a little attention, a little gentleness. Think of yourself as a powerful giver of gifts."

Veterans' Administration Medical Center in La Jolla, California, underscores the importance of shared activities. Working under a National Institute of Mental Health grant, Dr. Birchler found notable differences between the happy and unhappy (he calls them distressed) couples in his study. Happy couples went to sports events, movies and church activities together; they visited friends together; they had talks together; they went out to dinner together; they played Frisbee together—and they did these things far more often than the distressed couples. In fact, on a very comprehensive checklist of activities, happy couples checked off 500 such activities for a period of one month, distressed couples only around 300. The distressed couples were much more likely to do things alone or with persons other than their spouses.

"When a couple chooses to do things together rather than apart, I think it represents their interest in closeness as opposed to distance," Dr. Birchler says. It works both ways: Feeling close, a husband and wife want to do things together; doing things together makes them feel close—each reinforces the other.

"The happy couples don't deny they fight," Dr. Birchler explains, "but in contrast to the distressed couples they have fewer fights, their fights aren't catastrophic and they rebound much more readily. They might resolve a fight in a couple of hours as opposed to several days for the distressed couples."

In effect, their fights aren't shattering; if disagreements affect their level of intimacy adversely, it's for a very brief period of time.

## REALISTIC EXPECTATIONS

The wish to have—and maintain—a high level of marital intimacy also leads to a certain amount of confusion at times. Some people have the idea—the mistaken idea—that if you're in a good marriage, intimacy has to be at a peak all of the time. It disconcerts them when they go through periods when they feel less close to their partners—or sense that their partners aren't

# Getting Along with Co-Workers

Your co-worker is bugging you so much you find yourself contemplating the penalties for felonious assault. Or perhaps your co-worker is merely an annoying klutz. Whatever the details of the conflict, you can make a start toward solving it by writing an imaginary dialogue with your co-worker. According to Lawrence J. Weiss, Ph.D., a San Francisco psychologist, the made-up drama can be a chance to give the person a piece of your mind without a major breach of the office peace, or it can be a chance to rehearse a needed out-loud confrontation to make sure you will come across in a nonhurtful way.

Some people who have tried this method have discovered the source of their annoyance is something not relevant to the office situation, like their co-worker's politics. In such cases, says Dr. Weiss, options include avoiding the difficult subject or treating it humorously. But remember this is just a rehearsal for the most important step—open, honest discussion with your co-worker.

Sexual feelings may also show up, and a mental dialogue can help you work out the best way to handle these feelings before they get in the way of your productivity.

feeling close to them. They may even wonder, "Gosh, have I stopped loving my spouse?" Or, "Has my spouse stopped loving me?" They expect constant intensity.

Psychologist Jon Carlson, Ed.D., director of the Lake Geneva Wellness Clinic in Wisconsin and coauthor of a comprehensive couples' program, *Training in Marriage Enrichment,* says that's a pretty unrealistic expectation. "Marriage isn't a constant high; it isn't meant to be. We couldn't sustain that pace—nor would we want to," he explains.

Closely related to this misconception is another: that if you're in a deep, intimate relationship you lose your individuality, and if you want to preserve your sense of self, you had better keep some distance. Mental-health professionals refute this idea, too. Intimacy and individuality are not opposites. Dr. Carlson makes an analogy between intimacy and the hands—the human hands— we all possess. "Hands are apart or they're together, but they don't work very well in either position alone," he says. "To work well they have to be fluid, moving back and forth. It's that balance, moving in and out, that intimacy is all about. Life would really be difficult if our hands were always together. And life is really difficult if you're always together with your partner, just as it is if you're always apart."

In a healthy marriage there are times when we and our partners feel terribly close—when, in a sense, we "fuse." And there are times when we have a real need to be apart, to be by ourselves, independent. These fluctuations of mood and feeling are natural. The intimate moments give us the strength to enjoy the private times. And the private times recharge us for the pleasures of intimacy.

## SHIFTING NEEDS

We all have a need for contact, for closeness, for intimacy, but that doesn't mean we all have this need to the same degree or in the same way.

Simply because two people love each other, and marry, and live together, their individual needs for space and closeness don't necessarily jibe. One partner may need a lot more hugging and kissing than the other. One may need a lot more time simply sitting and talking than the other.

Ms. Hartman points out that the way we were raised and what we observed as children has a lot to do with the way we play out our

intimacy needs in adulthood. Suppose you grew up in a family in which everybody was warm and open and casual and affectionate. Most likely that's the way you are now. Suppose your spouse grew up in a family whose members (mother and father especially) were rather reserved—reticent about affectional responses. That's probably the way your spouse is now.

Apart from such childhood patterns, the temperaments we're born with also make us different in the way we see and need intimacy. So does the fact of belonging to different sexes. In general, men tend to view marital intimacy more in terms of sex. Women generally see it more as touching and talking.

All of these influences on marital intimacy are important to understand, because they can help couples get closer together. If, say, a wife wants more hugs and kisses than her husband is giving her, and she thinks he's being mean or withholding, her response is apt to be anger. Or she may keep on trying to get affection in such a way that he only backs off more. But if she understands that he isn't deliberately withholding—that to some extent this kind of kissy-huggy intimacy causes him discomfort, they have a better chance of working things out.

Dr. Carlson, along with other experts, offers several suggestions to couples who have intimacy problems, and to all couples who want to enrich their contact.

- Talk to each other about what you want with respect to closeness and distance. Often people assume their partners know their needs when they really don't.
- Allow for the fact that intimacy can be shown in many different ways. "Wives and husbands sometimes say their partners aren't being intimate with them when they really are—in their own ways," Ms. Hartman says. Thus, a seemingly undemonstrative wife who cooks her husband elaborate meals might be demonstrating her love in this way.

- If you seem far apart in your needs, have a negotiating session. Dr. Carlson says that when wives and husbands talk honestly and openly to each other about their differences, when they go from there to a search for areas of agreement, they usually find they agree on a lot more than they thought they did. "They really may not be so far apart," he says. "Both want to be touched. Both want time together. Both enjoy being with each other. Then the question becomes how often and how much, which is a lot easier to negotiate than when they create an either/or situation."

- Do more recreational things together. Dr. Birchler says that without even realizing it, a lot of couples work up such a hectic schedule with work-related activities, with friends, with relatives, that they spend very little time alone together. "Find something pleasurable that you can do together, just the two of you," he advises. "If you do fun things together, you become more relaxed, more open with each other, you have something more to talk about, something that lets you become more personal with each other."

- Recognize the fact that no one person—not even the most loving and devoted spouse—can fulfill all of your needs. Look to friends and relatives to provide you with some of the affection and emotional support you need. The most satisfied couples rely on each other *and* on the world outside.

## WEDDED BLISS

Our emotional and sexual lives are intimately bound together. If something goes awry with one, it often affects the other. In fact, when a sexual problem develops in marriage, it can trigger a great deal of worry.

Happily, this anxiety is frequently the result of jumping to the wrong conclusions. In the first place, no couple, no matter how close and loving they are, are *always*

## Handling the "Problem" Boss

Your boss comes into the office at 7 A.M. and stays until 7 P.M. The tyrant expects you to do the same. Or he undercuts your best efforts, or yells, or takes credit for your work, or sleeps in the kneehole of his desk. The bottom line: You have a problem boss.

Movies like *9 to 5* poke fun at the situation, but in real life a bad boss can create a real health hazard. Here's how the experts suggest you cope.

- Begin looking for another job immediately. That's the word from management consultant Jack Falvey. "Saying 'Everything's great except for this one person' is like saying 'I love living in this house except that it's on fire,'" he warns.
- Until you find a new job, keep out of harm's way. Don't argue or challenge unless you must. Power lies with the boss. You can't win.
- Don't be tempted to try to outmaneuver the boss. Aiming to get the boss fired is more likely to get you fired.
- Keep the relationship businesslike. Avoid the time-consuming and emotionally exhausting games of trying to play up to a bad boss.
- Make the best of it. Praise yourself lavishly for learning lessons in patience, how to handle adversity, and what *not* to do when *you're* the boss.

fulfilled, *always* problem free. As Dr. Carlson says, "It seldom happens that a couple doesn't have some form of sexual dysfunction at some point in time. That's perfectly normal."

In fact, that dysfunction may have nothing to do with the marital relationship. During periods of great stress, for example—when there's a lot on your mind and a drain on your emotions—some people simply don't feel sexy.

Dysfunction also may be caused by a medication. A wide variety of drugs create sexual problems as a side effect, something doctors rarely warn their patients about. "Drugs are one of the things I ask about early in our contact when couples come to me with a sexual problem," says Edith Szold. "They so often turn out to be the problem."

Sometimes what seems like a sex problem is, in reality, a problem of communication, says Dr. Birchler after studying happily and unhappily married couples. "Sex is the subject that people have the most difficulty communicating about," he says. People often find it hard to tell their partners what they want and don't want sexually, what's right and wrong with their sexual relationship. As Dr. Birchler puts it, "There's a big need, then, for better communication so that each partner knows what the other likes and doesn't like and is afraid and hopeful about."

In spite of what many therapists see as a national obsession with sexual performance, some couples with sex problems do lead satisfying married lives. This is the surprising finding of a study by Ellen Frank and Carol Anderson of the department of psychiatry, University of Pittsburgh School of Medicine. After studying the sexual relationships of 100 happily married couples, they learned that just because a couple is happily married doesn't mean they don't have sex problems—and just because they have sex problems doesn't mean they're not happily married.

In exploring marital conflict and sexual dysfunction—in exploring any problem, for that matter—communication is the key. As

Virginia Satir, a highly respected family therapist, has said, "Communication is to relationship what breathing is to life." Whether the problem is major or minor, whether it centers on sex or on something else, whether the exploration is done at home or with the help of a professional, you have to be able to talk about it. You have to be able to say what it is you feel or want or are troubled by. The first step in resolving *any* problem is to identify it. Then you can begin to work toward its resolution.

The problem doesn't have to be very serious or require extensive professional help. When husbands and wives really start the process of "conflict resolution," Dr. Carlson says, they often find that the conflict isn't as major as they thought, that they agree on a lot more than they disagree on and that when both really involve themselves in searching for solutions, they become amazingly good at finding them.

## GOOD MEDICINE

Family's always first, of course, but in terms of our relationships, friends are not far behind. California's State Department of Mental Health mounted an extensive advertising campaign, complete with radio announcements and bumper stickers, whose slogan was, "Friends can be good medicine."

The slogan is true. Friendships figure very early in the course of our development. Beginning with "parallel play," at around the age of two, we move toward developing a real best friend by the age of seven. Having a best friend makes the world more exciting and less scary. In adulthood, close friends give us pretty much the same things. They make our daily lives easier, smoother and more pleasurable.

With trusted friends we can let down our hair and talk about things that might not be of interest to our families. A friendship study by a well-known sociologist, Robert S. Weiss, Ph.D., of the University of Massachusetts, showed that even in the warmest, most compassionate marriages, "some important interests will not be shared within the marriage."

In friendships we can share hobbies, sports and other leisure-time activities. If we feel isolated and lonely, the easiest way to relieve that feeling is by visiting a friend or joining an activities group.

It's a funny thing about loneliness: People can feel lonely in a crowd or in a troubled marriage. Yet people can live alone and not necessarily feel lonely at all, though this isn't the common view of live-aloners. When Carin M. Rubenstein, Ph.D., and Phillip Shaver, Ph.D., of New York University looked into the relationship between living alone and loneliness, they found that many people who live alone aren't lonely—precisely because they've built up a network of friends. Of course, emotional health presupposes the ability to be completely alone at times, too, and enjoy it.

## PERENNIALS AND ANNUALS

It takes time to build solid, enduring friendships characterized by a strong emotional tie. Trust doesn't happen overnight. Yet it's a mistake to assume that deep friendships are the only friendships worth having.

"It's not a good idea to think of friendships too narrowly," cautions Ted Bowman, a family educator with the Family and Children's Service in Minneapolis. "Some people think of emotional closeness as the only meaningful kind of friendship, but there's a danger in that. One's circle of intimate friends is very small, and those friends aren't always available. Also, they may move away, something may happen to them, we may even have a falling out with a once-close friend. There are lots of other people, in a wider if less intimate circle, willing to spend time with us. These connections can also be quite useful, meaningful and fun."

Besides, Bowman points out, intimate friends don't just drop into our lives like manna from heaven. We have to cultivate them, which

# The Boss: Good Defense against Stress

Want to be thin, happy, disease resistant, have low blood cholesterol and a high energy level? Work for a good boss.

That's the voice of science based on several major studies of people's reaction to work stress. In one study of 170 AT&T executives during the tumultuous breakup period, those who felt their bosses were supportive suffered only half as many illnesses as others who believed they didn't have their bosses' backing. The unsupported group was also afflicted with twice the obesity, sexual problems and depression, in addition to their other health breakdowns. And psychological support from bosses was more important to workers' overall health than support from home, the study found.

Even blood cholesterol levels—risk factors for heart disease—climb when employees are under the thumb of an authoritarian fussbudget, a survey of 357 defense department employees discovered.

A good boss doesn't have to be warm, say the scientists. But he or she must make employees feel they are trusted to work out their own problems.

takes time. It means starting out on a casual, let's-play-together-and-see-how-we-like-each-other basis first. A study by two University of Utah researchers, reported in the *School Psychology Quarterly*, bears out Bowman's advice. According to this study, what draws people together in friendship most strongly is engaging in mutually pleasurable activities.

Bowman, a strong believer in the healing power of friendships, offers another important piece of advice. As you grow older, don't neglect forming new friendships. "We put such a premium on perennials, those friends who are long lasting, that we don't value the annuals—the briefer friendship experiences. But as we get into our fifties our circle of friends starts to diminish. The way to prevent feeling lonely or alone is to plant a new crop every season. In time, you'll see, they may turn into perennials."

**5**

# Ways to Overcome Stress

## While a little stress keeps you sharp, too much can cut you down. Here's how to cope.

Stress. You see that word all the time in newspapers and magazines, and sometimes it even makes the evening news. The stress of modern life. The stress of family life. The stress of work. The stress of living in the nuclear age. And, of course, the stress generated by the major events of our lives, like the birth of a child, marriage, divorce, illness or even winning the lottery.

Because emotional stress is so often fingered as the culprit in the disease process specifically and the body's breakdown generally, your immediate reaction might well be, "I'd better eliminate all the stress from my life!" But you know that's impossible. The events that bring on stress are as inevitable as death and taxes, both of which produce their own acute stress—sometimes just by thinking about them!

In fact, it's an oversimplification to view stress as "bad" and its absence as "good." It's both. As long as we're alive, we experience stress. We're even stressed when we sleep and dream. Just our bodily functions alone can be stressful. Stress mobilizes us; it enables us to achieve and compete. Stress—specifically, our physiological and mental responses to life's events—enables us to marshal our resources, make decisions and take action. The late Hans Selye, M.D., a pioneering stress researcher, has called stress "the spice of life."

Of course, to carry that analogy further, spices can electrify our taste buds or incinerate them, depending on how we use them. As this chapter will make clear, we can use stress as a positive force. We can learn to recognize the physical and emotional signs of stress—the telltale signs warning us that the tension we're under is working destructively on us. We can learn to defuse that destructiveness to a

# Three Steps to Happiness

Cha-cha-cha, do-si-do, or just boogie your blues away. As amazing as it sounds, simply moving your feet to the beat really improves your state of mind.

According to American Dance Therapy Association member Diane Duggan, who holds a master's degree in dance therapy, moving to music can be psychologically satisfying to many people.

"Dancing gives a sense of well-being," Ms. Duggan says. Anybody can get into a state of inertia. They feel down. But you can break that in a dance session, which leaves people feeling stimulated and invigorated."

Why? Because dance offers the opportunity for self-expression. Moreover, different forms of dance provide different benefits.

"Modern dance is good because it emphasizes expression," she says. "Folk dancing doesn't require much technical skill, it's extremely social and it's fun. And creative movement classes, which center around finding ways to express yourself, are also very good."

In addition to social dancing, people with mental or emotional difficulties that require professional treatment also can try dance or movement therapy. It's unlike most forms of dancing in that a therapist observes the patient in motion. Based on these observations, the therapist then designs an individualized program to solve various problems.

So, if you're feeling dreary, take these three steps to happiness: ONE-two-three, ONE-two-three, ONE-two-three.

significant extent—by taking care of ourselves, coping effectively with crises and setting time aside for relaxation and exercise.

## THE NATURE OF STRESS

As an old saying goes, to conquer an enemy you have to know him first. Destructive stress—Dr. Selye called it "distress"—is the enemy of physical and emotional health. Therefore, the more you know about it, the better.

Whether you're trapped, fuming, in a traffic jam or have just won a bet on the Indy 500; whether you're quarreling with someone or have just been given a surprise kiss; whether the stressful situation is painful or pleasurable—the interior physiological drama is the same. In simplified form, here's what happens: A portion of the brain—the hypothalamus—perceives the stressful event and immediately triggers an "alarm reaction." Electrochemical messengers race to various parts of the body, mobilizing it for action. Your heart (energized by a shot of adrenaline) beats faster. Your breathing quickens and becomes shallower. To give you added nourishment, your liver frees stored nutrients; extra blood carries them to the muscles and brain. This emergency delivery raises your blood pressure. Your eyes dilate, the better to see. Your muscles tighten. You feel tense. You're ready to spring, to act—to fight or flee.

For our ancestors, surrounded by predatory animals and other dangers, this instant mobilization was a biological necessity if our species was to survive. Today, we need to react instantly in sudden emergencies—a car accident, a fire, a burglar in the house. But most of the time the event that stresses us isn't that extreme, and neither is the degree to which our bodies mobilize. Feeling a little stress simply gears us up for the task ahead—studying for an exam, making a sales pitch, dealing with work pressures or whatever.

Just as the brain perceives the need to sound the alarm, so it also recognizes when the stress situation is over and thus that it's time to demobilize. Jeffrey Rudolph, Psy.D., director of the Multimodal Therapy Institute in New York City, points out that in the normal, healthy rhythm of our daily lives we go from being fairly relaxed to somewhat stressed (the alarm reaction), then on to a recuperative healing stage (once the stress has passed or we're dealing with it effectively). Eventually we're fairly relaxed, and the cycle can begin again.

When stress becomes *distress*, it's because we don't give ourselves the chance to heal or relax—or do so for too brief a time. It happens when we don't cope well with situations that generate stress. It also happens when, being the stressful type, we tend to overreact to situations, or when we feel trapped in high-tension situations. It's this *chronic* stress that's so detrimental to our health.

## WHAT NEXT? YOU ASK

Look for a life without changes and crises, and you'll have to look on another planet. From birth to death—which themselves are the most dramatic of all changes—we always have to cope with something. How we cope is, obviously, an individual matter. Some of us thrive on change; others find it extremely hard to adjust to alterations in the routine of our lives.

Coping is the crux of it, says New York psychotherapist Edith Szold. Cope poorly and you surely invite a crisis and its intensely stressful consequences. Cope well and you deal with the situation constructively and resolve it sooner. To do so, it helps to put "crisis" in its proper perspective. From a mental-health point of view, it's not the *event* that's the crisis, it's the *emotion* the event generates in us that makes it a crisis.

Here is what Mrs. Szold suggests.

**Minimize Disruptions.** No matter how chaotic the situation might be, try to lead your life as normally as possible. Follow your normal daily schedule; see friends, pursue your hobbies as before. The more custom-

# How Music Calms You

You settle back in your easy chair with your feet up and a pillow behind you. On the turntable is Pachelbel's *Canon in D Major.* As the celestial music fills the room, your body relaxes and your mind unwinds. The music holds you and lifts you, carries you beside beautiful wooded brooks and through cities of gold.

Physiologically, your heartbeat and breathing are both slowing down and becoming more regular, synchronizing themselves with the beat of the music. Your airways are opening up. Your blood pressure probably drops a few points to a more serene level.

The resplendent strains of Baroque music have a direct impact on your autonomic nervous system. Your heart, your smooth muscles (like your stomach), your gland system, even your metabolic rate, all respond.

Pitch, harmonics, tempo, melody—all contribute to the effect music will have on your mind and body. But the most important factor, says composer and researcher Steven Halpern, Ph.D., is your individual response.

Tempos of around 50 to 60 beats per minute are usually the most soothing. Some Researchers theorize that this tempo's calming effect may result from its similarity to our mother's heartbeat, which we heard in the womb.

Psychiatrists, who have successfully used music in place of sedatives and other drugs to reach and relax people with deep emotional disturbances, also point out that music touches us at our most fundamental level of feeling.

But how can we choose the music which will have the most calming effect on us? Simple, says Dr. Halpern. Just check your breathing. If it is deepening and becoming more regular, the music is relaxing you.

# Teddy Bears Forever

More calming than a hot bath, more cheering than a Walt Disney movie and more soothing than anything since getting a cuddle on your mother's lap—that's the teddy bear, to those who know and love it.

And teddy bear huggers are not all under the age of 5. Six out of 10 grown-ups recently surveyed said they owned a teddy bear (or wished they did).

What's the magic of a piece of plush-covered cotton batting with shiny button eyes? "Teddy bears give you comfort whenever you want it. They never criticize you. They always forgive. Teddy bears love you unquestioningly," says one 39-year-old who sleeps with Serenity, a formerly beige bear.

"Everybody should have a bear," maintains one psychiatrist who became an expert on stuffed animals when he studied their role in mental health. Paul C. Horton, M.D., author of *Solace: The Missing Dimension in Psychiatry,* says the "bear" may be any object or involvement that provides "instant soothing, calming and comforting." What that object is may change throughout your life. But no one ever outgrows the need for a bear of some type, says Dr. Horton.

"Everyone is confused and afraid once in a while," says Dr. Horton. "It's not childish to need to comfort ourselves. A teddy bear can work as well for a 60-year-old as it does for a toddler."

ary your routine. the more stable you'll feel.

"**Relabel.**" How we view things largely dictates our response to them. Call something a crisis and you've made it into something dangerous. Call it a problem and you're much more apt to bring your customary problem-solving abilities to bear.

**Gather Information.** Research thoroughly. Make a list of questions, read, talk to people, see that your questions are answered to your satisfaction. You'll gain at least four important benefits: (1) You'll feel less helpless—the very act of gathering information will give you a sense of taking charge; (2) you'll dispel any misinformation; (3) you'll develop options or courses of action to consider, then accept or discard; (4) you'll keep yourself from "catastrophizing."

Catastrophizing—assuming a worst-case scenario—is a common trap in a crisis and leads to needless anguish and panic.

Mrs. Szold adds. "So much of what we see as crises are really the products of our imaginations."

**Get Organized.** The more organized you are, the less overwhelmed or stressed you'll feel. Begin with—yes—another list. Fold a sheet of paper in half. Head the left-hand side, "Things I can do something about." Head the right-hand side, "Things I can do nothing about." List these things on both sides of the paper. Then tear off the right-hand side and throw it away.

**Establish Priorities.** You've gathered your information, you have your list of things you can do something about. Now jot down everything that has to be done to remedy your problem—the big, important, difficult things; the small, relatively trifling, easy things. Divide the list into two parts—what has to be done now, what can wait. Tackle something easy first, just to get started.

**Share Your Problem.** Choose someone you trust and whose judgment you respect, and tell them about your pain and fear. Expressing your feelings will help calm you. You may also get helpful suggestions.

**Control Anger and Blame.** Some people become very angry when faced with distress—they lash out. Anger in the face of something calamitous is a perfectly natural emotion, but lashing out only worsens personal relationships and does nothing to help the situation.

**Be Compassionate toward Yourself.** Many of us confuse self-pity with self-compassion, Mrs. Szold says. "Self-pity," she explains, "is wallowing in one's helplessness. Compassion for oneself is being able to define and understand when you're having a really rough time. Why shouldn't you be as kind to yourself as you are to other people?"

**Draw on Others.** Don't feel you have to go it alone. Accept help from friends, relatives, neighbors; turn to professionals—anyone from a doctor to a psychotherapist to a home-maker service—as you need them.

**Draw on Your Greatest Resource—Yourself.** You're not brand-new in the world; you have a personal history chronicling all the crises, troubles, shocks and disappointments you've weathered to this day. You've dealt with them all—and gone beyond them. And you will again.

## THE CHRONICALLY STRESSED

Developing a strategy for handling a crisis is good advice for most people. Yet some folks seem to be in a perpetual state of turmoil. They'd have to spend their lives charting a continuous battle plan. These chronically stressed individuals break down into two large groups: those whose stress is largely internal and those whose stress is external. The first group comprises those nervous, high-strung types—the natural worriers, the perfectionists. The second group is made up of people whose circumstances create enormous and constant tension. They live with bad marriages or bad jobs—and never do anything to improve their lot. Of course, membership in one club doesn't preclude membership in the other, as lots of chronically stressed people can verify.

How does someone qualify for membership? Group one people can look to their genes—and to their way of life, as well. "It's both nature and nurture," Dr. Rudolph explains. "Some persons are born high-stress types and remain that way because they haven't learned effective ways of mediating their stress. Instead, they do things to reinforce their tension and anxiety."

But there's a way to defuse chronic stress—chronic relaxation. Techniques include everything from Swedish massage to calling Dial-a-Trance.

## LEARNING TO RELAX

When you include a set of relaxation techniques in your life, you're doing something very positive emotionally. You're focusing your attention on your own welfare—being unselfishly good to yourself. As Dr. Elliott Dacher puts it, "People who learn to relax come out with a lot more than learning to relax. They develop an enhanced image of themselves, feel less helpless, more in control, capable of taking charge, of reversing disturbing facets of their lives."

And to people who say they don't have the time, Dr. Dacher rejoins, "What if you had a physical problem that required you to have bed rest twice a day in order to improve that condition? You'd do that, wouldn't you?"

## THE MEDIUM IS THE MASSAGE

Want to try your own brand of "therapeutic touch"—to ease tense muscles, get your blood flowing freely, move into a relaxed state and generally feel good? Then give massage a try.

Swedish massage is the best-known type. It's your basic rubbing,

## Pets of Old

The first household pet was probably scavenging garbage when the lady of the cave invited him in to sit by the fire. Thus began the enduring love affair between people and pets.

And what, exactly, do we get in return for centuries of feeding, brushing, walking and debugging? First and foremost, we get true love. But as a not-too-distant-second, we get certain health benefits. Stroking Fido's silky coat calms and relaxes us. In fact, it can produce the relaxation response—nature's antidote to stress.

stroking, kneading, tapping kind of massage that leaves you feeling peaceful and tingly all over. Shiatsu is a Japanese massage that uses

# What Is Shiatsu?

The feeling is both tingly and soothing as the thumbs press along your spine. But the strange part is that you notice other parts of your body responding. Your breathing slows and your mind falls into a more gentle rhythm.

You are receiving shiatsu massage. And according to the Oriental theory behind this ancient practice, the masseur's thumbs are stimulating points along lines of energy flow throughout your body—the same lines used in acupuncture.

The attempt to influence energy flow is what sets shiatsu apart from rubbing (or Swedish style) massage.

Though it may sound a bit exotic, or perhaps even a little scary, shiatsu—which literally means "finger pressure"—in Japan is nearly as routine a part of normal preventive medicine as tooth brushing.

And contrary to rumor, it doesn't hurt. Saul Goodman, president of the Pennsylvania Shiatsu Association, says most people experience no pain, but the ones who do think it's a "good hurt"—a healing sensation like stretching a ligament, which is, in fact, a part of the shiatsu routine.

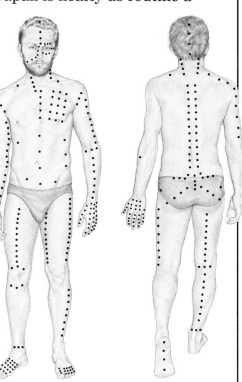

And almost everyone who tries it, likes it. "Relaxation is the number one benefit of shiatsu," says Goodman.

thumb and finger pressure. This pressure is applied to various points of the body, each designed to affect a different set of muscle systems. There are several shiatsu massage forms, each for a specifc purpose— for instance, one makes you feel serene; another makes you more energetic; a third increases sexual vigor; and yet another helps get rid of aches and pains.

How do you find a good masseur or masseuse? The best way is to get a friend's enthusiastic recommendation, or try your local physical therapist for a recommendation.

If you decide on a home massage, try the buddy system. Take turns with a friend giving and receiving a massage. This is all you'll need: a willing partner, your hands, some oil, and a couple of towels spread on the floor. (A bed isn't a good place for a massage. No matter how firm the mattress, there's not enough support.) Choose a comfortably warm room, avoiding chills and drafts. Begin by applying baby oil or vegetable oil to your hands to avoid friction during the massage.

When experimenting on your own, try a back or neck rub—areas of the body where tension so often settles. For a back rub, straddle your partner's thighs. Be careful not to rest your weight *on* your partner, otherwise she—or he—will tense up. Rub your hands briskly together to spread the oil and warm your hands. Place your hands on your partner's lower back, one to the left of the spine, the other to the right, and apply pressure firmly up along each side. When you get to the neck, brush your hands lightly along the spine until you get back to the base of the spine. Next, working slowly and as close to the spine as possible, use your thumbs to make short, firm strokes up along both sides of the spine. When you reach the neck, gently knead the muscles that curve from the neck to the shoulders between your fingers and thumbs.

As you work through the various steps, keep your hands relaxed. Don't assume positions that tense you up, because you'll communicate that tension to your partner.

Ask for, and be responsive to, feedback. The pressure you exert should come mainly from the weight of your body, not your hands or arms. Feel for knots, tight muscles and tender spots, and give those more attention.

## A GAME OF SKILL

"Step right up, ladies and gentlemen, and get it free—one of the most remarkable medicines of this or any other age. Taken as directed, it will make you more energy-efficient. Your alpha brain wave activity will increase—exactly the waves that are always present when you're calm and relaxed. Your blood lactate levels will fall—and if that's a lot of mumbo jumbo to you, ladies and gentlemen, be advised that scientists associate blood lactate, a substance produced by the skeletal muscle metabolism, with anxiety. And here's a case of less is better.

"Don't go away, folks; this powerful potion, this noble nostrum, has still more to offer you. It will slow your breathing and decrease your heart rate. Is that good? you ask. That's very good, I reply, for it means your sympathetic nervous system, the selfsame system that's activated when you're under stress, decreases its activity and puts you in that most desirable of states, the relaxed state.

"That's not enough, you say, you want a bonus. Very well, a bonus you shall have. This extraordinary elixir also will lower the blood pressure of people who have high blood pressure.

"What is this exceptional medicine? you ask. This is the best part, I answer. It is not a drug. It is not something you smoke or drink. Moreover, it is absolutely free. I repeat, free. The only cost to you is 20 easy minutes of your time a day. This curious cure-all is—*meditation!*"

## THE ART OF MEDITATION

If an old-fashioned pitchman were to sell this particular "medicine," that's how he might present it to the crowd—and he wouldn't be exag-gerating, either. In the East they've known about the tranquilizing benefits of meditation for centuries, but you don't have to be an Indian guru or Zen master to enjoy those benefits. All you need to do is to take a break (a relaxation break, not a coffee break) for 10 minutes a day, twice a day, every day.

The easiest, most popular meditation break is the one worked out by Herbert Benson, M.D., of the Harvard Medical School, and fully described in his best-selling book, *The Relaxation Response.* It was Dr. Benson's laboratory work with practiced meditators of the Transcendental Meditation school that first gave the Western world hard clinical data on the physiological effect of meditation.

Here, according to *The Relaxation Response,* is how to meditate.

Find a quiet place (that alone should have a calming effect in our noisy world!). Set a convenient time. Dr. Benson suggests waiting an hour or two after eating so that the digestive process doesn't interfere with your efforts. Sit in a comfortable position. Clear your mind, as much as you possibly can, of distracting thoughts. That's not easy to do; our minds tend always to be abuzz with things. Whatever thoughts, daydreams or memories cross your mind, don't hang on to them; let go, let go. Adopt a passive attitude.

So there you are, sitting comfortably, easily, being passive in the sense of being willing to let things happen to you. Now close your eyes. Relax all of your muscles as much as you can, starting with your toes and working up to your face. Breathe through your nose, focusing your attention on your breath. Each time you breathe out, say the word "one." Don't worry about whether or not you're relaxing sufficiently; worry will only keep you from the desired result.

Continue this exercise for 10 to 20 minutes. If that's too long to begin with, if you're going to fidget restlessly halfway through, some meditation instructors suggest working up to the full time. Start with 4 minutes, then 5, then 6, and so on. But don't stop before you've gone to

*(continued on page 92)*

## Rolfing: Getting Along with Gravity

Take a minute to watch people walking down the street. Most of them do not have good posture. The late biochemist Ida Rolf, Ph.D., believed this problem exists because gravity tugs the body out of alignment. So in the 1920s she developed Rolfing, a type of deep massage that firms and balances the body's structure.

In a Rolfing session, the tissue between the bones and ligaments, or fascia, is worked over by the fists, knuckles and even elbows of a certified Rolfer. The manipulation is said to release a great deal of tension—both muscular and emotional.

Rolfing is given in a series of 10 rather costly sessions, each focusing on a different area of the body.

While the treatment can be painful, certified Rolfers say that there is little chance of physical damage.

# How to Give a Great Massage

A massage not only feels good, it's good for you. "All massage is beneficial," says Patricia J. Eckardt, administrative director of the famed Swedish Institute in New York, who points to benefits both physical and psychological, such as increased circulation and a feeling of relaxation. "Massage," she says, "is an ancient form of healing." (A caution: People with phlebitis or serious illness need a doctor's okay for massage.) And it's not difficult to learn. The steps below can help you give a massage that feels good *and* does good. For equipment you need only willing hands, a light vegetable oil (preferably a fragrant one like rosemary or jasmine) and a flat, padded surface like a table or floor with a quilt on it. (A bed doesn't give good support for a massage.) After just a little study and a few sessions of practice you will have an always-welcome skill. And volunteers to practice on shouldn't be hard to find!

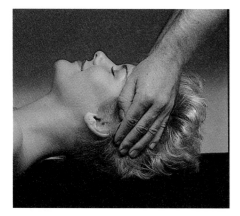

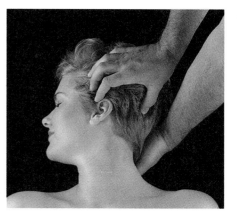

**1** Ask your partner to stretch out on his or her back. Start the massage by gently holding your partner's forehead in your hands. Take enough time to allow both of you to feel relaxed and comfortable.

**2** Next, press your thumbs down firmly in the middle of the forehead and let the pressure slide them down toward the side hairline. Bring your thumbs gently back toward the center. Repeat the process, lowering one thumb-space toward the eyebrows each time. Use harder pressure on the forehead, but ease up as you reach the temples.

**3** Using one hand to support the neck just below the base of the skull, lift your partner's head and turn it gently to the side. With the fingers of your free hand, work the scalp in tiny, firm circles, feeling the skin move over the skull.

**4** Ask your partner to slowly turn over so that you can massage his or her back. Rub a thin film of oil over the back, arms and legs. Shape your hands into V's and slide them firmly from the shoulders all the way down the back to the point where the buttocks begin. Bring your hands around to the sides and, pressing firmly, pull hard up to the armpits. Repeat the slide down the back several times, leaning so your weight adds pressure. Then, with your hands in the same V position, use your thumbs to make hard, slow circles in the furrows on either side of the spine as you work your way down the back.

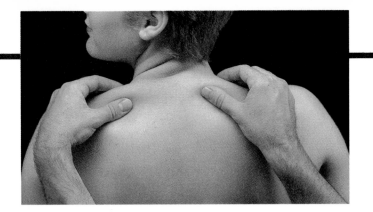

**5** Knead the muscles on top of the shoulders—a high-tension area—between your thumbs and fingers. The pressure should be gentle but firm enough to stimulate the circulation.

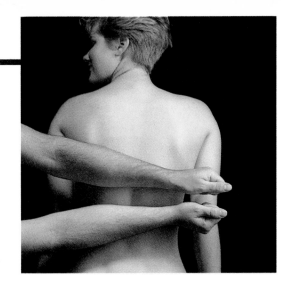

**6** Use your forearms to reach and relax a large area of the back. Pressing hard, slide your arms apart until they reach the top of the back and buttocks. Repeat.

**7** Massage up the legs and arms, first with long strokes. Then work up the muscled areas using your thumbs, slowly and deeply working a feather design as you go.

**8** Hold one of your partner's hands in both of yours and use your thumbs to massage and spread the palm with small, hard circles. Still supporting the hand, grasp each finger in turn and use it to shake the hand lightly. Slide off each finger, pulling as you go.

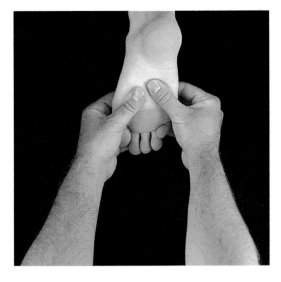

**9** Foot massage can be especially valuable because of the number of nerve endings there. Oriental theory says that pressure here can have a positive impact on all the major organs. Massage the sole of the foot as you did the palm of the hand and give the toes the same treatment you gave the fingers. Finish by holding the ankles gently for a few minutes. Then tell your partner to rest for a while before getting up slowly.

the end of the time you've set for yourself. If the word "one" doesn't feel right to you, choose another that you feel comfortable with.

Ted Smith, D.Min., director of the Central Counseling Service in New York City, encourages many of his clients to incorporate meditation into their daily lives. A pastoral psychotherapist, Dr. Smith suggests another easy and effective meditative technique; sitting comfortably, with your eyes closed, count from one to ten as you breathe, starting with "one" as you breathe in, "two" as you breathe out, and so on until you reach ten; then start over. Try to keep your mind from wandering; concentrate on the count, but if it does wander, don't scold yourself — just keep on. If you lose count because you're thinking of something else, go back to one. Start with a 5- or 10-minute meditation and try to work up to a half hour.

"Our minds are like wild horses," Dr. Smith says. "They want to take command."

Whatever the meditation, sit quietly for a minute or two after you stop.

## SELF-HYPNOSIS FOR STRESS

Betsy was tense. She was about to present a new ad campaign to a potential client. Though she was well prepared, being in the spotlight still made Betsy feel a little nervous. But she knew exactly what to do to overcome that nervousness.

She closed the door to her office. She sat comfortably in her chair. Consciously relaxing her body, she took some deep breaths and counted backward from ten to one while imagining herself walking slowly down, down, down a flight of stairs. Then she let her imagination take her on a walk through a sunny field in Brittany, France, where she had vacationed the previous summer. In her mind she roamed about the sun-dappled fields, picked a daisy, turned her face toward the cloudless sky and told herself that when she returned from this "trip" she'd make a marvelous presentation at the meeting. In a few minutes — the whole thing hadn't taken more than

a quarter of an hour — she was "back" in her office. Soon the meeting began — and a calm, self-assured Betsy did indeed do marvelously.

Betsy used self-hypnosis as her relaxation technique. Not only can it help to keep stressful events from overwhelming you, it also enables you to relieve pain and master phobias, as well as to break self-destructive habits such as smoking.

In order to use self-hypnosis effectively, you first have to believe it's something *you* can do. The second important element is suggestibility, or the power of suggestion. This element requires that you uncritically accept an idea you present to yourself while in the hypnotic trance. The more suggestible you are (or allow yourself to be), the better self-hypnosis will work for you.

According to Dr. Rudolph, your general life attitude is a factor, too, in whether you are a good or less-than-good hypnotic subject. People who feel somewhat defeatist or helpless sometimes sabotage their own efforts. People who feel they can effect changes in their lives, who can set goals and achieve them, tend to do better. It's the motivation they bring to the experience that counts. Estimates vary, but some experts believe that about 80 percent of the population can be hypnotized. In any event, it's the posthypnotic suggestion — which you give yourself while hypnotized, and which can be anything from "keep calm" to "stop smoking" — that's at the heart of the process.

It's best to learn self-hypnosis from a qualified teacher, such as a physician trained in hypnosis or a clinical psychologist or other qualified professional. Your local medical center, medical association or state psychological association should be able to refer you to such a professional. Hypnosis is fairly simple to learn; in fact, lots of people catch on to the basics in an hour or two. When a professional does the teaching, however, he not only shows you how self-hypnosis properly is done, he also puts you into a hypnotic state and gives you the posthypnotic suggestion that you'll be able to put yourself into a trance with a brief formula. Often that involves or includes a short breathing exercise and counting backward from 20 or 10 to 1.

Alternatively, you can learn self-hypnosis through self-help books and cassette tapes.

Dr. Rudolph, who teaches self-hypnosis as well as biofeedback, has a number of suggestions for the person just starting out to master self-hypnosis. First, if you're just beginning, don't expect too much. Don't get into a "How'm I doing?" frame of mind. Self-hypnosis is a passive process in which you're focusing your concentration on a suggestive phrase, therefore rating yourself can create tension, thus thwarting the process. Choose a quiet time and place. As in meditation, a comfortable position is also important. Don't wear clothes that bind. Many people who practice self-hypnosis do some muscle-relaxing exercises as part of the process. The more relaxed you are, the easier it is to put yourself into a hypnotic state.

And the deeper you get into the hypnotic state, the more effective the posthypnotic suggestion is going to be. One common way to go deeper is by using positive imagery. You think of a very pleasant, relaxing scene and imagine yourself right in it, experiencing the sensations you would if it were real. Lots of people who practice self-hypnosis do what Betsy did— they evoke images of a vacation scene they loved. Beach scenes are very often used because the setting lends itself so well to letting go and feeling relaxed.

Picture yourself lying on the white sand of a lovely Caribbean beach, for instance, with the hot sun beating down, the waves lapping gently at the shore, a soft breeze cooling you . . . . Such visualizations are for sale on prepared cassettes. Even better, you can make your own by preparing a little script that describes your personal relaxing scene and then reading that scene, in a calm, relaxed way, into a tape recorder.

# Dial-a-Trance

Three, then one, then two—my finger is rigid with tension as I punch the area code into the phone. In a blur of speed, I dial the rest of the Chicago number—792-1051.

Darn deadlines, driving me crazy. Pressure all the time. This office is Stress City. I clutch the phone between my shoulder and my ear. A muscle in my back begins to twitch. Now they want me to write about Dial-a-Trance, of all the dumb, silly. . .

"Thank you for calling Dial-a-Trance," says a soothing voice. "This is your hypnotist, Larry McManus. If this is your first hypnotic experience, relax. Nothing strange or unusual is going to happen. If you have had prior trance experience, you already know what a wonderful experience is in store for you."

But this is nonsense! I can't be hypnotized by phone!

The rhythmic, reassuring voice of Larry McManus tells me to get comfortable and instructs me to breathe deeply, slowly, evenly and to let my eyes close slowly, gently, naturally. I feel "deeply relaxed and comfortable in every way." I am, in fact, about twice as relaxed as I have ever been before. According to instruction, I feel negative emotions flow out. I feel positive emotions flow in. Nothing bothers me.

"*So* calm. *So* comfortable," he says. Now he makes some suggestions: I'll feel more mature and calm in every way. Yeah. Healthier in every aspect of my life.

He says I will awaken now, feeling "refreshed, relaxed and wonderful in every way!"

Odd, just a few moments ago I felt so tense. Now I feel refreshed, relaxed and wonderful in every way! And I deeply believe I'm getting healthier and more mature in every aspect of my life.

I will call you back, Larry McManus.

If you decide to learn self-hypnosis, be persistent. You'll need practice. The more you practice, the better it will work for you.

## BIOFEEDBACK: LEARNING SELF-CONTROL

Biofeedback is a technique that helps you learn about and gain control of those secret inner workings of your body. Using a machine that gives you instant feedback (hence the name), you can learn to recognize and then duplicate desirable body states, such as having low blood pressure or feeling relaxed. Complete success means weaning yourself off the machine after learning how to control these physical mechanisms.

Because biofeedback training can be a relatively expensive relaxation approach—especially in contrast to those that don't cost a cent—we'll give you both the pros and the cons in detail.

High drama accompanied biofeedback's entry into the world in the early 1960s. Hordes of medical writers and some psychologists pounced: Here, they seemed to say, was a miracle cure, electronics come to alleviate our pain and suffering. Predictably, it couldn't live up to inflated expectations, and in some scientific circles it has been relegated to the status of an expensive toy. As is so often the case, the truth falls somewhere between the extremes. A fair number of people use biofeedback, some in laboratory training sessions, others at home.

No cure-all, biofeedback nevertheless can help some people. Are you often tense and headachy? Through biofeedback you may learn to unstress yourself. Do you grind your teeth, either when you are awake and thinking nervous thoughts or when you're asleep and having nervous dreams? Through biofeedback you may learn to stop this stress-related habit, which can create serious dental and jaw muscle problems. Do you unconsciously clench your jaw muscles when you're feeling tense? Through biofeedback you may learn to abandon this automatic clenching, a bad habit that can bring on headaches and neck pain, and throw your teeth out of alignment.

## ON-LINE RESULTS

Biofeedback has helped people suffering from a variety of disorders. An example is Raynaud's disease, a circulatory disorder in which either emotional stress or exposure to cold constricts the blood vessels in the extremities, causing fingers or toes to turn icy and blue. Some people learn to warm their extremities through biofeedback. And biofeedback has controlled another circulation problem—high blood pressure.

Chandra Patel, M.D., of the London School of Hygiene and Tropical Medicine in England, headed a team of researchers working with a large group of people with high blood pressure. These people were offered a smorgasbord of relaxation techniques—breathing exercises, deep muscle relaxation and meditation, along with biofeedback training. Another group of hypertensives received only counseling and lectures. After two months, the biofeedback training group had a greater fall in blood pressure than the group who didn't get the training. They were also smoking less and their cholesterol levels were lower.

As that British study suggests, you don't just hook yourself up to a machine and start relaxing. What you do is hook up, practice breathing or one of the other techniques, and instantly get a signal that tells you how you are doing. Explains the Multimodal Therapy Institute's Dr. Rudolph, "The machine is not therapy. It's not an end but a means to an end. You get feedback—objective data. The machine also facilitates motivation and learning."

Let's take a look at a typical session of biofeedback. You have a chronic headache (or neck ache, or lower back pain)—muscle tension pain. The specialist takes your stress history, tries to get a sense of when the pain comes and goes, then hooks you up to an electromyograph (EMG). Specifically, he places

# Buying a Biofeedback Machine

If you're in the market for biofeedback equipment, check out the two types considered best for home use.

According to Tim Lowenstein, Ph.D., director of the Conscious Living Foundation, the first type measures small temperature changes in the body while the second reads changes in muscle tension. Your choice should be based on your stress symptoms. "If they include cold hands, migraine headaches or hypertension, then the temperature method is a good choice," Dr. Lowenstein says. "But if you are experiencing tight muscles or clenching your teeth, then a muscle tension machine is better."

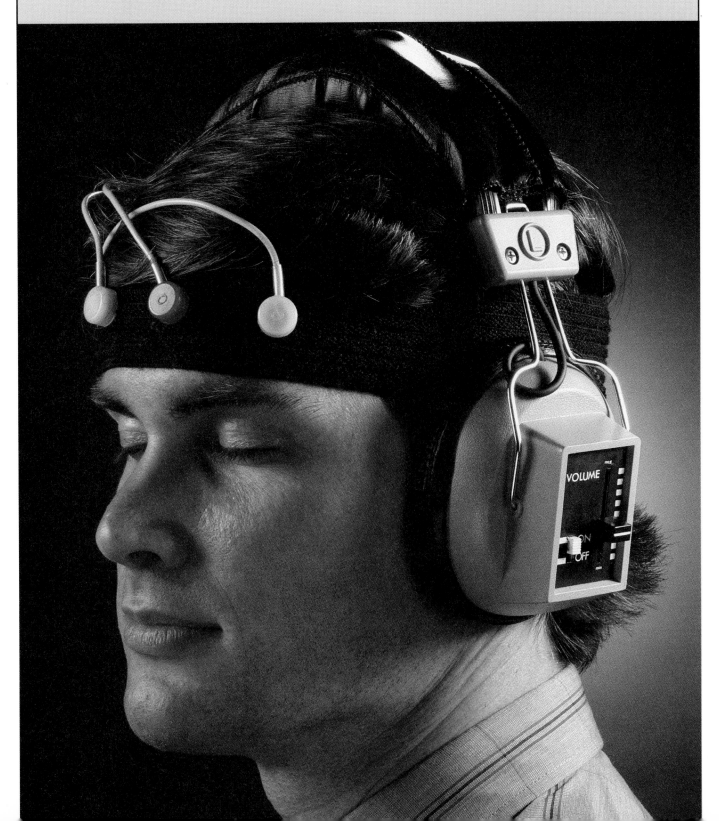

# Ma Bell Meditates

Busy schedules, approaching deadlines, high-pressured competition and even problems outside of the working environment are all causes of stress. But today some of our nation's companies are offering their employees programs in meditation, relaxation and other forms of stress management. Even Ma Bell meditates.

In fact, the New York Telephone Company (NYT) was a pioneer in the field of employee meditation programs. In 1978 Patricia Carrington, Ph.D., and a team of researchers from the department of psychology at Princeton University began a study on stress reduction using 154 NYT employees as guinea pigs. These employees were all self-identified as being under a great deal of stress.

At the onset of the study the employees were divided into four groups. Two learned to practice meditation techniques—Clinically Standardized Meditation and Respiratory One Method Meditation. Both are forms of meditation in which a selected sound is verbally or mentally repeated to achieve a calming effect. The third group was taught Progressive Relaxation, a muscle-relaxing technique. And the fourth served as a "waiting list" control group.

At the end of 6 months the results were amazing. All of the groups showed a marked reduction in stress; even the symptoms of the control group decreased, leading researchers to believe that a placebo effect had occurred. When tested for individual symptoms, the participants were less depressed, anxious, hostile, psychotic, paranoid and compulsive.

The meditating groups showed the most improvement, however. Many of the volunteers in these two groups said that they were able to think, remember and organize their thoughts better. They felt that they had a better handle on life's problems. They were even getting more enjoyment out of life. A more satisfied bunch of guinea pigs would be hard to find.

NYT, pleased with the study, continued the program and expanded it to include 8 of their branch offices. They believe—and it has been proven true—that happy employees lead to a happier and more productive company.

electrodes, held down by tape or an adjustable band, on the skin close to your forehead or the back of your neck. (That's for headache; other spots are used for other kinds of muscle tension.) Wires run from the electrodes to the EMG, where electronic wizardry takes place: The machine converts bioelectrical charges from the muscles into a biofeedback signal you can hear as a sound that varies in pitch, or as a series of clicks that go faster or slower, depending on how stressful you feel or how well you're able to relax. Thus, you immediately become aware of your body's stress reactions and the power you have to diminish or intensify them. You also can readily discover which kind of relaxation technique works best for you.

Another commonly used instrument is the temperature trainer, which reads minute temperature changes in the body, translating them into signals you can hear or see. A sensor slips over a finger, the wires run to the machine. It teaches you to control the temperature of various parts of your body, especially your hands. "It's used for all disorders relating to the heart and circulatory system," Dr. Rudolph says. And for migraine headaches. At least some people who suffer from migraines say they get cold hands prior to the onset of a migraine attack, and there are reports of migraine sufferers being helped by finger-warming biofeedback training.

The process becomes more understandable when you consider that tiny muscles surround your blood vessels. Relaxed muscles allow for a heavier blood flow and, thus, more heat. Constricted muscles reduce the flow, thus reducing heat. By learning to control these muscles— once thought involuntary—we can relax and warm up.

A third instrument you see in use a lot is the Galvanic Skin Response (GSR). Like the lie detector, it measures sweat gland activity through the electrical conductivity of the skin. The more activity, the more stress you're under. Again, you get instant auditory or visual feedback to let you know how you're doing. Like the EMG, the GSR can be used as a general stress monitor, showing you the level of stress you're under and helping you to retrain to lower levels.

These specific biofeedback machines are only some of the variations on this theme. Would one of them help you? It depends.

Biofeedback is not for you, for example, if you're in the small minority whose stress levels aren't picked up by the machines. This technique also is not for you if you start out being strongly skeptical, if you're easily frustrated or if you're going to become so dependent on it that you'll take your stress readings ten times a day. "People who take continuous readings keep resensitizing instead of desensitizing themselves to stress," Dr. Rudolph explains.

You absolutely also need stick-to-itiveness. Many people do a beautiful job of relaxing in the laboratory, but once they're finished with the formal training they put their newfound relaxing skills into the closet, never to look at them again. Or they buy an expensive machine and after a few tries put *it* into that closet, never to look at it again. Persistence is very important.

On the other hand, if you have persistence, enjoy gadgetry and learn well when you get instant feedback, biofeedback training may work for you.

If you decide to try biofeedback, should you go to a professional or buy a home-use machine? The professionals will say that one-to-one training, with extensive laboratory work and home assignments, does the better job. That's probably true, but finances can be a consideration. Working with a professional biofeedback trainer may involve 12 or more sessions, costing as much as $75 a session. A good home-use machine runs about $100. Some biofeedback enthusiasts do both—go to a professional and get their own instrument. Either way, the trick is to learn those relaxation technqiues

that work best for you, and learn them so well that in time they'll be part of your daily life and you'll no longer need a machine, either at home or in somebody's lab.

## USING THESE TECHNIQUES

Piano concertos to puppy dogs, and boogie to biofeedback—the ways to reduce stress in your life are very different, but also very effective. You may want to use some of them—or even all of them—to help you cope.

First, you might begin by scheduling time into your busy day for your antistress activities. Perhaps playing tapes of your favorite music as you commute to work, either in your car or—if you are a passenger and *only* if you are a passenger—directly into your ears. Make appointments ahead for your biofeedback or yoga classes. And remember, too, that just plain old exercise also helps you to release stress. Plan for some vigorous activity such as a brisk walk or a long swim three or more times a week. (Perhaps competitive games should be shelved during periods of tension, since even winning can generate a certain level of stress.)

Along with all this activity, remember also to be *in*active. Set up a time of day, every day—perhaps right before dinner—when you unplug the phone, close the bedroom door, turn off the light and sit, meditating quietly.

In addition to these techniques, it is important to remember that you have control over the stress in your life. You can work at destressing yourself the same way you can work at losing weight, building muscle or even weeding the garden. The secret rests in taking action. Inaction leads to becoming the victim of stressful circumstances. Applying common sense and stress-coping techniques leads to a winning attitude and a brighter life.

# Hotlines for Help

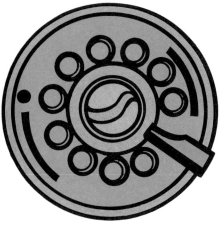

**W**here did you turn the last time you had a problem—a problem so serious or so personal that you chose not to discuss it with a friend, a relative or your family doctor? Maybe you reached out for your telephone—and a counselor manning the hotline at the other end.

If so, you made a wise move. Hotlines are available for almost every problem. They are found all across the country and some are open around the clock to help you in a time of crisis. And studies have shown these hotlines to be highly effective. In fact, one study reported that more than 90 percent of those who called a hotline were satisfied.

Much of this success can be attributed to those standing by

## Abused and Battered Adults

**Abused Women's Aid in Crisis**
9 A.M.-5 P.M., weekdays
New York City: 212-577-7777

**Battered Women Hotline**
24 hours, 7 days
Cleveland, Ohio: 216-961-4422

## Abused and Battered Children

**Child Abuse Prevention Effort (CAPE)**
24 hours, 7 days
Pennsylvania only: 800-932-0313

**Child Abuse**
Florida only: 800-342-9152

**Child Abuse**
New York City only: 800-342-3720

**Child Abuse Careline**
Connecticut only: 800-842-2288

**Family Crisis Center**
24 hours, 7 days
Denver, Colo.: 303-893-6111

**Child Abuse Hotline**
24 hours, 7 days
Missouri only: 800-392-3738

**Massachusetts Society for the Prevention of Cruelty to Children (M.S.P.C.C.)**
9:00 A.M.-4:45 P.M., weekdays (no holidays)
Boston, Mass.: 617-227-2280

**National Child Abuse Center**
Denver Colo.: 303-231-3963

**Parents Anonymous**
24 hours (daytime preferred), 7 days
Nationwide: 800-421-0353
California only: 800-352-0386

## Age-Related Problems

**Elderly Hotline**
8 A.M.-5 P.M., weekdays
Boston, Mass.: 617-722-4646

**Senior Citizens of Greater Dallas**
8 A.M.-5 P.M., weekdays
Dallas, Tex.: 214-823-5700

**Seniors' Resource Center**
8 A.M.-5 P.M., weekdays (no holidays)
Wheat Ridge, Colo.: 303-238-8151

## Agoraphobia

**The Agoraphobia and Anxiety Center of Temple University**
9 A.M.-5 P.M., weekdays
Bala Cynwyd, Pa.: 215-667-6490

**TERRAP**
Menlo Park, Calif.: 415-327-1312;
415-329-1233

## Alcoholism

**Al-Anon**
(Help for the families and friends of alcoholics.)
8 A.M.-5 P.M., weekdays
Worldwide: 212-683-1771
Southern New Jersey only:
609-428-0083

**Alcohol 24-Hour Help Line**
7 days
Eastern and Midwestern states:
800-252-6465
West of the Rockies:
800-ALCOHOL

**Alcoholics Anonymous**
(Offers information about AA chapters nationwide.)
9 A.M.-5 P.M., weekdays
New York City: 212-686-1100

## Breastfeeding

**La Leche League International, Inc.**
7 A.M.-3 P.M., weekdays
Franklin Park, Ill.: 312-455-7730

## Cancer

**American Cancer Society Information Service**
Nationwide: 800-638-6694

## Counseling

**CONTACT Teleministries**
24 hours, 7 days
Harrisburg, Pa.: 717-232-3501

**Women in Transition**
24 hours, 7 days
Philadelphia, Pa.: 215-563-9556

## Crime Victims and Witnesses

**Victim Hotline**
24 hours, 7 days
Manhattan, N.Y.: 212-577-7777
Brooklyn, N.Y.: 212-834-7400

## Crisis Intervention

**Crisis Center**
24 hours, 7 days
Detroit, Mich.: 313-224-7000

**Crisis Clinic**
24 hours, 7 days
Seattle, Wash.: 206-447-3222

**Crisis Line**
24 hours, 7 days
Miami, Fla.: 305-358-4357

**Rape Crisis Intervention Network**
8 A.M.-2 A.M., weekdays
Philadelphia, Pa.: 215-922-3434

the phones. While some counselors are professionals, others are simply caring people who have been trained to deal effectively with the problems they encounter.

Yet the hotlines are not without their problems. Because many callers remain anonymous, they cannot be reached for follow-up counseling.

Despite these difficulties, hotlines offer several real advantages. Many are free. All offer the opportunity to remain anonymous. And, perhaps most important, they bring the comforting realization that there is always someone available to lend an ear, just when you need it most.

## Drug Abuse

**Phoenix House**
24 hours, 7 days
New York City: 212-787-7900
California: 714-953-9373

## Drug Side Effects

**Office of Consumer and Professional Affairs**
8:00 A.M.-4:30 P.M., weekdays
Rockville, Md.: 301-443-1016

## Eating Disorders

**National Association of Anorexia Nervosa and Associated Disorders, Inc.**
9 A.M.-5 P.M., weekdays
Highland Park, Ill.: 312-831-3438

**American Anorexia Nervosa Association, Inc.**
Teaneck, N.J.: 201-836-1800

**Overeaters Anonymous**
Worldwide: 215-320-7941
Newtown Square, Pa.:
215-356-4099

## Gambling Abuse

**Debtors Anonymous**
New York City: 212-868-3330

**Gamblers Anonymous**
9 A.M.-5 P.M., weekdays
Los Angeles, Calif.: 213-386-8789

## Left-Handedness

**Left Is! Ltd.**
Hinsdale, Ill.: 312-789-3425

## Marital Problems

**Divorce-Anonymous**
9 A.M.-5 P.M., 6 days
Chicago, Ill.: 312-341-9843

## Poison Emergencies

**Poison Control Center**
(Gives emergency advice across the country, but check for the regional center nearest you.)
24 hours, 7 days
Seattle, Wash.: 206-526-2121

## Pregnancy

**Birthright**
9:30 A.M.-12:30 P.M.,
Monday-Friday;
7:00 P.M.-9:00 P.M.,
Monday-Thursday
Woodbury, N.J.: 609-848-1818

**National Pregnancy Hotline**
24 hours, 7 days
Nationwide: 800-238-4269
California only: 800-344-7211

## Rape

*(See also Crisis Intervention)*

**Rape Help Line**
(Listed in most cities as Rape Crisis Center.)
24 hours, 7 days
New York City: 212-777-4000

## Runaways

**National Runaway Switchboard**
24 hours, 7 days
Nationwide: 800-621-4000

**Runaway Hotline**
24 hours, 7 days
Nationwide: 800-231-6946

## Single Parents

**Parents without Partners**
9 A.M.-5 P.M., weekdays
Washington, D.C.: 301-654-8850

## Smoking

**Action on Smoking and Health (ASH)**
8 A.M.-5 P.M., weekdays
Washington, D.C.: 202-659-4310

**Office on Smoking and Health**
8:00 A.M.-4:30 P.M., weekdays
Rockville, Md.: 301-443-1575

## Suicide

**Suicide and Crisis Intervention Center**
24 hours, 7 days
Philadelphia, Pa.: 215-686-4420

**Suicide Prevention League**
(Will refer to help sources throughout the country.)
24 hours, 7 days
New York City: 212-664-0505

**The Samaritans**
24 hours, 7 days
Boston, Mass.: 617-247-0220

## Surgery

**National Second Surgical Opinion Program Hotline**
8 A.M.-12 P.M., 7 days
Nationwide: 800-638-6833
Maryland only: 800-492-6603

## Unwanted Pregnancy

**National Abortion Information Hotline**
9:30 A.M.-5:30 P.M., weekdays
Nationwide: 800-772-9100

## Venereal Disease

**National VD Hotline**
Nationwide: 800-227-8922

**Operation Venus**
9 A.M.-9 P.M., weekdays
Pennsylvania only: 800-462-4966

**6**

# Working through Negative Emotions

Our all-too-human failings can be turned around and used to our advantage.

Too many of us play both judge and jury to our emotions. Hauled before our mind's bench, some of them are judged to be errant muggers of our peace and tranquillity. Emotions such as shyness, anger, guilt, anxiety—all are held in contempt, then condemned as perpetrators of unhappiness and failure. These feelings deserve review by an internal court of appeals because, in actuality, they can be useful in our lives.

Take shyness, for example. Obviously no one wants to go through life tongue-tied and with a constant impulse to shrink from other people. That's shyness at its extreme; at that point it interferes with emotional health and daily functioning. But a little shyness can be a charming facet of personality, if we look at it that way. Observes Philip G. Zimbardo, Ph.D., a psychologist who runs a successful antishyness clinic at Stanford University, "Shyness makes one appear discreet . . . increases one's personal privacy . . . they [shy people] will never be considered obnoxious, overaggressive or pretentious."

There are positive aspects to all our feelings. Even envy, which has been called the meanest of emotions, can have its virtues in moderation.

These very human feelings usually become a problem when they become too intense or extreme. It's possible we aren't even aware of the intensity of the feeling; it may come out in disguised form. Anger does that a lot. These traits also cause us trouble when they are inappropriate to the situation we're in. (For example, feeling guilty about something you were

# Inheriting Shyness

If you hate walking into a party, it may be because your father dreaded public speaking. Scientists now think that a tendency to be shy can be inherited, says Stephen J. Suomi, Ph.D., National Institutes of Health researcher and the discoverer of genetic shyness in monkeys.

Monkeys with this trait are slow in exploring new environments and in leaving their mothers. Humans who have it show wariness and watchfulness. Both species have elevated heart rates and increased blood sugar levels in new situations.

Knowing that a tendency to be shy in new situations can be inherited should inspire people to be more accepting of this trait in themselves, says Dr. Suomi.

"High reacting" may actually be a favorable trait, thinks Dr. Suomi, if those who have it can be trained to use their extra energy.

"It's like a public speaker who uses his nervousness to get up for a performance. It's a matter of learning how to get up—without getting too up," he says.

And some of us might not want to change our shyness, says Harvard psychologist Jerome Kagan, Ph.D., who studies human inherited shyness. "Certain people cherish their solitude," he says. "They can get a lot done."

not *really* responsible for.)

It's important for us to know how to handle these feelings in a way that's healthiest for us. And most of us can turn potentially troublesome feelings around so they'll work *for* us.

## SHYNESS THAT SHACKLES

Do you find it fairly easy to talk to strangers? To make your entrance at a party when you know hardly anyone? To give a talk or make a presentation to a group of people? To be comfortable with members of the opposite sex? To involve yourself in new situations?

There's probably at least one no—maybe even a big, resounding NO—in your responses to these questions. We're all at least a little bit shy, depending on the circumstance, the situation. Says Gerald Phillips, Ph.D., a professor of speech communication at Pennsylvania State University and the author of *Help for Shy People,* "I know of no studies that show people existing who are *never* shy. All of us face situations where we can't cope or can't cope easily."

## THE OFFICIAL WALLFLOWER

Whether shyness matters depends on the person and the situation. "Shyness is of no consequence at all if it relates to something you don't have to do and don't want to do," Dr. Phillips says. He personally confesses to being "the official wallflower" on the rare occasions when he goes to country clubs, which he hates, but it doesn't bother him.

Many people feel shy in a variety of situations to the point where they consider it a real problem. Dr. Zimbardo conducted a large-scale study of shyness that included 6,000 people in eight countries. Eighty percent said they were—or had been—shy; most of these persons said their shyness bothered them greatly in their daily lives. Shyness can make it hard to form relationships. In your work life, no matter how good you are, if you can't communicate effectively it's apt to hamper you. Shyness causes anger, anxiety, depression.

In recognition of such facts, antishyness clinics and programs have sprung up all over the country. Dr. Zimbardo, for example, runs one at Stanford; Dr. Phillips conducts another at Penn State. They demonstrate that shyness can be shed, that very bashful people can go on to lead richer, happier lives.

Shy people sometimes have a tendency to feel, "There's something wrong with me." Not so, Dr. Phillips stresses. He finds that most shy people are no more psychologically distressed than anybody else. Actually, they're often especially bright. Their grade point averages at Penn State, for instance, are significantly higher than those of the rest of the student body. But they tend to take courses that don't require them to work in groups or give recitations, and to look forward to jobs that won't demand much contact with people.

Some experts say shyness is inherited (see "Inheriting Shyness"); other experts say they can find no evidence of that. But where shyness comes from is less important than how to get rid of it. Basically, what shy people lack is self-esteem and certain social skills. Overcoming shyness therefore is a two-pronged approach—building self-esteem and learning those skills. Here are ways to accomplish this.

**Don't Be Negative about Yourself.** Shy people tend to be very hard on themselves. They put themselves down, they predict failure at whatever they attempt—"prophets of failure," Dr. Phillips calls them. Joe Molnar, a psychotherapist who has given antishyness workshops at the New York University School of Continuing Education, says shy people often don't realize how often they do this. Listen to yourself talk. Consciously tell yourself to STOP each time you utter one of those self-critical remarks.

**Emphasize Your Strengths.** If shy people accent their faults or weaknesses, it's self-evident that they're prone to minimizing their strengths. Reverse the process. Try

this exercise: On one side of a sheet of paper write down your weaknesses, as you see them. On the other side, write down your strengths—those relating to your personality, your intellect, your physical self. "I show warmth," "I'm bright," "I'm well coordinated," might be three examples. Don't leave anything out. If you have much more trouble thinking of your strengths than your weaknesses, consult a friend or two. They're apt to see you more objectively and tell you your good points, those you can't tell yourself.

**Value "Small Talk."** Typically, shy people have trouble initiating and/or carrying on conversations. Many shrug this off with the excuse that small talk is unimportant—that most conversations just aren't worthwhile. But small talk is essential, Dr. Phillips stresses. It begins the process of conversation and provides the information that will guide it into more serious channels.

**Have Something to Say.** Some shy people feel they have nothing (or at least nothing important) to say. One way to overcome the problem, whether it is real or imagined, is to make yourself as interesting as possible. Read a lot and think about what you read so you can form opinions and develop interests and hobbies. Become as broadly informed as you can.

**Observe Role Models.** Role models are people who are successful in the way *you'd* like to be. Therefore, watching how they operate can teach you something. They're a resource. In the context of shyness, whatever social situation you're in, watch, listen to and study those lucky people who don't seem to have any trouble initiating or keeping up conversations.

**Use Professional Resources.** The best way to overcome shyness is in a systematic program specifically geared to shy people. Such a program needn't be expensive. Check with local colleges to see if any run a low-cost antishyness workshop or clinic.

## A MOTIVATING FACTOR

When shy people see someone who's outgoing, someone who's obviously at ease with others, they're apt to feel envy. This emotion is no stranger to any of us, whether or not we're shy. There's hardly a person alive who doesn't feel envious of someone, at least occasionally, for one reason or another.

Upon realizing they are envious of a friend or neighbor, most people tend to feel a little ashamed. They needn't. According to John Grace, a counselor at the Family and Children's Service of Minneapolis, by simply being ashamed they may be missing out on a good thing—namely, using that envy to clarify and further their life's ambitions.

"You can turn envy into a positive force in your life," Grace says, "by using it as a tool to define your own goals and aspirations. And if you decide you really want whatever it is you're envious about, you can use envy as a way of motivating yourself to get it."

Take a man who sees his neighbor driving a sleek, spanking-new sports car that talks about the condition of its motor and has all the other gadgets automakers dream up. Oh, how he envies his neighbor. How he wishes he had a car like that! Does he really, *really* want to own a car like that? If so, can he afford it? If not, is he willing to work longer hours, or get a second job, or give up some other things, in order to get it? If he's being honest with himself and the answer is no, his envy will disappear. If the answer is yes, he can begin to figure out concretely what he must do to get that car.

Envy that's chronic or intense is something else again. By its very nature it's corrosive; it has negative rather than positive effects on us.

## DANGER SIGNALS

Because this kind of destructive envy can sneak up on us without our realizing it, it's helpful to know what the danger signals are. According to Grace, these are often tip-offs:

- Being critical of or snidely gossipy about the person we envy.
- Being unaccountably angry—or dissatisfied—in general.
- Downplaying our accomplishments. "Some people are constantly picking up evidence that says, 'Other people have more than I do,'" Grace explains.
- Feeling "bad" or worthless for not having the things we want.

One other clue: People prone to chronic envy often tend to be perfectionists. "They may rate themselves as B or even B+, but they can never give themselves a perfect A," Grace says. "It's always the other person who gets the A. And it's that grade-A person whom they envy."

Envy of the person who gets the A is one of those difficult emotions we can obviously do without, especially when it starts to interfere with our relationships and our general well-being. What can we do about it? Psychotherapist Grace has some suggestions for people who tend to have a little trouble with envy.

**Be Clear What It Is You're Envious About.** Take an audit of your feelings. Are you discovering that envy is a more powerful element in your life than you had thought? Just making that discovery might well lead you to another— that what you envy isn't all that important.

Grace tells of a client who was terribly envious of wealthy people. Pretending to have money, he socialized with them to the extent he could. But he was constantly fearful of being found out. When he thoroughly analyzed his values, however, he discovered that material wealth wasn't really his top priority. What he found was not so much a desire to be "well connected" as a desire to just *be* connected in any way at all. He also discovered that being respected was more important than being "wealthy."

**Learn from the Person You Envy.** That person presumably has something—a personal quality, a material object—that you want. In a sense, "study" that person. Try to get to know him, or something about him. Maybe you can learn from him ways of getting the same thing that wouldn't have occurred to you on your own.

Another of Grace's clients, a woman in a therapy group, was snidely envious of another group member, a woman successful in her vocation. Says Grace, "Eventually we got the envious person to see that she was simply confused and unsure about how to reach her own career goals, and then she was able to ask the other woman for advice."

**Be Especially Good to Yourself.** To feel envious is to feel deprived. To feel deprived is to say, in effect, "I need something given to me." Doing something nice for yourself can help defuse envy. "When I realize I'm feeling envy, I try to figure out how to be kind to myself," Grace says.

---

### SEEING RED

---

Anger is a slippery emotion. It can disguise itself as shyness, envy, guilt, anxiety or frustration. Or it can be a straightforward response to a specific situation. It is a very difficult emotion for many people to acknowledge. Expressing it constructively is even more difficult.

Basically, there's nothing complicated about the effective handling of anger. As midwestern psychotherapist Nicky Bredeson puts it, "We know what we're angry about, who we're angry with, and then directly express our anger to that person."

Except, of course, handling anger is not that simple. Typically, we're taught—by our parents, schools, churches and society at large—that anger isn't "nice." We are, as youngsters, discouraged from expressing it. The result: Lots and lots of people are afraid of their anger. They fear (whether or not they realize it) going out of control. Or they fear that direct anger will bring them retaliation or rejection. "Anger," Bredeson affirms, "is a very powerful emotion."

But it's a fact of human life that we all experience the full range of angry feelings, from mild annoy-

# The Difference between Envy and Jealousy

Envy and jealousy are both reactions to a fear of loss, says psychologist Lee Gibson, Ph.D., of La Canada, California.

With envy, you fear the loss of status because someone has something you don't have. Jealousy, on the other hand, involves fear of losing the attention or affection of another person, usually by being dumped for someone else.

Envy can also awaken you to awareness of a want you didn't know you had, suggests another counselor. One way to cope is to figure out what you would have to do to get the thing you envy. Then you can decide if you're willing to work toward it.

Both emotions are linked to anger. And jealousy particularly reflects low self-esteem, say psychologists. "A person who has been rejected but who also has high self-esteem is more likely to say, 'Well, all other areas of my life are going pretty well, so if that's what you want to do, I'll just continue with the rest of my life,'" says Dr. Gibson.

It also may be helpful to remember, say therapists, that envy and jealousy are reactions *you* create. Another person doesn't "make" you envious or jealous—you "make" yourself feel that way.

ance to stomach-churning fury. And, whether we like it or not, anger is going to come out in one way or another.

## COUNT THE WAYS

John M. Curtis, Ph.D., of Pepperdine University in Los Angeles, made a study of the main ways people express anger when they don't express it directly. All four have serious drawbacks, but Dr. Curtis lists them from most destructive to least destructive.

**Evasion.** You automatically suppress or deny the fact that you're angry.

You don't even give yourself a chance to think about it. Of course, the emotion is still inside, festering. Denied expression, it finally shows up in headaches, ulcers or other psychosomatic illnesses, in sexual difficulties or in serious depression. Many experts feel that emotional depression is, in effect, unexpressed anger turned inward.

**Containment.** You do recognize your anger but deliberately choose not to do anything about it. Should this technique become a habit, it has a pressure-cooker effect. Charles is an example. Because he wants to be "nice," he tries hard not to show

---

# The Positive Side of Anger

"Think of anger as a form of energy," says Nancy Shiffrin, a counselor and author of *Anger: How to Use It.*

Anger provides the impetus for change—whether it's a major social movement like voting rights for women or just standing up to your mate.

First, anger signals that something needs attention—an injustice, for instance. Then it prepares the body for action by releasing adrenaline and other chemicals. But it prepares it *too* well for civilized life, says Ms. Shiffrin.

"You can't go beat up every tyrant you meet, though that's what your body may want to do," she says. Instead, try doing the "rational, assertive thing," which resolves the emotional side of anger.

Anger can also help you get close to others if you express it well. Distance won't grow between you if you give the other person the correct information.

" 'You dirty, rotten scum' is the wrong information," says Ms. Shiffrin. " 'I feel angry because you didn't return my book. I feel like you don't respect me when you do that,' is the right information."

anger. But the emotional pressure builds up inside him until eventually he explodes with a temper tantrum—often over a trifle.

**Displacement.** You're mad at your boss—but you take it out on your wife or child because it's not prudent to direct it at your boss. It's a way of getting rid of anger—but a destructive one. Taking it out on the wrong person generates guilt in the angry person and resentment in the one who's been unfairly targeted.

**Indirect Expression.** You're angry with someone but you don't confront the person directly with the cause of your anger. Instead, consciously or unconsciously, you show your anger in a roundabout way. Gary, for example, is angry with his wife for the way she overspends, but since he finds it difficult to talk about money he picks fights with her about the way she and her mother chat for hours on the phone.

## LETTING IT OUT

Aside from the other problems they create, all these evasive ways of dealing with anger have a major, basic flaw. The person at whom the anger should have been directed doesn't know of the other's anger. The angry person never comes to grips with the issues that created the anger in the first place. In his book, *The Language of Feelings,* David Viscott, M.D., says, "Expressing anger over the hurt that causes it allows an emotional wound to close." When we don't express anger directly, that wound never closes.

Since the direct expression of anger is so difficult for many people, here are some tips on the best ways to handle it.

- Admit to your angry feelings. As Dr. Viscott says, "The direct *appropriate* expression of anger . . . is a necessary part of a healthy emotional life." Reread Dr. Curtis's list of evasive tactics and see if you recognize your own way of dealing with anger. It's important to change circuitous expression to direct

## Hire a Crier

A man spent 3 long hours waiting to see his doctor, but he didn't complain. B. L. Ochman did it for him.

A woman was upset that her husband fell asleep in front of the TV every night. She didn't know what to do. B. L. Ochman got results.

And a group of roommates was angry that one of them would not do her share of the dishes. B. L. Ochman rode to the rescue once again.

B. L. Ochman is the president and Chief Kvetch (complainer) of Renta Kvetch, a New York City-based organization. Since its beginning in 1981, she has complained on behalf of hundreds of people who didn't have the nerve to do it themselves. She says her success rate is 95 percent.

Renta Kvetch delivers its complaints in letters costing $35 each. They take a light-hearted approach to the problems because Ms. Ochman believes that "you don't have to be nasty to get results."

Unlike many of us who don't like to complain, Ms. Ochman is proud of her work. "People don't realize that it's emotionally healthy to complain," she says. "If people complain they feel better. And by hiring me they also feel as if someone else cares about their problem."

expression because: (1) it eases your tension; (2) it helps resolve problems; and (3) it can, after the air is cleared, bring you closer to the person with whom you're angry.

- Get the anger out quickly rather than letting it fester. But

if you're so mad you think you'll fly into a rage or explode, that's not helpful. In that case, count to ten or take a few deep breaths— definitely bide your time. You want your anger to be productive, to express your feelings, not to be a weapon of revenge or intimidation.

- Sometimes a loud voice is appropriate, yet you can also convey anger—and the reasons behind it—calmly. But smiling or laughing when you talk gives a mixed message, and your anger won't be taken seriously.

- Know your audience. In some situations—a confrontation with an employer, for instance— anger as such may be self-defeating. Approach the boss rationally about the problem— after you give vent to your anger by telling a friend what you *really* think.

- Once you've expressed your anger, let go of it. Holding a grudge isn't fair to anyone, least of all yourself. It simply perpetuates the anger. Get it out, forget it, go on to more loving experiences.

## FEELING GUILTY

No matter how constructively you have expressed your grievances, you nevertheless may feel a little guilty about putting down a fellow human. And surely that's only natural. People who have absolutely no guilt are our society's psychopaths and sociopaths. They think only of themselves and their needs and will stop at virtually nothing to get those needs fulfilled. Therefore, explains Oscar Rabinowitz, executive director of the Whitehill Counseling Service in Hartsdale, New York, "Guilt is a civilizing emotion." It develops our consciences.

The threat of a guilty conscience may keep us from committing antisocial acts; the acute discomfort of a guilty conscience prompts us to make amends when we feel we've injured another person. We also can feel guilt for wronging ourselves— for not living up to our ideals. For

example, people who cheat on a strict weight-loss diet, or have a couple of drinks when they're supposed to have none, often say how guilty they feel afterward.

How best to handle guilt? "The healthy response is to deal with it as quickly and efficiently as possible," psychotherapist John Grace answers. That means: (1) analyzing the situation that triggered the guilt; (2) deciding whether those guilty feelings are really appropriate; and (3) if they are, taking responsibility for our actions by apologizing to a person we've wronged, say, or resolving to change if we've failed ourselves somehow.

Most of us know, though, that guilt isn't always handled or discharged so smoothly. As Rabinowitz says, "Guilt can be a healthy response to a situation or an awful psychological trip. Neurotic or unhealthy guilt can be very self-destructive. It's important to know one from the other."

These are the main patterns that indicate unhealthy guilt or shame:

- Almost always feeling at least vaguely guilty, even when there's nothing to feel guilty about.

- Feeling guilty out of all proportion to the event. "I tell a white lie," said one woman to her therapist, "and I practically can't sleep all night."

- Readily allowing other people to make you feel guilty without even examining the situation to see if you've been at fault.

- Personalizing your guilt. As Grace points out, it's one thing to say, "I made a mistake," and quite another to say—as do some people imbued with unhealthy guilt or shame— "I *am* a mistake."

- Feeling guilty about being happy, or about something good that's happened.

- Automatically turning guilt into anger or even rage. Anger and guilt are closely related, Rabinowitz says, because it's very common for someone who feels guilty, but doesn't want to admit it, to express that guilt with anger. Referring to his troubled college-age son, a father says, "He's nastiest to his mother and me when he's feeling guilty about having done something wrong."

Aside from making life very uncomfortable, unhealthy guilt has an unfortunate "can't-do-anything-about-it" quality. You're defeated before you start because there's that load of guilt, weighing you down. "I'm a bad person" doesn't allow for hope or action. "I did something wrong" is promising: "I can make amends, I can learn from my mistake, I can change."

Nobody needs to be stuck in a pattern of corrosive, unhealthy guilt. The experts offer the following suggestions for breaking out of that pattern and using guilt in a healthy, constructive way.

- Take a close look at what it is you're feeling guilty about. If it's simply a vague feeling, or you can't identify the cause, you're probably still carrying around some childhood guilt that never was resolved. In any event, if you can't find the reason, what's there to feel guilty about?

- The moment you call yourself shaming names or make blanket accusations against yourself —for instance, "I'm stupid"; "I'm unlovable"; "I'm bad" —stop. And, Grace advises, immediately change what you've said to something kinder: "I'm angry"; "I'm frightened"; "I'm confused"; "I, along with everybody else, am imperfect."

- To feel guilty about good things happening is to say, "I don't deserve them." But you *do* deserve them.

- Confession really is good for the soul. If you've done something of which you're ashamed, talk about it with someone you trust.

- Be compassionate to yourself. If you've done something you regret, make amends if possible. Try to learn from the event. And then forgive yourself.

## Avoiding the Guilt Trap

The key to sidestepping a guilt trap is to put on your thinking cap, says psychologist Salvatore V. Didato, Ph.D., author of *Psychotechniques*.

Guilt is tricky because it's subjective, says Dr. Didato. Sometimes it's okay for one person to make another feel guilty, as when a parent teaches a child. But some people use guilt skillfully and subtly to manipulate others.

"What you should do is ask yourself, 'Is what the other person is saying logical? Does it have merit? Is it motivated by something more than pure self-interest?'" says Dr. Didato.

For instance, if someone says to you, "I'll worry until you get home," ask yourself if the person really *will* worry. Then ask if there is justification for the concern.

If you believe the person really will worry but that you're doing the right thing, you can offer reassurances. But if you decide the other person is trying to use guilt manipulatively, just refuse to play the game. Display no guilt. If you display guilt, it gives the other person power. He or she wins—at your expense.

## HIGH ANXIETY

You know it because you feel it. Your palms dampen. Your stomach turns queasy. You're a little shaky. And the feeling that comes over you is awful—a feeling of dread, impending doom, disaster, or, at the very least, considerable apprehension.

That's anxiety.

Anxiety is a form of fear. The same physiological mechanisms are triggered—the racing heart, the adrenaline boost, the preparations for fighting or fleeing.

Fortunately, moderate anxiety can serve us well. For instance, it's a great spur for procrastinators and for people who have a tendency to put off difficult situations. Notes Atashi Acharya, director of treatment at the Family and Children's Service in Minneapolis, "If they weren't a little anxious about it, a lot of people wouldn't file their income tax forms on time." And a moderate amount of anxiety puts us in a state of readiness to deal with

# Performance Anxiety

Your stomach is in a knot and your knees are wobbly. You're not sure you can speak without sounding like Donald Duck. Slowly, inexorably, the curtains part and there you stand—alone, unprotected, totally exposed—before row upon row of people whose eyes are focused on you and you alone.

Old-timers called it stage fright. Today the phenomenon is known by a more sophisticated term—performance anxiety. And this anxiety occurs not only when you find yourself standing before a crowd, but also when you are in relative solitude. The symptoms can develop when your employer meets with you privately to conduct your annual job evaluation, and you ask for a raise. Or it can develop in very intimate circumstances—when you're trying hard to impress someone new.

According to Ray DiGiuseppe, Ph.D., of the Institute for Rational-Emotive Therapy in New York City, performance anxiety is a good thing. It sharpens the mind and can make you more alert. It's a matter of degree, he says. "At zero level of anxiety, there's no concern, no arousal and you don't do things very well. [In other words, there's no performance.] With moderate anxiety, you function much better. With extreme levels of anxiety, you don't function well."

How do you conquer performance anxiety? According to experts in public speaking, you must prepare thoroughly for your performance. Know your information inside and out.

Next, visualize the audience as a friendly group who wants you to succeed—because that is exactly what they are. Imagine the applause you will receive at the end of your performance. Feel positive. Relax.

potential emergencies.

Moderate anxieties are situational, external. We know their source. There's another kind of anxiety that's common enough, too, but much more disconcerting. This is the kind of anxiety that comes over us without an apparent reason. Life's going along reasonably well, you're grappling with garden-variety problems but nothing special, when all of a sudden that feeling of apprehension, dread or doom comes over you. This "free-floating" kind of anxiety can be like a dull ache that lasts for a few days, it can be chronic, or it can be an acute, abrupt panic reaction that seems overwhelming when it hits. Mercifully, it most often vanishes as quickly as it comes. Phobias—irrational fears about certain objects or situations—are also an exaggerated form of anxiety.

Where do such monster jitters come from? Since anxiety attacks often run in families, a genetic or biochemical factor may be at work in some cases. Physical causes—for example, hypoglycemia—can bring them on. So can withdrawal from caffeine and other drugs. Some psychiatrists believe unresolved internal conflicts are the cause. Ms. Acharya feels that anxiety often results from the fear of not living up to our own expectations. "We each have an 'ideal' self—how we'd like to be—and an 'actual' self—how we really are," she explains. "The greater the discrepancy between the two, the more anxiety gets triggered."

One facet of her own ideal self-image, she admits, is to be super-organized and competent. When she sees a lot of work ahead of her and doesn't think she'll get it done in the prescribed time, she becomes quite anxious.

Whatever the underlying reasons, a great many people have anxiety attacks, some of them serious. According to the National Institute of Mental Health, as many as 13.1 million Americans may suffer from anxiety disorders, and anxiety is the fifth most common reason people visit their family doctors.

## EASING OFF

How do we best deal with our anxieties? First, differentiate between ordinary anxiety that comes and goes and an incapacitating kind. Most of us feel anxious on occasion, with or without an obvious cause. While it's uncomfortable, our passing anxiety doesn't cause us any obvious harm. But if the anxiety becomes chronic; if it interferes with ordinary functioning; if it results in crippling fears; or if it becomes a steady drain on energy and fosters an inability to carry through with plans, it may be wise to see a doctor.

Most of us, however, can help ourselves in specific ways. Try these effective self-help approaches:

- Accept anxiety as a fact of life. In other words, don't be so anxious about your anxiety. "If I start getting anxious in the evening, I know the worst that will happen is that I might take a little longer to go to sleep," says Ms. Acharya. "And in the morning I'll be too busy getting ready for work to be anxious."

- If you've been feeling more anxious than usual, you might use the occasion as an opportunity for self-discovery. Maybe there's something bothering you that you haven't brought to light or a problem you've been avoiding.

- Exercise can help chase away those anxious feelings. Experiments at the University of Wisconsin showed that anxiety decreased in both normal and neurotic people following periods of exercise. Some people find that meditation and prayer also help relieve anxiety.

- Talk to friends about what it is that's making you anxious—or just about the fact that you *are* anxious. "Ventilating" this or any other feeling helps to reduce its intensity.

- Deep breathing helps a lot to reduce anxiety. If you feel anxiety coming on, draw a deep breath, hold it for a moment, then let it out slowly. Repeat the process several times.

The variety of negative emotions all of us experience from time to time should not rob us of our emotional well-being. Viewed dispassionately, they really are not all that bad. And, as we have learned from various mental-health experts, they often can be put to good use. Shyness becomes charm that engenders protectiveness in others. Envy becomes a motivator. Anger becomes a rage for justice and equality. Guilt becomes insight and forgiveness. Anxiety becomes a heightened awareness of surroundings and—eventually—a sense of being in control.

Not so negative at all, these human feelings.

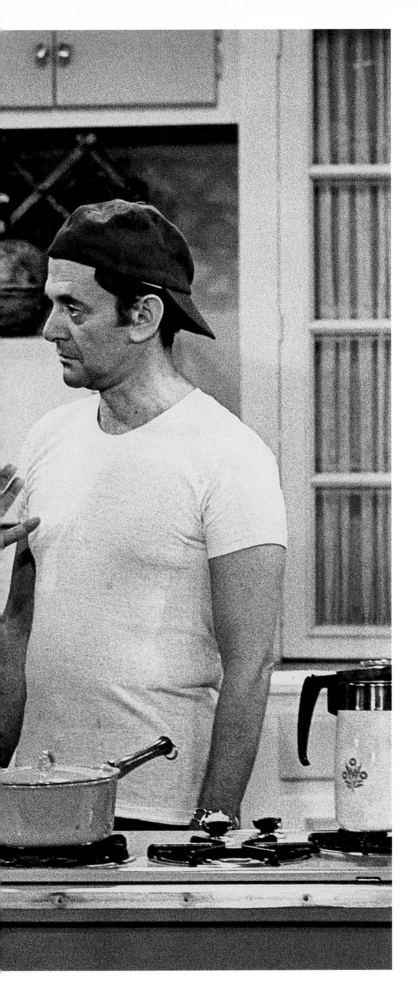

# Adjusting the Way You Think

It's possible to overcome mental "habits" that limit your capacity for happiness.

Bob was in high dudgeon. He'd jotted down the phone number of an important sales prospect, and now he couldn't find it. He specifically remembered writing it in red ballpoint on the back of a telephone message slip. He remembered leaving it on his desk the night he worked late last week—Wednesday. And now it had disappeared into thin air. Alison probably threw it out when she filed and straightened up.

"Alison, I can't find Fetter's phone number. Have you seen it?"

"Uh, I don't know. Where was it?"

"On the back of a while-you-were-out note. In red. On my desk."

"Well, there are lots of phone messages on your desk every day. Don't you throw them out when you return the calls?"

"Not this one, Alison. It was too important. You probably threw it out."

Challenged, Alison might have told Bob that she can't be responsible for every scrap of paper; that if the number were so important he should have taken better care of it. Instead, she began to scurry about the office, searching his desk, combing the files and scrounging in the wastepaper basket, trying to find it. If she succeeded, she'd get grudging thanks. If she failed, she'd carry the blame of losing that phone number till the day she retired.

Alison searched to no avail, and stoically accepted the blame. This incident was not unique, but one of a series of confrontations—at work and at home—in which Alison accepted the role of victim. She had, in fact, a mind-set—a way of responding to others—that often led her to become the patsy, the pushover, the victim.

Mind-sets are nothing more than long-held attitudes or internalized "programs." They can be positive and helpful, or they can be difficult—and make life difficult. Fortunately, once recognized, they also can be handled.

Difficult mind-sets come in a variety of guises, but all have a similar, limiting effect.

Fear of failure, for example, is a mind-set that keeps us from confidently trying new ventures. Why learn racquetball—we'd just be the court klutz. Why apply for a better job when we can't possibly get it. Fear of success is the flip side of this mind-set, keeping us from confidently trying to do our best. Should we blunder into success, we'd feel unworthy. Other mind-sets include a crippling need to be liked, or a compulsive need to be in control of people or situations, making us watchdogs over others and preventing us from enjoying life's spontaneous side.

You may find that none of these mind-sets causes you difficulties. If one or more do, however, you may want to take advantage of the various techniques provided by experts for effectively overcoming them. Important as these techniques are, though, what makes them effective is the determination of the person who uses them. The more determined you are that they will work, the better your chances of that happening.

## THE VICTIM SYNDROME

Ellen's friend Margaret borrows money without paying it back, cancels dates with her abruptly, and often asks her to babysit at the last minute. Ellen rarely says no, even though she agrees that Margaret "can get to be a bit much."

Therapist Oscar Rabinowitz calls people like Ellen "psychological victims—people who allow themselves to be used by others." Rabinowitz says we're especially vulnerable to being victimized when we're feeling blue, or are under a lot of pressure, or are ill.

There's a difference, though, between being an easy mark occa-

sionally and allowing yourself to be mistreated or exploited frequently. When being a chump becomes a behavioral pattern, it has consequences that can't be shrugged off. For instance, take somebody who's unfairly passed over for a raise or a promotion while another, less deserving employee gets it. If he says nothing about it, and doesn't even try to find out why it happened, he's therefore likely to be skipped over again.

New York City-based psychotherapist Claire Leighton says that victims often deny being victims. They make excuses for the people who victimize them. However, adopting a nice-guy attitude is just a way of not admitting you're being victimized.

## STAND UP FOR YOURSELF

Perpetual pushovers often feel helpless, sometimes as strongly as if they were born that way. But, stresses Janet Wolfe, Ph.D., of the Institute for Rational-Emotive Therapy in New York City, "We are definitely *not* innately helpless or fragile. Some of us just *see* ourselves that way. It's a matter of not functioning as well as we can."

To see yourself as not functioning so well is a message that implies several choices: "I can choose to remain a victim"; "I can take steps to stop being a victim." For people who want to change, the experts suggest the following:

**Shuck Off Destructive Labels.** As children some of us were called stupid or clumsy, or something similarly unfortunate, by parents, friends, teachers, whoever. The labels have stuck all these years. But now is the time to say, "That's what *other* people think. I don't have to think that, too."

**Check Out the Costs and Rewards of Being a Victim.** Remaining in a bad job or keeping up a relationship with an exploitative friend because you don't want to face the consequences of leaving? "Not leaving avoids short-term pain but maintains long-term pain," Dr. Wolfe

# Be Assertive

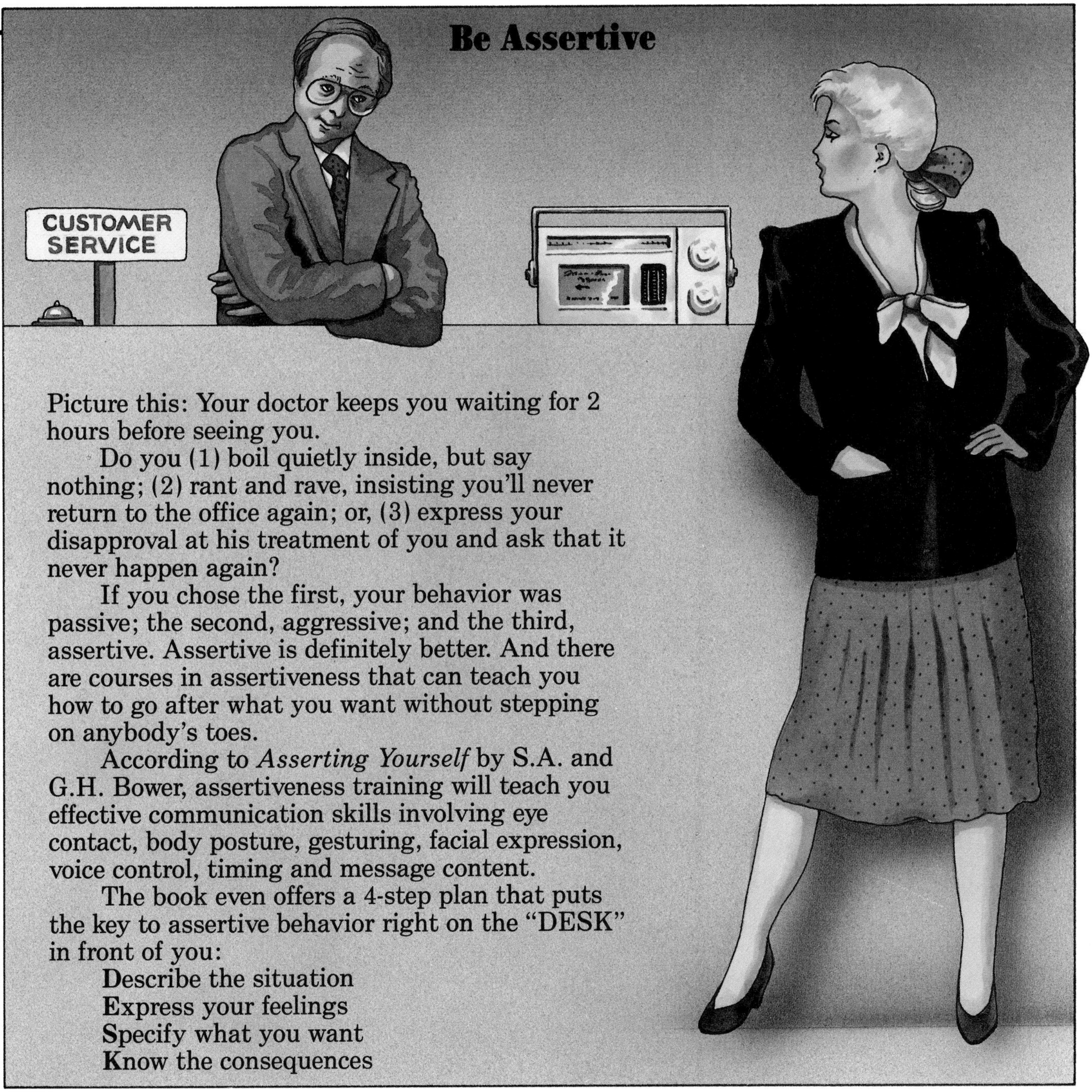

Picture this: Your doctor keeps you waiting for 2 hours before seeing you.

Do you (1) boil quietly inside, but say nothing; (2) rant and rave, insisting you'll never return to the office again; or, (3) express your disapproval at his treatment of you and ask that it never happen again?

If you chose the first, your behavior was passive; the second, aggressive; and the third, assertive. Assertive is definitely better. And there are courses in assertiveness that can teach you how to go after what you want without stepping on anybody's toes.

According to *Asserting Yourself* by S.A. and G.H. Bower, assertiveness training will teach you effective communication skills involving eye contact, body posture, gesturing, facial expression, voice control, timing and message content.

The book even offers a 4-step plan that puts the key to assertive behavior right on the "DESK" in front of you:

**D**escribe the situation
**E**xpress your feelings
**S**pecify what you want
**K**now the consequences

---

points out. Reluctant to speak up for yourself? Yes, you avoid the risk of anger or rejection, but it's costly, too, in terms of loss of self-confidence and self-respect.

**Learn to Acknowledge Your Strengths and Capacities.** Try this exercise. Write three headings on a sheet of paper: one for relationships, the second for work, the third for hobbies and other interests. List all of your strengths and skills in each of these areas. Don't leave anything out. A store manager with a shaky self-image became much more pleased with herself when she came up with 58 items, among them warmth, helpfulness, enthusiasm and good organizational skills. Psychological observations repeatedly show that the more we recognize our strengths, the less we see ourselves as helpless.

**Banish "I Can't" from Your Vocabulary.** Don't say "I can't make up my mind"; "I can't complain to the boss," etc., etc. There's very little we truly can't do. Most of the time we're really saying, "I'm afraid to," or, "I don't want to take the chance." From now on, consider "I can't" to really mean "I'm not ready." Then work up a plan so that finally you'll say "I can."

## TOO DEPENDENT ON OTHERS

Dependency is a loaded word. It implies infancy. Even though we adults have come a long way from our helpless infant days, we're still not totally independent. Studies have shown that we all have what the psychologists call "dependency needs"—which include everything from needing love to occasionally needing a friendly, sympathetic shoulder to cry on. As Susan Hartman, a psychotherapist at the Family and Children's Service of Minneapolis says, "We can't fulfill all our needs by ourselves."

But there's healthy dependency and excessive dependency. The distinctions are very great and extremely important to our happiness, our relationships, our emotional health. Healthy dependency works like companion planting. American Indians always sowed the seeds of beans and corn together. As the plants grew, the tall cornstalk provided support for the beans. The leaves of the bean plant, in turn, shaded the ground, keeping down weeds and conserving the soil's moisture for the plants' roots. While the plants were dependent on each other, they were also strong individually.

"Excessive dependency," explains Ms. Hartman, "means wanting to be taken care of—not every once in a while, which is common to all of us, but as a way of life. People who are too dependent don't believe they have enough strength of their own, enough personal power. They tend to believe that somebody else will 'give' them happiness instead of taking responsibility for providing their own happiness."

Relying on others inevitably leads to disappointment, frustration and unhappiness. Moreover, it's a psychological rule of thumb that

# Declare Your Interdependence

Following the "Me Decade" is the "We Decade," a trend toward considering some of the 4 billion people on earth with whom we must interact to survive.

The switch from *in*dependence to *inter*dependence requires learning to understand and respect the needs of others. In return, your own needs will be better respected and understood.

While "doing your own thing" might have had its benefits, California psychologist Stephen Johnson, Ph.D., says that interdependence is the key to determining who we really are. He explains that total dependence fails because it sacrifices self-esteem and total independence fails because it sacrifices communication.

Interdependence also may be the key to developing deeper, truer relationships with others.

excessive dependency breeds resentment: The dependent one resents having to lean all the time and the other person eventually resents being leaned on so much. And, not the least of it, being too dependent just doesn't feel good. As an exclient of Ms. Hartman's, a woman who overcame her excessive dependency on her husband and children, put it, "It's like there's a big hole in a little you—and you keep waiting for people to fill it up."

## TAKE COURAGE

It's not easy to break the bonds of excessive dependency and learn to rely on your own capabilities. It takes strength and courage.

In his book *Compassion and Self-Hate*, psychiatrist Theodore Isaac Rubin, M.D., points out that many seemingly dependent people actually haven't allowed themselves to see their real strength and competence. Step one to independence, then, is to find the areas of your life where you exercise your capacity for independence. Credit yourself fully.

Two, take a hint from Wall Street. Don't keep all your eggs in one basket; don't look to one person or setting to be your everything. Diversify. Let many different sources nourish you.

Three, break the habits common to more dependent people—such as deferring to others in decision-making, frequently asking for reassurance, saying yes when you mean no.

Your dependency on others may have kept you from realizing talents or ambitions now buried deep. Think about yourself in a new way, as a person apart. "It's important to diversify our activities, too," Ms. Hartman stresses. "Think of yourself as a many-sided jewel and start satisfying all those sides."

## BURIED TREASURE

Many people remain hidden treasures, buried in a protective cave that keeps them from sparkling in the spotlight of attention. These people are afraid to shine because they are

## Building Your Self-Confidence

From Denise Lyons, who teaches a course in confidence building, come 10 ways to build confidence.
- Set a realistic goal and fulfill it.
- Think positive thoughts about yourself.
- Spend time with people supportive of you.
- Take a reasonable risk.
- Do something just for yourself.
- Spend peaceful time alone.
- Accomplish something you've been avoiding.
- Maintain yourself physically through good nutrition, regular exercise and sleep.
- Make a list of 10 personal strengths. Don't be humble. If it helps, imagine you are reporting objectively on someone else.
- Complete the phrase "I feel best about myself when _____." Give a few different responses. Then try to regularly include these situations in your life.

afraid to fail. In fact, in our competitive society, fear of failure is relatively common. As career counselor Daralee Schulman of New York City points out, fear of failure dampens our initiative, makes us afraid to take risks, lowers our self-esteem and keeps us from learning from our mistakes.

Respect the adage, "Nothing ventured, nothing gained." Say you want to learn to sail. If you think,

"I'll never get the hang of it," and don't make the effort to try, of course you'll never learn to sail. You'll never know what a wonderful sailor you might have been.

To get over a fear of failure, Ms. Schulman suggests, begin by becoming *process oriented* instead of *goal oriented*. For instance, the process of learning to sail is fun, even if you don't become a wonderful sailor. Also, before attempting something, always have a contingency plan just in case the attempt doesn't succeed. And don't do a con job on yourself about having to be perfect. Some people think, "Being second-best at something makes me second-best as a person." That's a totally unwarranted leap.

Sometimes failure has serious consequences, but often we exaggerate the effects. Take a tip from the Phillies' relief pitcher Tug McGraw. When he really fails to strike 'em out, when the game is over and lost, he wonders if, when the world has turned into a giant snowball, this loss will still seem important. In other words, put failure in perspective.

Learn from your mistakes. Don't agonize over them—analyze them. The more you learn, the better your chances for a successful outcome next time.

## AFRAID TO SUCCEED

Achievement studies reveal that some people fear success rather than failure. Such people show their fear by holding back on their talents, by not calling attention to themselves, by pretending to be less bright than they are, by sabotaging themselves when they approach success or by dismissing the importance of their actual successes. "But my brother is the *real* artist in the family," a man developing into a fine painter of seascapes kept telling friends.

What's behind this fear of success? It could be fear of the consequences—success might cost them friends or (in the case of married women) might upset their husbands. The cause could be insecurity about their worthiness—"I don't merit success, I'm really a fraud." Such factors are largely unconscious, of course, but they do

keep people from either reaching their goals or enjoying their achievements.

What happens to people who keep on thwarting their own successes? They eventually become angry, discouraged, and, ironically, in time begin to feel like failures.

Emotionally and practically we're served best, Ms. Schulman says, "by doing the best we can and, whatever we've accomplished 'earning to enjoy the satisfaction we have earned."

Remember, good guys come in first, too!

## NEED FOR APPROVAL

We all want to be liked, appreciated, sought after and admired. While wanting to be liked is normal, a problem arises when we make social approval *too* important.

"Too much emphasis doesn't really mean *wanting* to be liked, it means *needing* to be liked," family educator Ted Bowman of the Family and Children's Service in Minneapolis points out. "And, from the point of view of mental health, there's an enormous difference between the two. Wanting to be liked, I can still be myself. Needing to, I have to be something else—what I think other people want me to be. Who I am becomes tied to how other people respond to me."

We don't really relax and have fun if our intent is always to make a good impression, Bowman says, because we become too busy and too careful watching our words. We're too busy trying to please, like the person who never says what's actually on his mind about politics or anything else for fear of offending someone. Ironically, this "tactfulness" can backfire and cause disapproval from others who expect more genuineness.

For people who tend to need approval overmuch, Bowman has this advice:

**Don't Demand Too Much of Yourself.** None of us is so flexible or adaptable as to be liked by everyone; it's no more realistic than expecting ourselves to like everyone else.

**Focus on Activities, Not on Yourself.**
When at a party, a class, in the office
or other setting, concentrate on the
people and the goings-on, rather
than on how others react to you.
You'll have a better time—and,
being spontaneous, a much better
chance of being liked for your true
self.

**Be Your Own Best Friend.** If you
truly like and accept yourself, others
will, too. And chances are that
there's a great deal about you to
like, because if you concern yourself
so much with other people you're
likely to possess vast funds of
friendliness, helpfulness and concern for them.

## TOTALLY INTO CONTROL

Asked whether you want to be in
charge of your life and your
environment, you'd probably say
yes. Asked if that control was
emotionally sound, you'd probably
say yes again. And, of course, you'd
be right—up to a point.

Being out of control—impulsive,
undisciplined, indecisive, direction-
less—is hardly a shining example of
mental health. Yet wanting and
trying to be totally in control can
become a real problem for us and for
those around us.

"We wouldn't feel comfortable in
our daily lives if we didn't feel in
charge of our lives to some degree,"
says Mardene Eichhorn, a
Minneapolis-based psychotherapist
in private practice. "But part of
being truly healthy is also having
flexibility—having enough trust to
give up control to some degree.
Marriage—and most other relationships, too—really work well only
when each person can let the other
be in charge to some extent."

People with a tendency to
control are often natural leaders.
They are—or have a potential for
being—very well organized and
hardworking. But this energy can
become excessive. For example, a
controlling husband might never
agree to a joint checking account. A
controlling wife might "supervise"
her husband's weekend work around
the house. A controlling person

## Through a Woman's Eyes

Have you ever wondered why men believe they
have a right to feel good about competitive
success, while women often feel bad about besting
someone? And why men tend to steer clear of
emotionally self-sacrificing actions, while women
seem to thrive on them?

The answer is a simple one: Because men and
women have psychological differences, they have
different outlooks on life.

Harvard University associate professor of
education Carol Gilligan, Ph.D., explains in her
book, *In a Different Voice,* that these differences
develop during childhood and adolescence, when
girls strive to be like their mothers—caring and
giving—while boys strive to differ from their
mothers by separating themselves from caring
relationships.

What results is that women develop different
values and different measures of success. Because
society often reflects a strictly male point of
view, caring, self-sacrificing women are sometimes
seen as second-rate nonachievers. Dr. Gilligan's
work takes a woman's stand to prove that being
*different* does not necessarily mean being
deficient.

might make a date with a friend and
independently plan what they should
do rather than discussing it together.
"They can have a hard time listening
to and entertaining other people's
opinions," Ms. Eichhorn says.

However, having to be in control
is ultimately counterproductive—
and illusory. People resent always
being told what to do or think or in
other ways being dominated. A
controlling father may find that his
children will have little to do with
him once they're on their own. An
entrepreneur may do a brilliant job
of starting a company—and see it
fail when he can't delegate
responsibility. Besides, with so
many unknowns in life, with so
many surprises around the corner, at
best we can be only nominally in
charge of our environment.

## BREAKING LOOSE

To break the control habit, Ms.
Eichhorn suggests the following:

# Make Friends . . . With Yourself

How do I love me? Let me count the ways.

Many people don't realize how important loving or liking yourself really is. But, in fact, some authorities feel that you must like yourself before you can learn to like others. According to clinical psychologist Robert Mendelson, Ed.D., "liking yourself gives you the emotional strengths you need to be able to give to others."

Dr. Mendelson adds that there is a great difference between liking yourself and being stuck on yourself. "Liking yourself means feeling good about the things you can do for yourself and for others; it doesn't mean having a sense of false pride."

Learning to like yourself more isn't a difficult process. One technique, says Dr. Mendelson, is to "begin by adding a positive statement to every negative statement that you utter. Soon you'll be able to see the positive in the world."

And once you feel more friendly toward the world, you'll not only be a better friend to yourself, you'll be a better friend to others.

**Change Control to Trust.** "I trust myself to handle life's surprises"; "I trust you to take care of yourself," and so forth.

**Practice Simple Behavior Changes.** For example, ask your friend what movies he or she would like to see.

**Really *Listen* to People.** Listen to their ideas, to their expressed needs and desires, to their attitudes. You don't have to feel compelled to agree, but do consider what they have to say.

**Develop a Faith in Something outside Yourself.** Faith in religion, a philosophy, a higher power will help loosen up the need to be too much in control of the world around you.

## ACCENTUATE THE POSITIVE

Do you see the glass as half full or half empty? An honest answer may be as revealing as a whole battery of psychological tests. If the glass is half full—if you think positively—you're likely to be spirited, energetic, gutsy, determined, self-assured. If the glass is half empty—if you think negatively—you probably lack the determination and confidence that characterize the optimist.

"People who think negatively tend to limit their options," says Bowman. "If they've unsuccessfully tried plan A, they feel stuck, don't see any other directions to go. And so much energy goes into their negativity, there's little left for positive action."

In other words, think defeat, be defeated—it becomes a self-fulfilling prophecy.

How do you switch from negative to positive mind-set? Begin by making a commitment to consciously resist negativity, says Bowman.

Never say disparaging things about yourself, either to yourself or to others.

Never assume that other people possess so much more in the way of attributes than you do. Everybody has strengths, flaws, fears, heartaches.

Never dwell on problems and failures when you're with friends. The more negatively you talk, the more power you give to your negativity. As Bowman says, "Connect with others around hope rather than despair."

## MONEY MATTERS

Money is more than dollars and cents; it's power, influence, a measuring stick of our importance. It can add to our happiness, make us miserable or drive us a little nuts. And the way we handle money may reveal a lot about our inner workings.

This facet explains why novelists often use money attitudes as a way of depicting character. In Henrik Ibsen's play *The Doll's House,* Torvald wields the upper hand over his wife, Nora, by making her flirt and dance in order to receive the weekly household stipend. This display of dominance—fueled by money—allows Torvald to feel like a real man. Macho money.

Money can be a substitute for love, self-esteem, or emotional security. But putting cash where your heart should be can lead to problems. For instance, a person whose sense of self-worth comes from his bank account frequently has a hard time sharing or spending it; often he can't even treat himself to a vacation and enjoy it. The emotionally healthy way of using money is being able to spend, save and share it reasonably, and not use it as a substitute for personal warmth and caring.

Observes Mary Lou Magnuson, a counselor who has worked with many clients on money-related emotional problems, "It's important that you feel you have a choice about how you handle money, not that any one way becomes a compulsion."

Examine your money attitudes. Do they work well for you and those around you? If not, maybe it's time to overcome your money mind-set. For example, if you're an extreme saver, try this experiment: Make a list of things you'd like to have and buy just one thing on that list. See how it feels. If you're an extreme spender, make a similar list but buy only one item (and make that an inexpensive one!) Master your spending habits, instead of having them master you.

# Let Go

Do you have to call all the shots—not only in your life but in the lives of those around you? In business, at home, at play, do you assume all authority? Do you find it difficult to relax and unwind even during your free time? Must you direct your children's every move and "supervise" your spouse?

If the answer to these questions is yes, you show the signs of being an overly controlling person. And your behavior could be hindering your family's growth, your managerial abilities and your own emotional stability.

According to one psychologist, the easiest way to release control is to imagine yourself letting go, and then put these fantasized scenarios into practice.

For example, Dom I. Nate, an overly controlling person, usually reigns supreme when he and his wife go out for dinner. He calls for reservations. He picks the wine. He chooses the meal for himself and his wife. He pays the bill and leaves the tip. But tonight, after rehearsing the evening over and over in his head, Dom will give control of the evening to his wife. She chose the restaurant and phoned for reservations; she will select the wine and maybe even pay the bill.

A simple exercise like this one can lead you into a freer, easier world.

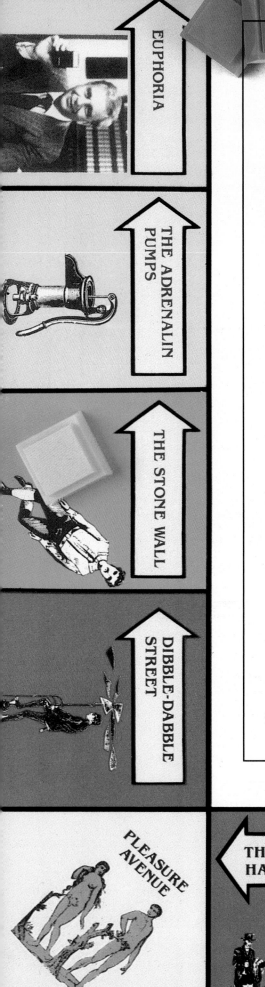

EUPHORIA

THE ADRENALIN PUMPS

THE STONE WALL

DIBBLE-DABBLE STREET

# Victor Kiam Defines the Entrepreneurial Personality

"An entrepreneur is an individualist who has ideas that he believes in and wants to implement, who's willing to try, who won't be afraid of the risks and who is willing to ride with the punches. It's somebody who is ready to overcome *any* roadblock and strive for success. Business is a roller coaster. You've got to have a pretty strong stomach to accept the problems and hard knocks that occur.

"I think anybody can be an entrepreneur. That is, if he or she is willing to devote the time, the energy and the interest that are necessary. You see, there are a lot of things in life that can give you pleasure. But no matter how alluring, you've still got to throw yourself into your business fully. Otherwise—don't do it. Don't dibble and don't dabble.

"If I personally have a weakness of which I'm aware, it's the fact that I won't give anything up. And sometimes it's wrong, because you might be able to better spend your time doing something else; you end up beating your head against a stone wall. But I just don't like to lose.

"Being a true entrepreneur is a question of approach. For example, I think of my business as a game—a game with no time-outs. You play to win. You play fair. You play by the rules. The money you make is just the scorekeeper. When you're working at business, you devote yourself fully to it, just like you would to a game. You don't fool around. You spend all of your time in constructive endeavors.

"And when you win, you get a euphoric feeling. For example, my son and I just won the Eastern Clay Court Father and Son Tennis Championships. We've been competing for 12 years. I was on such a high. I thought, 'My gosh, we worked at it, we kept at it, and I'm an old man now and we finally did it.' I was really ecstatic, it was like adrenaline was pumping in the system.

"If you go into an account, or a store, and set up a program . . . and you convince other people that your program is right for them . . . and the whole thing gels . . . well, you get this feeling of accomplishment; and the adrenaline pumps there, too.

"When I started out in the business world, I had to earn a living. So, I said, 'Gee, it looks like I'm going to spend more of my waking hours working than doing anything else. And if that's what I'm going to do, then by gosh, I'm going to do it as well as I can . . . and win the game.'"

*Victor Kiam II*
*Chief Executive, Remington Products, Inc.*
*(He liked the shaver so much, he bought the company.)*

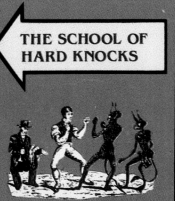

PLEASURE AVENUE

THE SCHOOL OF HARD KNOCKS

RIDE THE ROLLER COASTER

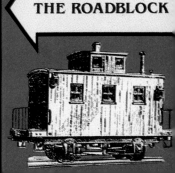

THE ROADBLOCK

# Can Money Buy Happiness?

In a way, it can. Sure, we all know money can furnish you with Caddies and condos, and maybe those things make you feel pretty good.

More important, money can buy a certain kind of security. For example, it can get you the best in health care, or a college education, or a fascinating hobby. And those things, too, can make you feel pretty swell.

But, fact is, you don't *need* money to be happy. What you need is your health, a loving family, some close friends and the *desire* to be happy.

Certainly life is more pleasant if you are not living in fear of a car repair bill. But *happy* is when you wake up to a sunny morning, heart bursting with fullness to start the day. And money doesn't buy *that!*

RULES

THE KEY TO FREEDOM

THE BEST HEALTH CARE

HIGHER EDUCATION

POWER

PLEASURE AVENUE

HAPPINESS

A CONDO

A CADILLAC

For Love or Money

**8**

# Climbing out of Depression

**Everybody gets the blues now and then. Here's the experts' advice on how to dump the slump quickly.**

You feel draggy, listless, tired—or, at the other extreme, a little frantic. You sleep fitfully and wake up in the early morning hours. You eat too much or too little. You probably find it hard to concentrate, make decisions, remember things. Your sexual drive may wane. There may also be some physical distress—headaches, backaches, stomach disorders. And, most of all, you feel sad—maybe so sad it hurts a little.

You're emotionally depressed.

And you're not alone.

The National Institute of Mental Health (NIMH) notes that over a lifetime some 25 percent of us will suffer at least one serious depression; as for the mild ones, most of us are familiar with them. Observes psychologist Lesley Hazleton, author of a *The Right to Feel Bad*, "That basic feeling of emptiness, exhaustion and meaninglessness is universal, crossing all borders of age, sex and nationality."

There's a lot about depression that's controversial among the experts. Its biological and psychological origins still aren't clearly understood. Some researchers believe serious or chronic depressions result from a malfunctioning of the neurotransmitters, the brain chemicals that send signals from one cell to another. Studies show that the tendency to depression may be inherited. A depression could, however, be due to a glandular problem or result from food allergies or nutritional deficiencies.

How to treat depression, especially if it's serious and prolonged, is also a matter of disagreement. Drugs, shock treatment and psychotherapeutic approaches all have their champions. Since serious depressions sap their victims' energy, spoil their days, disrupt their nights, seem without end and may even bring on suicidal thoughts, people with such symptoms shouldn't hesitate to seek professional help. Here we'll deal with the depressions most of us know, the mild and fairly fleeting ones. You'll learn the many possible reasons we feel blue and the many constructive things we can do to lift our spirits again.

## DEFINING DEPRESSION

Some people say it feels like being shut inside a black box. Others say it's like carrying a heavy stone, or having to fight lump-in-the-throat tearfulness all the time. However you might experience it, depression certainly doesn't feel good. Abraham Lincoln, who suffered many bouts of depression, once wrote, "If what I feel were equally distributed to the whole human race, there would not be one cheerful face on earth."

Lincoln didn't anticipate modern psychologists; some see mild depression as serving positive functions. According to Ms. Hazleton, ordinary depressions—mild depressions—often play significant roles in our lives. When emotional in origin, they can help us understand ourselves better. They can play a healing role in times of pain. They can bring us to greater appreciation of the happy, vibrant phases of our lives.

Though many depressions have an emotional basis, not all do. When a gloomy frame of mind seems to come from nowhere and hangs on like a low-grade fever, the cause may be physical. Possible physical causes include:

**Hormonal Problems.** Stephen Langer, M.D., a holistic physician practicing in Berkeley, California, says that when patients tell him they're depressed he routinely checks their thyroid and adrenal functions. "Low thyroid function, especially," he says, "is one of the great undiagnosed causes of depression."

**Hypoglycemia.** Otherwise known as low blood sugar, it can bring on mood changes such as depression and irritability. Detected by a glucose tolerance test, hypoglycemia is usually controlled by a diet that eliminates refined carbohydrates like sugar and emphasizes lean meats, low-fat dairy products and high-fiber foods like whole grains and beans— all of which help keep blood sugar balanced.

**Vitamin Deficiencies.** Studies at McGill University in Montreal have suggested a link between a marginal deficiency of certain B vitamins and emotional depression. Marginal vitamin deficiencies (where you're getting enough of the vitamin to keep going, but not enough to feel your

# Color Me Happy

Want to think more highly of yourself? Wear a red scarf or tie. Red raises self-esteem, say psychologists who've conducted thousands of dollars' worth of research on the impact colors have on feelings and actions. Here are other clues to using colors to change moods.

Bright reds, oranges and yellows invigorate. They measurably lift body temperature and stimulate circulation.

Hot pinks, reds, oranges and yellows also turn on your tummy, say experts. In a red room, food looks tastier and conversation sparkles. Combined with other bright colors, red alters time

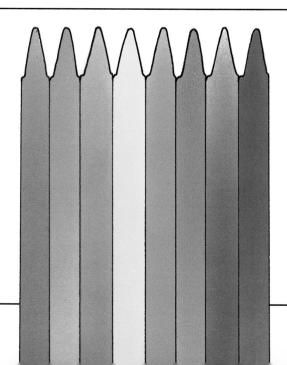

best) are fairly common, Dr. Langer says, because of poor diet or stress. Foods rich in the B's are whole grains, eggs, fish and green vegetables. Many nutritionally oriented doctors suggest taking a B complex supplement daily if you feel your diet is inadequate in these crucial nutrients.

**Drugs.** Taking a medication? Feeling depressed? Your medicine might be the culprit. Drugs containing reserpine (used for high blood pressure), the benzodiazepine family of tranquilizers (like Valium), and some sleeping pills are examples of drugs that can bring on depression as a side effect. If your problem *is* caused by your medication, your doctor may be able to switch you to a comparable one that won't have you singing the blues.

The emotional causes of a depression are less easy to narrow down. There are loads of possibilities, yet what depresses one person may simply sadden (or barely touch) another. While we often have a very good idea why we're depressed, sometimes the reasons are as elusive as the solution to a clever mystery. Consider the following factors.

## LOSS AND DEPRESSION

If you think "depression," also think, "What's been lost?" Very often that's what depression is all about—a loss in our lives. But, cautions Manhattan psychoanalyst Stephanie Goldenthal, Ph.D., don't automatically equate grief or mourning with depression.

"Though many people think so, these emotions are not the same," Dr. Goldenthal explains. "You can grieve over a serious loss in your life without getting depressed over it. Grief leads to depression when it's accompanied by a feeling of helplessness and lowered self-esteem."

In other words, to feel mournful when a close friend moves away, or that hoped-for job doesn't come through, or we lose someone dear through death is one thing. Painful but not depressive. It becomes depression when we go further and attack ourselves: "Not getting the job means I'm no good." Or, "I won't be able to cope." Or, "I'll never be happy again."

Also watch out for losses that don't seem at all obvious, because they create a kind of "mystery" depression. For example, the aging process is sometimes overlooked as a cause of the blues. Some people have a hard time coming to terms with wrinkles, eyeglasses and "middle-age spread." Mourning their lost youth, they mark the passing of the years with at least mild bouts of depression. There are other people, of course, who see life as an ongoing adventure, who keep their gaze on the road ahead and rarely look back.

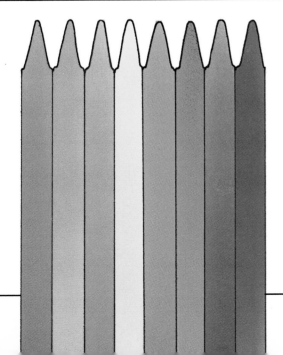

perception. Fast food restaurants take advantage of this phenomenon to get you to eat and leave quickly.

Red turns the brain on, too, provoking new thoughts. But to develop, nurture and apply your new ideas, you'll want a green or blue environment, say psychologists. Blue and green will also calm down your appetite if you're trying to lose weight.

Green's a good color for year-round clothing. Except for the always-cool pale mint, green looks warm in winter, cool in summer. That's because it's a "living" color, say experts.

## SAD MEMORIES

Another kind of depression is called an anniversary reaction, and is caused by an event in the past.

Psychotherapist Susan B. Shor of New York City gives a typical example. Ms. Shor's client—let's call her Wendy—was feeling very low. She couldn't understand why; nothing unusual was going on in her life and she was in good health. What could be wrong? Noting that the month was May, Ms. Shor asked Wendy, "Did anything important ever happen to you in May?"

Wendy looked at her in astonishment. "Of course," she exclaimed, "my mother died in May. But that was five years ago!" As it turned out, she'd mourned her mother's death the year it happened, but during the past four years had avoided painful thoughts of her mother's death. Yet her grief wouldn't stay buried; each May it surfaced.

This "anniversary reaction" is just what its name implies—a depression that occurs on or around the anniversary of a traumatic event. It's as if a psychic beeper goes off, reminding people of the event they might consciously wish to forget. "When they realize what's happening, they say, 'No wonder I'm feeling terrible!'" Ms. Shor says. "Everything becomes evocative of that month—even the smells seem the same." Anniversary reactions tend to be most powerful when people avoid acknowledging or dealing with their feelings of grief, as was the case with Wendy. Otherwise they're usually mild.

Thus it seems that our minds won't let us get away with a thing. We make believe we don't feel bad about a loss in our lives but our feelings surface anyway, in the form of an anniversary depression.

## HAPPY-DAY BLUES

Even if it feels bad, at least there's some kind of internal logic to a depression brought on by sad events. Far more disconcerting, to some people, is the depression that comes on after something *good* has happened. Yet there's nothing mysterious about it. Usually, despite the happy nature of the occasion, a loss is also involved. For instance, while moving to a better neighborhood *is* a positive step, it also means saying goodbye to dear old neighbors and leaving familiar surroundings.

You'd think that people who strive and strive for success, then actually achieve it, would be happy. Well, success can also bring on a psychic slump because here, too, something has been lost—the challenge and purpose that gave them their drive. To emerge from the slump, Ms. Hazleton says, such people need to redefine their goals. In other words, they need to create new challenges for themselves.

## HABITS THAT MAKE US BLUE

Can the way we habitually think about things lead to feelings of depression? Definitely, according to a fairly new theory that is gaining widespread acceptance as a way of understanding and treating the blues.

"We all have a guiding philosophy in life," says cognitive therapist Patricia Lacks, Ph.D., of Washington University in St. Louis, "and if that philosophy is self-defeating, it can lead to depression or anxiety."

According to Dr. Lacks, the habit of thinking, "Everyone has to like and approve of me," is one of those self-defeating mind-sets. "I can't make mistakes; everything I do has to be perfect," is another. Some people also may go into a depression, she says, because their families aren't perfect. "They grew up watching 'The Waltons' and become depressed because their own families aren't kind and sweet like that."

Many people also develop depressions because they automatically assume that whatever they tackle won't work out well. They blame themselves when things go wrong, even though they may not be at fault. And, in a double whammy to their psyches, they fail to give themselves credit when things go right.

It's important to realize that self-defeating thoughts may accompany depression. A man whose business has just gone under may be very upset about it but nevertheless optimistically think, "I've started from scratch before. I'll start again." Depressed, that same businessman is likely to think, "I've failed, I always fail, what's the use of trying?" Because clouded judgment is so common when we're depressed, the experts advise us not to make any major decisions just then.

Finally, there is "depression" that is really something else. "People often say, 'Oh, I'm so depressed!' and it turns out they're dampening—shutting down—other feelings," Ms. Shor explains. "People who feel very angry or scared or anxious, but can't admit it to themselves, will call it depression."

## DEFUSING DEPRESSION

Blue moods are like colds—even if we do nothing about them they usually go away in time. But, as with colds, we can employ remedies to ease the discomfort, to keep it from worsening, to possibly rid ourselves of depression sooner and to keep it from coming back. How? The "cures" are as varied as the causes. Here's the experts' advice.

**Accept the Blues as a Fact of Life.** Consider these important lines from a National Institute of Mental Health study of depression: "Feeling sad, blue, down and dejected is a normal part of the spectrum of human emotions . . . Transient unhappiness follows many of life's disappointments, losses and letdowns . . . But most normal people bounce back from these experiences with renewed enthusiasm and gusto."

So, don't be hard on yourself for being depressed. Depression isn't a sign of weakness. Accept the fact that you're feeling down, then take action to help yourself. A study by psychologists Constance L. Hammen and Christine A. Padesky of the University of California at Los Angeles showed that men in particular are apt to deny their depressions—and therefore fail to do something about them.

Granted, a case of the blues isn't much fun. But depression is a universal experience; it helps, therefore, to keep it in perspective and view it as an aspect of being human.

**Avoid Drugs.** The NIMH study suggests that some people—men, in particular—are prone to drink to avoid acknowledging or dealing with their depression. Alcohol can give a lift, but only in the short run. Basically it's a central nervous system *depressant,* which means that after the high wears off the depression actually may intensify.

Many experts also frown on the use of antidepressant drugs for mild depression, even though some family doctors prescribe them. The drugs have potentially serious side effects. On a psychological level, they have a negative effect because, Dr. Goldenthal says, "They contribute to feelings of helplessness. Moreover, they mask our feelings so that we never really learn how to deal with them."

A research project headed by George E. Murphy, M.D., of Washington University School of Medicine, shows that cognitive therapy is just as effective as drug therapy in treating moderately to severely depressed people.

**Be Good to Yourself.** If you wake up one morning feeling very down and wanting to hide under the covers—well, go ahead. "Getting away from it all can be helpful if it's done occasionally. It's one day in an otherwise healthy and active life," Dr. Goldenthal says. But don't mope around too often during a depression, even though that's what you might feel like doing most. Include some fun activities in your schedule—see a happy movie, buy some new clothing, take a hike in the woods, do whatever you really enjoy. Most important, do things that will give you a sense of accomplishment and raise your self-esteem. "Even if it's only cleaning out that messy drawer you've been meaning to straighten up, it will make you feel better," Ms. Shor says.

**Analyze Your Depression.** This is especially helpful if there is a recurrent problem in your life. Sometimes simply knowing where depression comes from is enough to clear it up. At the very least, you may learn what makes you depressed and what you can do about it. Ask yourself these questions:

- Has there been a recent loss in your life?
- Has there been a recent change?

- Did you suffer a major loss around this time of year earlier in your life?
- Are there problems, conflicts or powerful feelings you've avoided dealing with?
- Do you tend to engage in negative thinking?

**Fight Those Negative Thoughts.** Remember, distorted thinking produces depression and depression produces distorted thinking. Here are the steps Dr. Lacks suggests for overcoming that kind of thinking.

Step one: Catch yourself whenever you think or say something that's sad, gloomy, negative or hopeless—for example: "I just know it's going to be an awful day"; It's hopeless"; "Everybody always takes advantage of me." Write down your thoughts, along with the circumstances that produced them.

Step two: Challenge their irrationality. Make a real effort to dispute them. Taking the above examples: How do you know beforehand what the day will be like? Of course it's not hopeless. You just have to pump up your energy to turn the situation around. *Sometimes* people take advantage of you, perhaps; it's very, very unlikely that it happens on every single occasion.

Step three: Work hard on those distorted thoughts to turn them into healthier, more positive ones: "I'm going to have a fine day"; "I'll deal with the situation as constructively as I can"; "I'll do my best to speak up when people take advantage of me."

**Become Physically Active: Exercise.** Studies at Duke University Medical Center and other prominent research centers all point to the same heartening conclusion: Physical exercise has a significant antidepressant effect. Some researchers speculate that exercise may produce the same kind of changes in the chemistry of the brain that antidepressant drugs do, changes that result in an elevation of mood. Aerobic exercises in particular— running, swimming, biking, brisk walking—do a very good job of restoring both flagging spirits and

## Smilin' Through

People respond to us in some unexpectedly positive ways when we smile. Smilers are perceived as more friendly, more likeable, nicer and warmer. For some reason they are also seen as more intelligent. Smiling, apparently, can boost our "face value."

And, even more surprisingly, we respond to our *own* smiles. Positioning the facial muscles into a smile—even on a purely mechanical level, with no joy or happiness involved—sends a message to our autonomic nervous system, the system which controls heart rate, breathing and other vital involuntary functions. According to the findings of Paul Ekman, a psychologist at the University of California at San Francisco, the physical changes are the same as those which occur when we actually do feel happy.

In other words, if you want to lift your mood, try fixing your face into a warm, sunny smile. Your nervous system will begin to think you're having a great day. In addition to the physical changes taking place, people you meet will smile back in response. Warm, likeable, friendly old you will soon be humming, "Let a smile be your umbrella . . . "

flagging energy. In order for it to work, though, the exercise has to be done regularly and consistently—at least 30 minutes a day, three days a week. If you're over 30 and out of shape, get your physician's okay before embarking on an exercise program.

**Try Meditation or Progressive Relaxation.** Dr. Goldenthal advocates both as effective ways of relieving depression. Meditation works beneficially on all the areas, both physical and mental, affected by depression. Progressive relaxation dissipates anxiety, which often accompanies depression. Furthermore, it promotes a sense of well-being that counters many of the negative effects of depression.

**Get Out and Socialize.** When you're depressed, that's probably the last thing you want to do. In the interest of fighting that depression, make it one of the first. Being with other people—especially people you like—keeps you from concentrating too much on yourself. You can get some soothing hugs. You can get the healing that comes with knowing other people care about you. You can talk about your innermost feelings with a trusted friend or relative. And friends or relatives can provide companionship as you pursue those fun activities you've scheduled as another way of fighting your depression.

One caution, though, from Ms. Shor: It's easy to advise, "Be with other people," but do give some thought to whether those people are going to make you feel better or worse. If being with sunny types will make you feel better, fine. Otherwise, avoid them for the time being. On the other hand, if being with people who are dispirited will only intensify your own blue mood, stay away from them just now. Socializing—and picking the right people to do it with—is another important way of working through to a happy, cheerful frame of mind.

## How to Cheer Someone Up

Got a friend who's down in the dumps? Showing you care will make your friend feel better. Even if it doesn't, the effort will improve *your* spirits.

Here's a handy list of some basic give-your-friend-a-lift ideas:

- Tell a joke.
- Give a small, unexpected present, like a card or a flower. (Men particularly get a kick from flowers.) Because it's alive, a plant is an especially cheering present.
- Write a letter just to say hello.
- If your friend's an animal lover, take your dog or cat to visit.
- Declare a holiday. Ask your friend to help you celebrate Wednesday. Or declare it National (your friend's name) Day and put up a sign that says so.
- Sponsor an outing to the movies—perferably a light comedy.
- Take your friend out for a walk.
- Send a bunch of balloons or a "gorilla-gram."
- Have your friend "kidnapped" and taken to a lavish party.
- Cook a special dinner or arrange for breakfast in bed.
- Lend an ear. Sometimes we all just need someone to listen, say psychologists.

# Fears and Phobias

Sometimes we all feel afraid, and that's perfectly normal. But sometimes a fear gets out of hand. Here's how to regain control.

In his most famous speech, President Franklin Roosevelt was rousing and articulate, but wrong: Fear itself is not the only thing we need to fear. Not by a long shot. We actually need to fear a whole host of things. Take rattlesnakes, for example. They can bite. So, too, timidity in the presence of live electric wires and death-defying highway traffic are both healthy and commendable.

In fact, anxiety and fear are among the most natural, universal and useful of emotions. All animals know—and need—fear. Only one living creature glides through life blissfully panic free: the shark. Imagine a similarly fearless rabbit. In a world ridden with hounds and snares, how long would it survive?

The same physiological responses that help your typical, twitchy rabbit run—the elevated adrenaline levels, increased heart rate and rapid breathing—are likewise beneficial to people. Actors and politicians, for example, perform more expertly while in the grips of mild stage fright.

Fear is also a normal part of human development. No one, at any age, is fearless. Almost from birth, infants react to loud noises with anxiety. As we grow, our fears change, but they also persist.

## WHITE-KNUCKLERS, ALL

And all of us have such fears, in varying degrees of intensity. Usually we handle them by grimacing or flinching but then forging ahead. We fly from city to city, though we shut our eyes and pray during take-off. We go for walks after rainstorms, though the thought of worms makes us shiver. We are, many of us, what Jerilyn Ross, senior clinical associate of the Phobia Program of Washington, calls white-knucklers—people who know real, often intense, fear and panic, but must continue to function regardless.

Imagine, though, just for a moment, your worst fear, magnified. And not merely magnified a little, but taken to triple, quadruple, one hundred times its normal dimensions! Face to face with what you fear, you feel your heart begin to beat wildly. You can hardly breathe, your chest aches, your palms sweat, your legs sway and buckle beneath you, your head spins, you feel faint. You're just sure that you are about to lose control. You no longer know fear: you know PANIC! And you know how it feels to have a phobia!

The difference between fear and phobia is one not of kind but of degree. Charlotte M. Zitrin, M.D., director of the Phobia Clinic at Hillside Division of Long Island Jewish-Hillside Medical Center in New York, says, "A phobia is an irrational fear. It is realistic to fear actually walking up to a hungry lion and shaking its paw." It is not realistic to worry, in suburban America, that a hungry lion is likely to walk up to you, especially if such a worry keeps you at home, doors locked against lions. This would be a full-blown lion-phobia.

## FEAR VS. PHOBIA

Alan Goldstein, Ph.D., director of Temple University's Agoraphobia and Anxiety Program, agrees. "A clinical phobia interferes with your life," he says, by prompting you to avoid what you fear and any place where the feared object might be. People afraid of dogs won't visit public parks. People afraid of moths won't go to evening barbecues. And people afraid of bridges will detour 150 miles around the formidable Chesapeake Bay Bridge near Baltimore. Hundreds of other drivers, who do attempt the span and become terror-stricken, must be driven across by members of the overburdened Chesapeake Bay police department.

Called avoidance behavior, it knows no boundaries of occupation or income. Science fiction writers Ray Bradbury and Isaac Asimov—

men who, in their books, travel to the farthest reaches of outer space— refuse to fly on airplanes.

Sound odd? Well, it's not. Yet one of the most insidious things a phobia does is make the fearful person (and often his family or friends, too) believe that he is "crazy." As Isaac M. Marks, M.D., author of *Living with Fear,* writes, "The more common and familiar the phobic object, the greater the incomprehension and lack of sympathy. Most people cannot understand how anybody can be scared of a playful puppy, a fluttering bird or going outside the home."

Unfortunately, persons with phobias often feel the same; their fear is as incomprehensible to them as it is to others. As a result, typical phobics spend ten years and as many thousand dollars trying to find a *physical* cause for their fear, to prove to themselves and others they are not crazy but curable—if only a doctor could find the cause.

Yet, people with phobias aren't crazy. In fact, they seem almost immune to insanity. "Phobics can't and won't go insane," Dr. Goldstein says. "It's not as if there were some sort of continuum, with panic attacks leading into insanity. They are completely separate conditions." In fact, people who develop phobias are usually "highly competent, take-charge types," according to Jerilyn Ross. "They frequently handle normal situations and crises very well. They're the ones that everyone else turns to during a fire. It's just that, for some reason, they freeze at the sight of, say, crickets."

## WHO'S AFRAID—AND WHY

The "typical" phobic, then, as described by Ms. Ross's colleague, Robert L. DuPont, M.D., director of the Phobia Program of Washington, is "healthy, perfectionistic, eager to please, sensitive to feelings . . . and successful in school, work and interpersonal relationships."

Some 80 percent of phobics who seek treatment are women, and their phobias usually began sometime between the ages of 15 and 30, very

# Fear of Driving

Getting there. If, for you, that means a constant chorus of "aarghs" ("a bridge—aargh!") and knuckle cramps from gripping the steering wheel like a chinning bar, then, like millions of Americans, you have a fear of driving.

Luckily, it's a fear that can be easily braked, says Jerilyn Ross of the Phobia Program of Washington. Begin by asking yourself what, specifically, you're afraid of.

Have you lost confidence in your driving ability? Then take a driving refresher course. If you're scared to drive over a bridge, grab a sympathetic friend and practice driving over one. Most important, once you do feel comfortable in a car, congratulate yourself. How about driving out for your favorite meal, "to go"?

often following within a few months of a stressful incident such as childbirth, separation or the death of a loved one.

But the debate in the medical community over what actually *causes* phobias is intense. Only in the last decade or so have significant amounts of research been done. Most phobia specialists agree that there are multiple possible causes. The first of these, they say, is a bad experience. Typically, but not always, it occurred in childhood: Maybe a hulking brute of a dog snarled at you long ago, while you were still young. If you then developed a fear of dogs, your phobia was caused by a bad experience. It would be classed a "simple phobia," because it involves only one feared object.

## FEAR OF FLYING

One common simple phobia is the fear of flying. It affects some 25 million Americans. Fortunately—in part because the airlines have been so eager to help—treatments have been developed.

One treatment, some counselors say, is to alter your diet. Captain T. W. Cummings, who leads The Program for the Fearful Flyer in Florida, and Lucienne Skopek, Ph.D., who leads a similar program in McLean, Virginia, both recommend that, if you're afraid of flying, you *not* drink coffee or eat highly sugared foods before a flight. Get to the airport early, watch the planes land, ask plenty of questions and let yourself relax.

Most important, though, *do board.* Because that is, really, the big "breakthrough" that has been made in the treatment of simple phobias: A phobia can be overcome if you can somehow *cease to avoid* what you fear.

More complex phobias require more complex explanations and treatments. By far the most complex, debilitating—and studied—phobia is agoraphobia, literally, "the fear of the marketplace." The name, however, is misleading; what the agoraphobic fears is not a place, but fear itself. "The agoraphobic—usually a woman—fears being away from a safe base, usually their home," explains Dr. Zitrin, whose clinic treats 40 to 50 agoraphobics a week. "That's because

# Computer Phobia

Though a computer can be intimidating, you *can* deal with one. No, not by kicking it or, like a frustrated sheriff in California, filling it full of buckshot. Instead, Cathy Shankweiler of the Lehigh Valley Computer Learning Center suggests you get hands-on experience in the company of a computer consultant.

Familiarity with computers breeds content, for once you're Master of the Machine and not vice-versa, you'll find it a cooperative tool. With your new know-how, you can just feed it an impossibly time-consuming task and watch it eagerly flash out the answer for you. Who could feel intimidated after that?

they're afraid that if they're in an unprotected situation, they'll have a panic attack and/or lose control."

Each time an agoraphobic has a panic attack somewhere, in a grocery store, her automobile or wherever, that place becomes "unsafe," somewhere to be avoided, until finally she draws her life inward, to within the narrow confines of her own safe home. Until recently, as publicity brought the problem to light and let agoraphobics know that they were neither alone nor crazy, some would live almost totally housebound for decades.

## WHAT TO DO

Today, many agoraphobics are successfully treated, despite raging controversy among researchers. Some believe the phobia is caused by a genetic predisposition in certain people that leads them to experience crippling panic attacks in situations where other people don't. Therefore, the reasoning runs, agoraphobics must have some sort of biological difference, a condition that could be treated with drugs.

Wrong, other researchers cry. Though many agree that there is some sort of genetic susceptibility that leads certain people to become agoraphobic, they don't see drugs as part of the treatment.

Indeed, others believe that certain *foods* may affect a person with agoraphobia so that anything that makes them especially nervous, and that includes substances like caffeine, can lead to agoraphobia. Caffeine? You mean drinking coffee can contribute to agoraphobia?

Indeed yes, say these researchers. One woman, for example, whose phobia was resisting treatment, was finally discovered to be drinking in excess of ten cups of coffee a day. After she cut back to no more than two cups, her anxiety leveled off and she could overcome her fear.

In fact, your overall nutritional level may determine whether you develop the phobia or not. A study by New Jersey nutrition counselor Laraine C. Abbey, R.N., showed that all of her agoraphobic clients had severe vitamin deficiencies of one kind or another, due in part to poor diet.

---

# Hyperventilation Can Cause Panic Attacks

Remember Mom's advice to "breathe deep and count to 10" whenever your terror of spelling tests loomed large? Well, Mom should have opened a phobia clinic and become famous, because she was exactly right.

New research has shown that people often react to stress by overbreathing. This reaction produces feelings of dizziness, unreality, choking and chest pain. Not surprisingly, such symptoms worry their sufferers, who suspect they're having a heart attack. They panic, and this increases their symptoms and a vicious cycle results. Such may be one of the origins of panic attacks, wherein a person repeatedly has attacks and begins panicking at the mere thought of one. But the cure for hyperventilation is simple and effective: When you feel panicky, *breathe slowly* and the panic will soon pass.

---

Many of her patients got three-quarters of their calories from processed, "junk" foods. Moreover, genetic abnormalities made it difficult for the agoraphobics to metabolize sugar well or kept them from absorbing certain vitamins, contributing to the problem. But she also found that she could bring about dramatic recoveries by replenishing her patients' nutrient stores. One woman with a thiamine deficiency, who wouldn't leave her chair at times, lost virtually all her phobic symptoms, including severe depression, after only three months of supplementing her diet with thiamine.

Treatments for phobias only recently have become so easily accessible. Until the early 1970s, phobias were usually treated with psychotherapy, with therapists delving deep into the phobic's unconscious for the buried traumas believed to lie there. However, "There is no need to look for hidden origins of phobias and obsessions. They do not point to dark, unconscious secrets which have to be uncovered," Dr. Marks says. "The anxieties can be cleared up by working on the assumption that the sufferer needs to get used to the situation which troubles him, without any need to reconstruct his personality."

## MAKE YOURSELF DO IT

In other words: Face what you fear.

This approach is the basis for the treatment first practiced in 1971 by Manuel Zane, Ph.D., at his phobia clinic in White Plains, New York. But it is neither as dictatorial nor as painful a program as it might at first appear to be. Others, building on Dr. Zane's work, adapted behavior modification techniques to the treatment of phobias, using a practice known as desensitization. Since the "flash-point" of a panic attack usually lasts a few seconds, if a person can be taught to endure whatever he fears for 15 to 20 seconds, the panic will subside and so, finally, will the phobia.

In practice, this kind of program requires the person with a fear of elevators to ride one; the agoraphobic to go to a shopping mall; the person frightened of worms to touch one. Virtually all phobia treatments are based on desensitization, sometimes combined with psychotherapy or drugs. But the process is carefully controlled. Until a person is ready, he or she may be encouraged simply to imagine meeting up with the feared object.

The success rate for this type of treatment has been excellent. Jerilyn Ross reports that a Washington, D.C., clinic had a 92 percent "recovery" rate without using any drugs. "Recovery, of course, doesn't mean the person feels no fear. But it means they can now lead a normal life without avoidance behavior," she explains. Similar, if not quite so spectacular, success has been reported at other clinics across the nation.

## STEP BY STEP TO FREEDOM

The same principles that got Ms. Ross's head gloriously into the clouds can help you to overcome your fears. The first thing you have to acknowledge, though, is that it is going to be hard work and will require both commitment and discipline. Still, "just about anyone with a phobia can get over it if they're motivated to," Ms. Ross promises.

The first step, according to Dr. Marks, is to isolate what it is that you're afraid of. Be as specific as possible. Are you afraid of driving? Or only driving alone? Do dogs frighten you? Or only schnauzers?

This careful pinpointing of what makes you panic is important, because the next step in overcoming panic is to induce it. Yes, *induce* it. As part of a phobia program, you do that by imagining yourself confronting whatever you fear.

The philosophy behind imaging is that, since phobias are built on anticipation—"What if I see a dog?"; "What if I faint?"; "What if I can't get away?"—you learn to anticipate a positive outcome. Instead of panicking at the mere thought of seeing a schnauzer, try closing your eyes, relaxing and imagining yourself walking up to that dog, patting it on the head, then walking calmly by, whistling.

Keep this in mind as you begin the toughest part of your program—exposure. Experts suggest that, before you begin, you might learn some relaxation or deep breathing techniques. These help you control the physical symptoms of panic. Then, go out and find what you fear. But, slowly. The idea is to desensitize yourself step by step, over as many days or weeks as needed.

If you totally panic on the first day after only a few seconds, fine. The next day, as you feel your panic mount, try counting backward from 50. See if, at the end, your panic isn't less intense. What you need to do is to face the panic, even welcome it. You'll discover that, in fact, the panic passes, and a new, stronger you survives.

At this point, Ms. Ross says, congratulate yourself! Too many people feel so embarrassed by their fear that they can take no pride in overcoming it. "How can I be proud of becoming able to leave my house?" they ask. "It was silly to be afraid in the first place."

Well, that attitude is wrong. Fear is natural; fear is not silly. We

## Phunny Phobias

A quick glance through a listing of the nearly 300 phobias that have been clinically identified is an experience likely to make the most sympathetic among us smile. Phobias, if you don't share them, can seem pretty phunny.

Take Genuphobia, for example. It's the fear of the knees. Or Dexterophobia, the fear of objects on the right side of the body. Or Blennophobia, the fear of slime. Yes, slime. These fears are hard to understand. Certainly not many of us would *welcome* slime into our lives, but neither would we actually sit and brood darkly about a chance encounter with some.

Of course, something like Bacilliphobia, the fear of microbes, is perfectly reasonable. Our world's teeming with the tricky little buggers. But since you can't see them, you probably never know exactly when to panic.

The same rationale applies to Anglophobia, Gallophobia and Germanophobia, the fear of England, France and Germany respectively. These, after all, are countries far, far away, where the Fourth of July and Thanksgiving are not paid holidays. Such behavior is inexplicable and suspect. Why shouldn't it be viewed with suspicion?

Other fears, though legitimate, must be awfully difficult to live with. Anthropophobia, the fear of human beings, for instance. Granted, there is much in human beings to make us nervous. But, since you are one yourself, you must feel pretty jumpy. In fact, by definition, you'd have to have Autophobia, the fear of oneself. (No mirrors in this person's home!)

Nor can there be peace of mind for the person with Barophobia, the fear of gravity. Named, maybe, in commemoration of what its sufferer grips as he waits for his hopes to be fulfilled and gravity to be no more? Because, at that point, without a bar to hold on to, he'd bolt straight into space, there doubtless developing Meteorophobia, the fear of meteors, or Auroraphobia, the fear of auroral lights, or maybe just Hodophobia, the fear of travel. Or Acrophobia, the fear of heights.

And now—*surprise*! (If you have Phonophobia, the fear of loud talking, stay calm.) Having smiled over our imaginary Barophobic wafting away to shrink in the face of meteors, you have just taken part in one kind of phobia treatment program. Many clinics try to get patients to see the humor inherent in fearing, say, heredity (Patroiophobia). So, whether you have a phobia or are helping someone overcome one, smile! And rejoice that the phobia you face isn't Cherophobia, the fear of gaiety.

live with it, but some of us live with a weight of it that threatens to crush us. To instead crush the fear is to re-affirm how marvelous the human will is. So, take a deep breath, open the door and step into a freer, fuller life.

**10**

# Techniques for Living Happily

**Living well is an art that you can enhance by learning the skill of communicating well.**

Picture yourself bound and gagged, unable to convey your thoughts or share your feelings; unable to express any of your needs, physical or emotional; unable to meet the needs of others. You'd be effectively isolated. The very idea is chilling.

Some people who have trouble communicating might just as well be gagged. Yet, the ability to communicate is essential to sound emotional health. Unfortunately, many of us don't communicate as well as we might—or even as well as we think we do.

"If you've ever completely misunderstood what somebody else said when you thought you understood perfectly, or if you've ever been misunderstood when you thought you were being very clear, you might benefit from improved communications skills," says psychotherapist Muriel Reid.

This description of miscommunication probably includes most—if not all—of us. Luckily, we all can learn how to communicate more effectively, in both personal and business situations.

Effective communication is, obviously, the most invaluable of our personal tools for happy living. But it's far from the only one. What good is it to know how to get your ideas across if you find it very hard—or nearly impossible—to speak up for yourself in difficult situations? What's needed here is the art and skill of assertiveness.

Or take another kind of situation that requires another special skill. Say you're having a fight with somebody—it doesn't matter who—but while you have no trouble speaking your piece, the words may not be right. It's one thing to fight, it's another to fight fairly. Then there's the resolution of a fight or conflict. Sometimes people fight endlessly because they simply don't know how to resolve issues.

Your emotional tool kit also should contain a couple of additional implements for effective living—the ability to take risks and to make decisions. As author Gail Sheehy discovered in her major study of change and transition, *Pathfinders,* people who know how to risk and how to make effective decisions are successful in life. These skills, too, can be readily learned.

## SAYING WHAT YOU MEAN

There's nothing complex or difficult about communicating effectively. You know what you have to say. You deliver your message in a clear, straightforward way. You listen carefully to the response. You respond to the reply if one is needed.

If only communication were really that simple! We wouldn't have misunderstandings. Missed messages, mixed messages and other confusions wouldn't be as common as they are. Communications often do go awry, however, sometimes because we're not using the right approach, sometimes because of the power of the emotions generated and often for both reasons.

Fortunately, communications specialists have worked out a variety of techniques that solve these problems. The benefits that come from this improved skill are enormous. When we communicate effectively we make a very good impression. Our self-confidence is boosted. We have the best chance of getting our wishes and desires met, as well as meeting those of others. And our relationships, both personal and professional, are improved. A study reported in the *Journal of Consulting and Clinical Psychology,* for example, showed that the higher couples rate their communication before marriage, the more satisfied they are with their marriages years later.

Here are the experts' rules for effective communication.

**Think about What You Have to Say.** "Organization is the key," advises Dorothy Sarnoff in her helpful guide to public speaking, *Make the Most of Your Best.* That's excellent advice whether you're talking to an audience of a thousand or just one. Far too often people have something to say and think they "know" it well—yet it somehow comes out a bit fuzzy, with thoughts tumbling out in random order, vague references or lack of a clear conclusion.

"We have a harder time being precise when we're talking about an emotionally charged issue," explains Susan Hartman, former director of a popular communications program called UNITE for the Family and Children's Service of Minneapolis. "That's when we need to be most careful about organizing our thoughts ahead of time."

An emotional issue can be anything that raises *your* emotional temperature from its normal state—talking with your spouse about a marital problem, with your doctor about your physical condition, with a department store clerk to whom you're returning an unsatisfactory item. Prepare yourself: Before talking, mentally rehearse the important points you want to make and questions you have. Jot them down if that will help. The more prepared you are, the more certain it is that you will come across clearly, logically, effectively.

**Fit Style to Mood.** According to communication specialists Sherod Miller, Ph.D., Elam W. Nunnally, Ph.D., and Daniel B. Wackman, Ph.D., who developed the communications program upon which UNITE is based, everything we say can be fitted into four main styles. Style One is a conventional, superficial, let's-talk-about-the-weather kind. Style Two is an assertive, commanding style—for instance, "Tony, answer the telephone," or "Please hurry, they're expecting us at nine." Style Three is a speculative style, in which we question, explore, make tentative suggestions. Style Four is a direct, open style which we use to express our feelings and solve problems.

We get ourselves into trouble when we don't match our style with our intention. Say a couple is trying to figure out where to go for their vacation. If they use Style One, they're apt never to leave their house. If they use Style Two, they're likely to have a huge fight. Styles Three and Four are best for dealing with major issues.

**Fit Body Language to Verbal Language.** We're always speaking. Of course we use words, but we also use tones of voice, expressions, gestures, postures and the glint in our eyes. Often, without realizing it, we're very eloquent even in silence. Picture yourself at a party watching somebody sitting there utterly bored; you "know" just what he's feeling though he doesn't say a word. Studies have shown that we can look at photographs of people and correctly identify the emotion conveyed by their facial expressions from 60 to 80 percent of the time.

To communicate effectively, you have to be aware of your nonverbal signals. A job interviewer will tune out no matter how good your credentials are if your voice sounds bored and disinterested. Tell someone you're angry—but do it with a little smile on your face—and the other person will conclude that you don't mean it. The closer the match between the verbal and nonverbal you, the more powerful your message will be.

**Use Clarifying Techniques.** Sometimes misunderstandings occur and tempers flare, even when two people start off wanting to have a civilized discussion. It happens most when the topic is an emotional one. With the following UNITE techniques, however, two people can talk about any sensitive subject and still keep even-tempered.

*Speak only for yourself.* Don't tell your partner what he is—or should be—feeling. Stick to your own thoughts and feelings; begin most of your statements with "I." For example, you'll generate less heat if you say, "I feel left out of your weekend plans" instead of "You never want to spend time with me."

As much as possible, back up your statements with examples and illustrations. Demonstrate why you feel the way you do.

*Listen well.* Really consider what the other person says, rather than interrupting or formulating

---

## On Listening Well

Though your ears may be as big as Dumbo's, the most important equipment for operating those flaps is found between them, say experts on listening.

And learning how to listen can improve both your business and personal relationships. What's the secret of good listening? It's paying attention.

For example, although white-collar workers spend about 40 percent of their working time listening, according to Ralph Nichols, Ph.D., professor emeritus of rhetoric at the University of Minnesota, only about 25 percent of what they hear registers.

To improve your listening, first ask yourself, "*Why* am I listening?" says Dr. Nichols. If you're listening to a friend, the answer might be not only that you want to help, but also to learn how someone else sees life.

Don't interrupt, offer advice or spend time formulating a response, say the experts. If you do, you're not really listening. Instead, fight a wandering mind by mentally summing up what the speaker is saying and by listening hard for what's being communicated between the lines.

---

your reply while he's still talking.

*Give feedback, get feedback.* Miscommunications usually occur because the other person isn't being clear or because we (without realizing it) hear what we want to hear, or make assumptions about what is meant. It helps if each of you "checks it out"—repeats, in your own words, what the other has just said. Don't hesitate to ask questions. For instance, "Do I read you correctly?" and "How do you feel about what I've just said?"

*Be respectful and straightforward.* Being threatening, manipulative or evasive has no place in effective communication. Neither do "double messages," in which a person says something that sounds straightforward but which he immediately contradicts either verbally or nonverbally. If you share your feelings and intentions openly, you encourage a like response.

*(continued on page 146)*

# Body Language

**O**ften unconsciously, we "talk" to each other with our bodies. It's known as "body language," and its messages are fre- quently more meaningful—because they come from our heart and gut—than what comes out of our mouths.

## Power Seats

The head of the table traditionally belongs to the leader, whether it's of a family, a company or a country. The second most powerful seat, although it suggests competition, is at the opposite end of the table. Even if the table is round, wherever the boss sits becomes the head, and seats nearby are the next most potent spots.

## I Agree with Him

Watch for this "identical twin" posture. It announces a shared point of view. But if the listener stops mirroring, it means his opinion differs, too.

## Steepling

Holding the hands in this position indicates a desire to dominate. It's a sign that a struggle for control or supremacy is going on. And, in effect, it says, "I'm on top. I'm above you." This gesture often shows up when executives are pitted against each other in debate or a contest of wills. As each struggles to dominate, the steepled hands attain new heights. The executives are vying with body language for the top position, and saying with their fingers, "I'm higher than you are."

## Preening

Gestures like stroking, patting or fluffing the hair signal courting behavior and sexual attraction—it's the result of an upsurge in sexual self-awareness.

## Leave Us Alone

A group of friends in a public space will often use limbs and posture to form a human barrier, clearly communicating that no intrusion is wanted.

## Anger

A person with fists on hips appears angry to us, especially if the elbows are forward and there's intrusion into our "body buffer zone"—that space, usually about 1½ feet, that we need around us to feel safe.

## Closed Up

Tightly crossed arms and legs may not afford any real protection against anger, aggressive curiosity or unwanted sexual approaches. Nevertheless, most of us will automatically assume a stance that could protect our bodies from blows even though the danger we fear—real or not—is purely emotional.

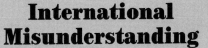

# International Misunderstanding

A friendly American gesture can translate into a dastardly insult abroad. Our advice: Play safe. *Don't* let your fingers do the talking when you travel.

"A-okay, everything's great." That's the approving message this sends in the United States. But in France or Belgium, the natives will react to a different meaning. You'll have said, "I think you're worth zero."

V is for victory—maybe. Nixon and Churchill both used the palm-forward V-sign to spell w-i-n. But turn it palm backward in England, and you're sending a very hostile "message" where the sun never shines.

Tap your index finger to your temple in the United States, and you have indicated braininess. In Europe, however, the translation is exactly the opposite. It signifies a judgment of stupidity.

Nodding the head means "yes" almost everywhere. *Almost* everywhere. In parts of Greece and Turkey, a nod communicates "no," especially if you also click your tongue.

Both hands clasped in front of the body or over the head mean, "I'm the champ," in America. But a Russian making this gesture signals not triumph but friendship.

## A FAIR FIGHT

Few of us go through life without exchanging some loud words with another. Some of us become too heated, others remain reluctant to express themselves. Most of us would like to keep our disputes from getting out of hand. There are ways of fighting constructively and destructively; these ground rules are designed to take the destructive sting out of verbal battles.

# The Battle of the Sexes

Does your mate's battling behavior puzzle you? Wives, do your jaws drop when your husbands stop fighting promptly at 11:00 and start snoring at 11:10? Husbands, are you stunned when your wives bring up wrongs you did them 7 years ago?

The answer is that men and women fight differently, says psychiatrist H.G. Whittington, M.D.

Men fight on a sports contest model, says Dr. Whittington. Society teaches them to ritualize combat, to fight by rules, to limit the time of the fight, to put hostility aside after "game time," but to be openly aggressive during combat.

Women, on the other hand, are not taught rules to fight by. Instead, they learn to control or repress their hostility, especially when fighting with men, who are usually larger and stronger. Nor do women see a fight as a separate event with a clear-cut end and a clear-cut winner.

Acknowledging the disputational difference between the sexes can help you resist anger over matters of style—and stick to substance.

**Give Yourself Permission to Fight.** Some people believe it's wrong to fight. While there's certainly something amiss when a person constantly quarrels, an occasional argument can be constructive. It can dissolve tension and ready us to resolve a conflict. In fact, a number of psychologists believe occasional heat is healthy in close relationships because it shows there's real warmth and feeling there. Referring specifically to husbands and wives, George R. Bach and Peter Wyden write in their best-selling *The Intimate Enemy*, "We have discovered that couples who fight together are couples who stay together— provided they know how to fight properly."

**Know Why You're Fighting.** Sometimes we fight about one thing when we're really angry about another. For example, a wife may trigger an argument with her husband when she complains about the way he leaves his clothes lying around, when she's really upset about their not having made love for three weeks. If your fights just seem to go round and round, maybe you're not talking about the real issue. Be clear about the reason for the fight.

**Establish a Goal.** Don't just fight. Use this occasion to accomplish a specific goal—to express your displeasure about something; to get past anger to an easing of tensions; to prepare the way for a resolution of the fight, either then or later. To go into a fight with the attitude, "I'm going to win!" is definitely not helpful. As Herbert Fensterheim, Ph.D., and Jean Baer put it in their assertiveness-training book, *Don't Say Yes When You Want to Say No*, "You don't fight to win, but to clear the air, find a solution, share feelings, gain greater understanding of each other, and thus both of you win."

**Fight according to the Rules.** The rules of fair play, that is. Don't bring up sensitive issues that have nothing to do with the fight at hand just because you know they will hurt the other person. Don't be sarcastic or belittling. Don't "mind read" by telling the person what he's thinking or feeling. Don't make threats or bring other people—say children, friends or parents—into the quarrel. All are low blows; just as important, they're self-defeating in that they simply incur anger and defensiveness. When people become defensive they're too busy nursing their wounds and thinking up counterattacks to hear the points being made.

Also, stick to the point of this particular quarrel; if you fire a broadside of grievances, none will make the impression you want.

**Be Forthright.** State your grievance clearly; don't keep your partner guessing. Express your feelings directly. Listen to the other person. Acknowledge it if he scores a telling point. The point of a successful fight is to clarify issues, not prove one person right and the other wrong.

## FINDING YOUR STRENGTHS

Sometimes people should fight but don't. Instead, they knuckle under. They say yes when they really want to say no—lending out a record they know won't be returned or baby-sitting for kids they can't stand.

If your most fervent wish is to be able to stand up for yourself without feeling guilty about it, you need lessons in assertiveness. Here's a quick test to see whether you need help.

Can you calmly tell someone who's snide or rude to you to stop talking to you that way?

Can you ask for something you really want?

Can you defend yourself against an unfair accusation?

These questions all relate to your ability to be assertive. If most of your answers are in the "yes" category, you're most likely an assertive personality. In fact, a study by researchers at Southern

Illinois University at Carbondale showed that people who are responsibly assertive are better able to cope with life's stressful events than those who aren't.

If you want to be more assertive than you are, you *can* be. First, be clear about the differences between being passive, aggressive and assertive, because confusion on this point can cause problems.

# You Can Take It!
# CRITICISM

How do you react when your best friend finds you guilty of every fault in the book? Do you take it lightly, brushing it off like a bit of lint on your shoulder? Do you take it seriously, vowing not to rest until every last fault is corrected? Do you not take it at all, throwing each item back in his face?

As painful as it may seem, there is value in criticism. That is, *if* you know how to handle it.

According to Hendrie Weisinger, Ph.D., psychologist and author of *Nobody's Perfect*, when being criticized, do not defend yourself. Instead, think of the criticism as new, incoming information that should be listened to now and assessed later. Get specific details of the problem, then ask for possible solutions.

Take time to carefully analyze the criticism before you decide to change your behavior. Look at the source of the criticism and at the situation in which it occurred. Weigh the importance of the issue. Ask yourself if similar opinions have been offered before. Then decide if the benefits you would derive from correcting the criticized behavior would be as great as the energy needed to make the change.

If you've decided to put a change in the works, the following few steps might help. Draw up a specific contract with yourself, complete with rewards and punishments for good and bad behavior. Or break down the objectionable behavior into a list of smaller behaviors; work through your list slowly, changing each behavior as you come to it. Also make sure to record your behavior and feelings during the period of change—just keeping track will make the struggle a little easier.

## Are You a Procrastinator?

**Do you send Christmas cards in February? Celebrate the 4th of July on the 7th? Haven't yet mailed that wedding present to your niece, now the mother of 3?**

You're not alone. There's even a group for you—the Procrastinators Club—if you can get around to joining it. And maybe you should,

because putting things off is no laughing matter, according to William J. Knaus, Ed.D., author of *Do It Now: How to Stop Procrastinating.* Procrastinators, he says, "often live encapsulated in a teardrop of misery. Bit by bit, they kill off their hopes, dreams and wishes."

Want to be a doer instead of a stewer? Dr. Knaus suggests a simple technique for getting yourself into action. Instead of trying to force yourself to do the task you've been avoiding, commit yourself only to 5 minutes on it. At the end of that time, decide if you're willing to give it another 5. Eventually you'll get it done.

Being passive is timidly waiting for things to happen rather than initiating them. It's also ducking out of unpleasant situations. Being aggressive is bullying to get your way, riding a bit roughshod over others, disregarding their rights and feelings. Somewhere between these two extremes is assertiveness. Being assertive means being clear, direct and open about your feelings and desires; it also means being respectful of your rights *and* the rights of others. Basically, it means functioning at your best.

One good way of overcoming a reluctance to be assertive is to practice doing things you find inhibiting. For instance, speak to a stranger a day, tell the noisy moviegoer to stop talking, ask a waiter for something that's not on the menu, disagree with somebody's opinion, ask a store cashier to give you change even though you aren't buying anything. The more you practice speaking up in situations that are difficult for you, the easier speaking up will become. Just remember, other people have the right to say no.

## ENFORCING YOUR BILL OF RIGHTS

Another important way of learning to become more assertive is to take your rights to heart. Yes, rights. We hear a great deal about our duties and responsibilities, but much less about the rights that are ours by virtue of being human. If you believe in these rights—and stand up for them—you'll have no problem being assertive.

- The right to feel good about yourself.
- The right to be treated with respect.
- The right to express your feelings.
- The right to say no without feeling guilty.
- The right to stop and think before responding to another person.
- The right to make mistakes.

Of course, as with any other

rights, these have to be used with judgment, cautions psychotherapist Joe Molnar, an assertiveness-training workshop leader. You have to take circumstances and consequences into account. In a work situation, for example, it's not always wise to express certain feelings very directly. You don't tell the client he's a jerk. And a surgeon should certainly not take upon himself the "right" to make mistakes when he's operating. Use your judgment—but commit these rights to memory. They'll serve you well.

## MAKING FIRM DECISIONS

Sandy will spend hours in the supermarket; with so many brands and products to choose from, she can never make up her mind.

Whether the decision is major or minor, many of us have the same problem: We can't make up our minds. Gordon Miller, Ph.D., president of Decision Training Systems in Pelham, New York, notes that even people with very high I.Q.'s often are "awful decision-makers."

Why is decision-making frequently such a problem in one way or another? "Lack of skill and practice is a very important reason why people have trouble reaching decisions—or making good ones," Dr. Miller explains. Fear of making a mistake is another. Fortunately, both can be overcome, and here are Dr. Miller's suggestions for doing so.

Determine how important the decision is. Does it have possibly serious long-term implications? Don't spend much time and energy on relatively trivial decisions.

Get all the information you need. You'll be that much more confident in reaching a decision. Don't make collecting information a lifetime task, however; then you're procrastinating. When do you have enough information? When you have alternatives to choose from (even if they're just yes or no). Work out the pros and cons on paper.

You may be in for surprises. Dr. Miller tells of a friend who went through this decision-making process and bought a sports car instead of the station wagon he first

# Negotiate for What You Want

Life is one big negotiating table, says Herb Cohen, author of *You Can Negotiate Anything*. Skillful negotiating can get you more love, money, prestige, security, justice, freedom—things obtainable only through the favor and cooperation of other people.

"Negotiating shouldn't be 'I win, you lose,'" says Cohen. "It should be 'I win, you win.' You and I are not exactly alike. What we want may be complementary."

Another approach to successful negotiating, he says, is to ask, "'How can we get together and make the pie bigger?' not, 'Who gets the biggest piece of the pie?'" And don't forget to express confidence that you *will* end up agreeing.

considered. He discovered that in his heart of hearts he wanted a fun car and could always rent a station wagon when he needed it.

## FOUR STEPS TO RESOLVING CONFLICT

Whenever we're in a conflict with someone, we have a clear decision to make. We can avoid the issue or choose to resolve it.

Like every other aspect of successful communication, resolving conflicts takes thought, care and skill. Consider two people and their approaches. Whenever Wanda is upset she plunges right in, says what's on her mind and hopes for the best. Nina, on the other hand, is more careful. For example, when she wants to talk to her husband, friend or boss about something that has the potential of causing a blow-up, she waits until they're both fairly relaxed.

Who's most successful in easing discord and settling problems? Nina, of course. She's conscious of timing, a very important point. Don't engage in a delicate problem-solving talk when either you or the other person is tired, preoccupied, intoxicated, in a hurry to go somewhere or extremely angry.

In addition to timing, surroundings are also important. The fewer distractions the better. A blaring television set is not conducive to clear, calm thought.

If the time and place are good, a four-step "conflict resolution"

approach can settle many disputes. Developed by Don Dinkmeyer, Ph.D., and Dr. Jon Carlson as part of a marriage enrichment program, its elements can be used in many nonmarital situations as well.

**Show Mutual Respect.** Don't blame, accuse, demean or insult. Don't try to determine who's right or wrong. Listen with care. In sum, as Dr. Dinkmeyer and Dr. Carlson put it, seek to understand and respect each other's point of view.

**Pinpoint the Real Issue.** Often we have "surface" fights that don't touch the basic issue. Feeling

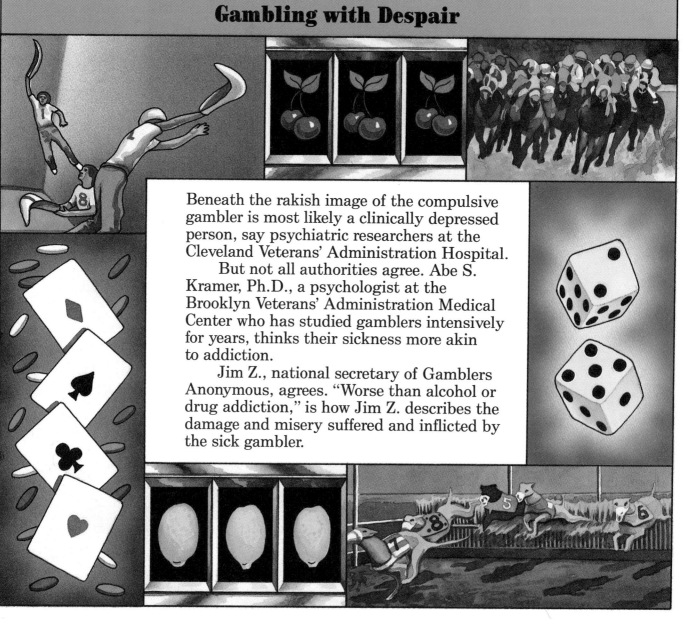

## Gambling with Despair

Beneath the rakish image of the compulsive gambler is most likely a clinically depressed person, say psychiatric researchers at the Cleveland Veterans' Administration Hospital.

But not all authorities agree. Abe S. Kramer, Ph.D., a psychologist at the Brooklyn Veterans' Administration Medical Center who has studied gamblers intensively for years, thinks their sickness more akin to addiction.

Jim Z., national secretary of Gamblers Anonymous, agrees. "Worse than alcohol or drug addiction," is how Jim Z. describes the damage and misery suffered and inflicted by the sick gambler.

unfairly treated, feeling your judgment questioned and resenting it, feeling vengeful and needing to retaliate may be the real basic issues. Look for what the conflict is really about; that's what has to be resolved.

**Seek Areas of Agreement.** When two people are very angry with each other they often think there's absolutely nothing they agree on. Prove each other wrong. "Most couples agree on a lot more than they disagree on," Dr. Carlson says. Find areas of agreement, even if it's only that you don't want a permanent break. Using that as a springboard, you'll find lots of other things to agree on.

**Mutually Participate in Finding a Solution.** Since the conflict involves both of you, it's most helpful if you both seek possible solutions. Says Dr. Carlson, "If both parties offer suggestions on ways to improve things, they have the best chance of reaching an agreement."

## REACH FOR THE STARS

Here you are, communicating effectively, resolving conflicts, getting along—still, something's wrong. You feel in a rut. Rooted to the same neighborhood, chained to your job, bored beyond reason, yet afraid to move from either home or job. Why? Most likely, you're afraid to take risks.

Taking a risk, taking a chance, reaching out for the stars, is the surest way to feel most keenly alive. Risk-taking doesn't mean trying your hand at hang-gliding, or quitting everything to tend sheep in Vermont. Some risks are sound and some aren't. As General George S. Patton, the daring World War II military commander, once wrote, "Take calculated risks. That is quite different from being rash."

Plenty of risks confront us in our daily lives; in one way or another we often say, "Dare I? Dare I not?" And when we don't dare we sometimes feel diminished. Says California psychiatrist Dr. David Viscott, author of *Risking*, "Not

risking is the surest way of losing. You never learn who you are, never test your potential, never stretch or reach."

It's important to note that even people who see themselves as very timid take risks. They get married, have children, buy houses.

In fact, most of us take some significant risks, but recoil from others. It's those we don't take that can make us feel we're missing out on some of what life has to offer. There are businessmen who think nothing of risking hundreds of thousands of dollars in venture capital, but shrink from the emotional risk of love.

## THE RULES OF RISKING

Take note of the risks you have no trouble with and those you do in order to gain a better perspective on your risk-taking abilities. As for those you have trouble with, Ms. Reid suggests a process that will help you overcome your fear.

**List All Your Apprehensions.** Say the risk entails buying a house. Your fears might have to do with meeting mortgage payments, judging whether the house is sound, the neighbors friendly, the schools good. Jot down all your concerns.

**Draw on Past Experiences.** Look back on how you've handled things in the past. "Get in touch with your abilities," Ms. Reid says. For instance: You've moved before, made friends before. You'll see that some of your apprehensions are eliminated.

**Get All the Facts You Can.** As with decision-making, the more you know, the better you can judge whether the risk is worth taking. An engineer will tell you whether the house is sound, some mathematics will tell you whether you can afford it.

**Seek Alternatives.** If you pinpoint a major problem, is there a way around it? For instance, if you can't afford a house right now, can you get a second job, rent out a room, cut down on other expenses?

**11**

# Creating Your Own Happiness

**Don't wait to find happiness. Seize today. Use it. Love it. Make it work for you. Here's how.**

You're eating the right foods and sleeping well. You're mastering those quirks of personality that have always gotten the better of you. You're handling stress and working on overcoming that irrational fear of helium balloons. All the negatives, in other words, are being neutralized. But the positives—the joy and optimism—are still elusive. Why?

It could be that you're making one of the most basic of all errors—you're waiting for someone or something to *make* you happy. Fortunately, happiness does not rest in anyone's hands but your own. We all generate our own good feelings—mostly by the way we react to what's around us. (Corny, but true!)

Of course, life isn't all skittles and beer. Most of us slam into that brick wall called bad luck from time to time, and nobody's recommending that we enjoy the experience. But on a very basic, day-to-day level, we're entirely capable of creating our own happiness just by sheer force of will. If you *want* to be happy you *can* be happy. Take the start of any workday, for example. You can have a wretched little breakfast and a gloomy commute to work, or you can slice some berries into your cereal bowl and read a whodunit on the bus.

Likewise, you can phone friends to make weekend plans, or you can spend all day Sunday alone, sulking that nobody likes you. You can plug into fake adventure every weekday night, or you can get out of the house and have some real adventures of your own. You see, it's all up to you.

Certain character traits seem to foster the ability to create your own happiness. Emotional maturity, for example, allows you to keep jarring events in perspective. Creativity allows you to

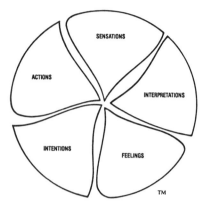

THE AWARENESS WHEEL

SENSATIONS

ACTIONS

INTERPRETATIONS

INTENTIONS

FEELINGS

™

transform the ordinary into something that's really fun. In addition, there are techniques that allow happiness to grow—techniques that smooth the way at work and allow you to get the most from your leisure hours.

## TRAITS TO DEVELOP

To be emotionally healthy requires a certain amount of maturity. But if you don't feel like the wisest, most grown-up person in the world, don't let the term scare you off. Emotional maturity isn't something you reach one fine day in spring. It is, both

philosophers and mental-health experts tell us, a process—something we continue working on our whole lives. Here, as many experts view it, are its main aspects.

**Awareness of How Our Actions Affect Ourselves and Other People.** "Whenever we give expression to our feelings and wishes, it has its effect—good or bad," notes psychotherapist Claire Leighton, who has a private practice in New York City. "We can't predict every possible outcome in every situation, but we can try—and try hard—to think of the consequences of our actions on ourselves and other people, and to act accordingly."

## Find Your Inner Self

You'd looked forward to dinner with an old friend, but the evening left you disappointed and depressed. And you haven't a clue about why you feel that way.

If you'd like to know more about your mental inner workings, try using the Awareness Wheel.

Use your imagination to place any personal issue or event you'd like to examine at the "hub" of the wheel. Then apply information on that issue to each of the wheel's 5 "spokes." As the information comes together, you'll develop a true picture of how you feel about the issue being explored.

Write out the entire process the first few times you use the wheel. Slowly, the technique will become a natural part of your thinking process.

| | |
|---|---|
| **Actions** | Gestures, expressions and other outward signs of what is happening inside. We don't always notice our own actions, but they color how others perceive us. |
| **Sensations** | The messages our physical senses relay to us. Be careful not to confuse what you sense (see, hear, touch, smell, taste) with what you think. |
| **Interpretations** | Our thoughts, opinions, impressions, conclusions, attitudes and beliefs. They are influenced by your expectations of each situation. |
| **Feelings** | On-the-spot emotional reactions to the experiences we encounter. It is common to have several at once. Don't deny these—accept them and deal with them. |
| **Intentions** | Our wants, goals, objectives, desires and wishes. The things we want to *be* and *do*. Look carefully—these may be hidden. |

**Ability to Tolerate Frustration.** Everybody's life has its share of irritations, annoyances, problems. Not overreacting to each unpleasant incident is another important way of keeping control. Humor helps. "We take things too seriously," says Dr. Ted Smith, director of the Central Counseling Service in New York City. Tolerating frustration also means *not* giving in to every whim we have. Instant gratification is definitely not compatible with maturity.

**Mastery of Our Emotions.** "We can certainly experience emotions without acting on them," Dr. Smith points out. "We don't have to be pushed around by our feelings." One way to help counteract a strong feeling is to contradict it with the opposite behavior. Whistling in the dark when you're afraid is a good example, or being pleasant to someone you'd really like to kick. Try it; you'll feel the emotion weaken—and feel yourself become more in charge.

But counteracting a strong feeling is only a short-term palliative, Dr. Smith points out, and not particularly useful if you're often gripped by a powerful emotion like anger or fear. In that event, figuring out what causes the emotion to reappear is the first step toward getting rid of it permanently. Look for patterns. Do you usually experience a specific strong emotion under similar circumstances? What are they? Next time you find yourself in a like set of circumstances and you feel the emotion coming on, consciously stop yourself. Pause to determine exactly what triggered the emotion. That kind of understanding is the way to master the emotion.

Also master your emotions by not personalizing situations that are difficult for you. That rude person, for instance, may not be intentionally rude to *you*, just in a foul mood. "Fundamentally, experience is an event plus an interpretation," Dr. Smith points out, "which is why two different people can go through the same situation and experience it quite differently." Two people, two interpretations. Reinterpret the event,

## Big Boys Should Cry

The U.S. Men's Gymnastics Team stood on the top platform to receive their Olympic gold medals. As "The Star Spangled Banner" began, the television camera focused on the face of veteran Olympian Bart Connor. The 26-year-old gymnast wiped the tears from his eyes, showing the whole world that it *is* all right for a man to cry.

Not only is it all right, but many experts believe it can be good for you. Clinical psychologist and psychophysiologist Alan J. Fridlund, Ph.D., assistant professor of psychology at the University of Pennsylvania, explains that although it isn't known *why* people cry, the process has its merits.

"Both sexes report feelings of relief when they cry," he says. "There are also reports that state that crying lowers stress, possibly because it causes a reduction of bodily activities associated with stress. And there is a hypothesis which contends that when people cry they secrete by-products of neurotransmitters that are related to mood changes, bringing about a calmer state."

see it in a less egocentric way, and you avoid a lot of unpleasant emotions and reactions.

**Being Empathetic.** Empathy, the ability to put ourselves into other people's shoes, is what makes mature adults different from small children. Maturity, Ms. Leighton says, entails seeing others as "whole people with needs and feelings of their own."

**Being Altruistic.** In studying mature and immature ways of coping with life, George E. Vaillant, M.D., found that altruism—giving to others—is one of the most "mature" ways of coping. Even people in inner turmoil stay more emotionally stable.

**Taking Care of Our Own Needs.** Just because giving to others is mature doesn't mean giving to ourselves is immature. "I see a lot of people who view their own needs as selfish, even sinful," says Washington University's Dr. Lacks, "but that kind of thinking leads to resentment, depression and general unhappiness. We call taking care of your own needs 'enlightened selfishness.' It involves being aware of what you need to make you happy, letting other people know what it is and then bringing it about. When you are being your own best friend, then you can actually be a better friend to others." One important way of being your own best friend is to lead a creative, nourishing life. Many people have a mistaken idea about creativity. "Oh, it's something artists and writers and musicians have," they think. "What's it got to do with me?"

Everything. Writers and other such imaginative folk are obviously and directly creative; they channel their artistic energies into one specific field. But that doesn't mean the rest of us aren't—or can't be—creative in our own particular ways.

## LIVING CREATIVELY

"Look at children," Dr. Smith says. "They're wonderfully creative and imaginative when they're young. The problem is that society, with its expectations, demands and judgments, stifles that sense of mental freedom."

For famed English zoologist Desmond Morris, Ph.D., author of *The Human Zoo,* one of childhood's richest qualities is the urge to "seek and find the test," to explore and discover. These are the qualities the lucky ones among us carry into adulthood—the qualities we then call creativity. As Dr. Morris says, "The child asks new questions; the child is inventive. The childlike adult is inventively productive."

If all of this suggests that you don't have to be a genius in order to be creative, you're perfectly right, J. P. Guilford, Ph.D., a psychologist at the University of Southern California who has done a great deal of research on creativity, is only the latest scientist to affirm the fact that many people with average intelligence score high on tests for creativity.

Other scientists tested painters, sculptors, designers and artists to see if there was a close connection between the quality of their work and their measured intelligence and no such match could be found! Also, creativity isn't restricted to the arts. Whether you're a scientist, school-teacher, businessman, businesswoman or retiree, you can be richly creative.

## OPENNESS AND INVOLVEMENT

Then what's creativity all about? For one thing, that joyful spontaneity children have, which Carl R. Rogers, Ph.D., a humanistic psychologist and author of *On Becoming a Person,* has called "openness to experience." It means not taking things for granted, being alive to many experiences which fall outside the usual categories. Trees are green, Dr. Rogers points out, but *this* tree may be a lovely lavender.

When we create something—a poem, a sketch, a handsewn garment— we're not too concerned with what other people think or the value they place on our creation. Rather, we're concerned with its value to us. As Dr. Rogers puts it, "Have I created something satisfying to me? Does it express a part of me—my feeling or my thought, my pain or my ecstasy?" It doesn't matter what the creation is, just that it nourishes and rewards you.

Whatever the creative activity, really become absorbed in it. *"Be* there," Dr. Smith advises. "Follow your heart and put yourself completely in it. Involvement is an important element of the creative life."

## NEW WAYS TO THINK

When you're creative you're not a stodgy thinker, you don't see things in the same old way. Scientists have discovered that our thought processes occur in two ways. "Convergent thinking" involves starting with broad perspectives, eliminating possibilities, narrowing down to a solution. "Divergent thinking" is expansive; you begin with a problem or goal and generate all kinds of options and possibilities. The journalist Bill Moyers, who produced a television series on creativity, points out that divergent thinkers "make a series of breaks with the past." By

## Break the TV Habit

Do you allow your television set to control your life? Do you deliberately schedule your day around "Phil Donahue," "General Hospital," and "The 6 O'Clock News"?

If so, you are showing signs of TV addiction, and it's unfortunate because you could be *living* life instead of just watching it. If you want to break the habit, here's how.

• Plan your viewing time, scheduling each show you're going to watch a week in advance. Limit your total hours of weekly viewing time.

• Ask yourself if you need to watch each show and why. If you can't come up with a good answer, skip it.

• Limit the number of television sets in your house. If you have one in the kitchen, the living room *and* the bedroom, you'll tend to watch more often.

not going at something the same old way, the new approach can lead to something unpredictable. Some of humanity's most awesome creations have come about in this way.

A lot of us have trouble making that break and being more original. Here are some ways you can loosen up to think more divergently: Visit and browse in a type of shop you've never been to before. Break the age barrier—become acquainted with someone much younger or older than you are. Take a course in photography, creative writing, yoga, needlepoint—whatever you think you'd enjoy. Study the customs, history or language of a foreign country. Allow yourself to daydream; it does wonders for creativity. Break

the daily routine—if you've been reading contemporary novels, try nonfiction; take a new route to work; listen to a different radio station; outlaw television. Have fun!

Actually, no matter who you are or what you do, you can lead a more creative life—at home, at work, at play. Follow your heart, open your mind—give yourself over to the wonder of things.

## CREATIVE CAREERS

Not everybody can have a highly creative, exciting job. And apparently not everybody wants one. Job dissatisfaction in our country isn't as rampant as some downbeat social

## Stress-Free Commuting

You love your suburban home, but you hate the daily commuting. Before you put your house up for sale, try these tricks to make your trip stress free.

• Arrange your own comfort. Prop your feet up on your briefcase. Use your coat as a pillow or bring an inflatable one along.

• Wear comfortable clothing. You can always change when you reach the office.

• Don't get involved in the hustle and bustle around you. Relax instead by reading, writing a letter, listening to music or meditating.

observers would have it—at least not for people who look upon even seemingly ordinary jobs as careers. This is the surprising result of a recent study by SRI International, an influential California-based think tank. Among those interviewed, 81 percent of the women and 78 percent of the men said they enjoy their work. (Jobs ran the gamut from office clerks to career professionals.) Some people enjoy working so much that 57 percent of the women said they'd keep on working in their present jobs even if they got paid for *not* working; 48 percent of the men also said they would.

There was, however, general dissatisfaction with salaries and promotions. Even these highly satisfied people didn't claim their jobs were problem free. That's the way it is with most of us; there are aspects of work we enjoy and others we'd change, if we knew how.

"Some people feel helpless to change what they don't like in their workaday life," career counselor Daralee Schulman says, "but they're usually not as powerless as they think. We can do something about most work-related problems." Other experts in the field of work relationships concur—and prove the point by offering solutions to some typical work-related problems.

## Personalize Your Workspace

Today's business world is just that—busy, busy, busy! A person working 9 to 5 (or 7 or 10) is under a lot of pressure. While you can't drop your "in box" out the window, experts do have a few suggestions for making your total work experience more pleasant.

Make your workspace your own. Personalize it with family photos and other items from your private life.

Be firm about your need for privacy. If your work area has a door, use it. If not, arrange your desk so that it doesn't face others. Don't look up when co-workers pass by; that's an open invitation for invasion. And if necessary, tell co-workers that you'd rather not be bothered.

It helps to escape from your working environment (whether it's your office building or just the chair at your desk). So get up and stretch, walk down the hall, or just let your mind wander several times during the day.

When lunchtime rolls around—cut loose! Get some fresh air. Walk, run, have a leisurely lunch, or just sit and soak up the day.

**Your Job Is Boring or Repetitive.** You can make it more interesting. Richard P. Smith, Ph.D., a professor of psychology at the University of Louisville, Kentucky, recalls work-

## For Low-Cost Vacations, There's No Place Like Home

That vacation you've been waiting for has finally arrived, but you find yourself a little short of cash. Don't worry. Take a wonderful vacation anyway — just take it at home.

Alan J. Tuckman, M.D., coauthor of *Time Off: A Psychological Guide to Vacations*, recommends that you plan a daily itinerary. Remember that you are on vacation, so forget the lawn and the laundry and fill this schedule with things that you enjoy.

For example, allow yourself to sleep late. Then do a little shopping (window shopping will do) — on a weekday, when the stores aren't crowded. Or take a day trip; play tourist somewhere near home that you've never explored. Plan exciting nighttime activities: Get theater tickets. Hit the latest foreign film festival. Or don jeans and sneakers and head to the nearest park for a stroll in the moonlight.

"Remind yourself that if you had gone away it would have cost anywhere from $700 to $1,000," Dr. Tuckman says. "Then give yourself $150 and go out and buy some new clothes to wear on your vacation at home. Take another $100 and hire a babysitter for the entire week. The sitter can pick up the kids after school and you'll have the evenings free to do whatever you wish. You can have a wonderful vacation without going anywhere and still save money."

ing on a mass production line making toys one summer; he was bored to tears. The regular workers weren't. When he asked them why, they said their jobs gave them time to think, plan, daydream. "They enriched their own experiences," Dr. Smith concludes.

Among truckers, he says, the safest drivers are the least bored. And the least bored are those who notice everything on the road, play mental games, keep themselves so mentally active that boredom rarely becomes a problem. Of course, they keep a sharp eye out for road hazards; they don't daydream, but they don't let monotonous driving get them.

**People Take Advantage of You.** Suppose a co-worker has been taking credit for your ideas. What to do? The experts say be closemouthed; put everything in writing and give it only to your superior. Suppose your boss is snide or rude to you. Don't take it personally, especially if he's that way with everyone. Tell him, nicely but firmly, that you'd appreciate feedback without condemnation. Suppose a co-worker dumps work on you. Tell him over lunch — a neutral setting, where the talk is less apt to get emotional — that you don't have the time to do his work and your own. Try to work something out together. In other words, be assertive without seeming uncooperative.

**You Feel Burned Out.** Make a real effort to develop a more detached view of your job. Whenever possible, delegate responsibility — don't feel you have to accomplish it all yourself. Be time efficient. Limit the amount of time you give to a project; for instance, avoid reworking and reworking a proposal when it was fine the first time. If a draft is called for, don't try to make it into a perfect document; by definition, a draft is rough. And be sure to do a lot of relaxing things outside the job.

**You Want a Raise or Promotion but Aren't Sure How to Go about Getting It.** Prepare yourself ahead of time, advises Sharon Bermon, a New York career counselor and

# Make Your Vacation
# a Learning Experience

If you think vacations are just for mindless pleasure—think again. A new breed of vacation that incorporates learning into fun is rapidly gaining in popularity. And if you're a person who likes structured activities as well as the challenge of conquering a new subject, a *learning vacation* might be the perfect way to spend your time off.

Psychotherapist Stephen A. Shapiro, Ph.D., coauthor of *Time Off: A Psychological Guide to Vacations,* explains that learning vacations have several advantages over regular, open vacations.

"First of all, they provide the structure that some people need," he says. "Second, the mastery aspects of such a program can increase a participant's self-esteem. Third, the product of a learning vacation might be of use in a person's social, recreational and work lives. Finally, learning vacations can be fun."

Programs are offered by many colleges, universities and museums, as well as by vacation and travel companies such as Club Med.

Because they are so readily available, Dr. Shapiro emphasizes that any learning vacation be researched by gathering information about the organization sponsoring the trip, vacation leaders and accommodations.

Some of the most popular learning vacations involve athletic instruction, offering lessons in tennis, sailing, scuba diving, yoga, even mountain climbing. Others focus on glacier study, wilderness survival, archeological digs and cultural expeditions to other parts of the world. Other popular vacations are based on self-improvement programs, such as those teaching weight reduction, stress management and sensitivity training. And one popular newcomer on the scene is computer camp.

## Do Nothing—Effectively

It's been called vegging out, bumming around, goofing off and loafing. You'd think that with so many synonyms, it would be a common practice. Surprisingly, it's not. Many people find that doing nothing is one of the most difficult things to do.

It all goes back to the fable of the tortoise and the hare. We are afraid that if we stop "doing" we're going to lose the race—of life. We're also plagued by a constant stream of guilt-inducing "shoulds" that tell us that until our lives are *perfect* we "should" be doing this and "should" be doing that.

The problem is that most of us don't realize that loafing is good for us. It has both mental and physiological benefits. For example, studies indicate that it can lower both stress levels and blood pressure.

If you find that you can't do nothing, try turning nothing into something. Say to yourself, "While I'm relaxing, my body is healing and my mind is rejuvenating." Then find a place—any place—that feels good and do whatever you want to do. Try daydreaming, talking to yourself, soaking in a hot tub, reading a magazine, watching TV, flying a kite, anything. Just remember, the time you *enjoy* wasting is not wasted time.

management consultant. Keep notes about the work you do, your on-the-job accomplishments. Review them from time to time. The idea is to *document* your readiness for the raise or the promotion. Just saying you deserve it or need it is not good enough. Rehearse your spiel with a friend ahead of time. What if your documentation is good but you're turned down anyway? Don't just let it go—ask why. It may be that you need to improve your skills. It may be there's a company policy against giving raises at certain times of year. It may also be that you're in a dead-end job.

If the job proves to be a dead end, or if the burnout is taking too high a toll in terms of stress-related illnesses, depression or high anxiety, this may be the time for a change. Consider it carefully. Being in charge of your work environment can also mean, at times, leaving it for something better.

## RE-CREATING THE LEISURE ETHIC

How would you like to pop a pill that lets you blow off steam, gladdens your senses, gives a shot of adrenaline to your creative powers, offers a change of pace and just generally makes you feel good physically and emotionally?

You have that pill. It's called play.

Experts in child and developmental psychology know how important play is to children. It helps them blossom, heals their hurts, tempers the serious side of life. In much the same way, play is important to us as grown-ups, too. The trouble is, many of us have forgotten how.

"We in this country need to develop a strong leisure ethic to go with our work ethic," notes Tony A. Mobley, Re.D., dean of Indiana University's School of Health, Physical Education and Recreation. "When you start seeing leisure as something that you must use effectively and productively, it becomes a trap. You're superimposing the work ethic onto leisure. This time isn't only hours to spend engaged in an activity, it's also a state of mind."

To make some sense of your leisure time, Dr. Mobley suggests analyzing your daily time. Keep a log, breaking it down into work time, maintenance time (eating, sleeping, going to the grocery store, etc.), and free time. Once you know how much free time you have, think about what you want out of your leisure time—for instance, to gain a skill, to become fitter, to meet more people. Then, tailor your free time to meet those goals.

With the smorgasbord of free-time activities available to us these days, from biking to books and back, it's more important than ever to fit our leisure to our needs. Vacations, too, offer a diversity of opportunities. Adventure, fitness, learning, foreign travel and plain old lying-on-the-beach-somewhere are all available to us. If you're very work oriented and would feel too anxious being away from the job for a couple of weeks, go on a number of three- or four-day minivacations throughout the year instead.

Work oriented or not, be sure to also take do-nothing breaks. As Dr. Smith says, "People need to learn to waste time. We don't need to be accomplishing something all the time." Dr. Mobley says he looks forward to some completely unstructured hours. "I may just sit and do nothing—it's reflective, dreaming time," he says.

## THE NEW, IMPROVED YOU

If you can accept the paradox that doing nothing is really doing something—recharging your batteries and giving yourself a break— then you probably can accept all the other paradoxes that help make you a happy, emotionally healthy person.

Remember that exercise energizes you while too much rest can make you bored and cranky. Search for meaning in life, but don't take things so seriously that you can't laugh about them—or at yourself. Live one day at a time, but plan for the future. And remember, giving to others promotes emotional health, but so does loving yourself.

## Spread Your Wings —Try New Things

Take this oath: "I declare, in my own best interest, that when I get bored or tired with my life, I won't give in to it! I'll just develop a new interest to put a little fun back into my world."

Live by this oath and watch it work wonders. Psychologist Philip Nastasee believes that trying new things, or experimenting, can lead to happiness because experimenting is a sort of playing—and we all know that playing is fun. There is also evidence that people who play tend to live longer and more fulfilling lives.

To introduce new experiences, experiments and adventure into a world-weary existence requires some creativity and effort—but these new endeavors don't have to be major undertakings.

Learn a new sport, adopt a stray cat, throw a party, take up the banjo—let your creativity make your life a never-ending series of adventures. If you need a big boost, try floating in a hot-air balloon. And remember, the sky's the limit.

## Source Notes

### Chapter 3
#### Page 40
"Caffeine Scoreboard" compiled from information supplied by the U.S. Food and Drug Administration, Food Additive Chemistry Evaluation Branch, the National Center for Drugs and Biologics and the National Soft Drink Association, Washington, D.C.

#### Page 45
"Food Sources of Choline from Lecithin" adapted from "Sources of Choline and Lecithin in the Diet," by Judith J. Wertman, *Nutrition and the Brain*, vol. 5, 1979.

#### Pages 50-52
"Mental-Health Side Effects of Drugs" adapted from *Physician's Desk Reference*, 37th ed. (Oradell, N.J.: Medical Economics Co., 1983).

### Chapter 11
#### Page 154
"Find Your Inner Self" adapted from *Straight Talk*, by Sherod Miller, Daniel Wackman, Elam Nunnally and Carol Saline. (Canada: McClelland and Stewart, 1981). "Awareness Wheel" diagram reproduced by permission of the authors and publisher.

## Photography Credits

*Cover:* Margaret Skrovanek.
*Staff Photographers*—Christopher Barone: pp. 28, top; 62-63; 74, bottom; 75, bottom. Angelo M. Caggiano: pp. 16-17; 28, bottom; 90-91; 131. Carl Doney: pp. 105; 108-109; 148. T. L. Gettings: p. 36, top. Ed Landrock: p. 61. Mitchell T. Mandel: pp. 74-75, top; 117. Margaret Skrovanek: pp. 2, center; 10; 64; 67; 73; 77; 84; 102; 116; 120; 122-123; 144-145. Christie C. Tito: pp. 57; 149; 162-163. Sally Shenk Ullman: p. 76.

*Other Photographers*—Carl Dyke: p. 68. Jerry Howard (copyright 1981)/Positive Images: p. 27. Marcia P. Huttner: p. 36, bottom. Mark Lenny: pp. 35; 48; 57, top; 85; 86. Michael Norcia/Leo de Wys, Inc.: p. 29. George Shal: p. 2, bottom. Joseph Skrovanek: p. 2, top.

*Additional Photographs Courtesy of*—The Bettman Archive: pp. 152-153. Club Med: p. 161. Frederick Lewis Photographs: pp. 58-59; 132-133; 140-141. The Free Library of Philadelphia: p. 106. Movie Star News: pp. 38-39. Movie Still Archives: pp. viii-1. Olan Mills Portrait Studio: p. 87. Photofile International Ltd.: p. 23. The Sharper Image: p. 95.

## Photographic Styling Credits

Anne Hakanson: p. 73. Renee R. Keith: p. 144; p. 145, top left and bottom left.

## Illustration Credits

Bascove: pp. 41; 50-52; 139. Susan Blubaugh: pp. 24-25; 33; 130. Lisa Gatti: pp. 122-123. Susan Gray: pp. 46-47; 49; 121. John Knutila: sculpture, p. 120. Jerry O'Brien: pp. 107; 158-159. Mary Anne Shea: pp. 8-9; 12; 40; 56; 110; 115; 126-127; 135; 150; 160. Elwood Smith: pp. 31; 79; 136. Chris Spollen: pp. 70-71; 93; 98; 157. Carl Weisser: pp. 20; 146. Wendy Wray: p. 88.

*Special Thanks to*—Morna Holden, National Zoo, Washington, D.C.; Kahle's Musical Instrument Repair Service, Emmaus, Pa.; Nestor's Sporting Goods, Whitehall, Pa.; A. Pomerantz & Co., Allentown, Pa.; Dina Porter—The Gallery For Fine Gifts, Allentown, Pa.; Sports Chalet, Allentown, Pa.

# Index

maintaining individuality in, 78
problems in, hotline for, 99
sexual problems in, 79-80
Massage, 87-89, 90-91
Maturity, emotional, main aspects of, 154-56
Meditation
effects of, 89, 92
employee programs for, 96
use of against depression, 131
Memory(ies)
effect of choline on, 44
effect of iron deficiency on, 43
effect of smoking on, 48
sad, depression and, 128
Migraines
drugs for, possible side effects of, 50
use of biofeedback for, 96
Mind
benefits of aerobic exercise for, 57
body and, link between, 15-37
body's power over, 39-57
healing ability of, 35, 37
minerals important for, 43
Mind-sets
definition of, 114
depressing, 128-29
money and, 121
overcoming, 113-23
switching negative to positive, 120
Minerals, important for emotional health, 43
Minivacations, value of, 163
Money
attitudes toward, 121
happiness and, 123
Mood(s)
blood pressure and, 21
effect of alcohol on, 47
effect of drugs on, 44
effect of herbs on, 46
effect of physical activity on, 52-53
Mother, working, benefits of for child, 67
Muscle relaxants, possible side effects of, 52
Music, calming effects of, 85

N
Narcolepsy, 30
Needs
satisfying own, 66
self, importance of, 155
shifts in during marriage, 78
Negative emotions
benefits of, 101
fighting, 8, 120, 130
working through, 101-11
Negotiation, value of, 149
Nervous system
effect of caffeine on, 48
effect of music on, 85
Niacin, use of for mental disorders, 44
Nicotine addiction, 48
Noise pollution, 55-56
Nonverbal communication, 143
Nutrients
effect of on behavior and mood, 39
importance of to health, 36, 40-43
phobias and, 137
role of in brain chemistry, 43-44
use of for severe mental disorders, 44

O
Oral contraceptives
depression and, 42
side effects of, 46, 52
Organization, importance of
in communication, 142
against stress, 86
Orthomolecular psychiatry, 44
Overeaters, hotline for, 99
Overprotectiveness, problems with, 64

P
Pain, postsurgical, relief of, 33
Painkillers
effect of on emotional health, 45-47
possible side effects of, 50
Parent(s)
acceptance of, 65
clashes with, 65
parenting of, 66
single, hotline for, 99
Parent/adult child relationships, 62-66, 72-73, 74-75
Parent-child relationships, 66-68, 73-75
power struggles in, 68-69, 72
Parenting, 66-68
during teenage years, 68-69
etiquette of, 72-73
Performance anxiety, 110
Persistence, importance of in stress management, 97
Personality
effect of birth order on, 62
entrepreneurial, definition of, 122
tips for changing, 5
Pets, health benefits of, 87
Phobias, 111, 134, 136, 137
fears and, 133-39
recovery from, 138-39
unusual, types of, 139
Placebos, 33, 37
Play, importance of, 36, 162-63
Poison emergencies, hotline for, 99
Positive thinking, benefits of, 120
Postsurgical pain, relief of, 33
Potassium, 43
Potential, human, views of, 2-5
Power games, problems with, 68-69, 72
Power of suggestion, 92
Power struggles, minimizing during teenage years, 72
Pregnancy, hotlines for, 99
Preoccupation
accidents due to, 25
bodily, 33-34
Priorities, establishing, 86
Prisoners, effect of diet on, 41
Privacy, maintaining in adult child/parent relationships, 65, 70
Problem boss, definition of, 79
Problems
ability to recognize, 12
benefits of sharing, 86-87
preoccupation with, 25
resolving, 80, 150
work-related, 159-60, 162
Procrastination, 148
Productivity, importance of, 8
Progesterone, effect of on emotional health, 49
Progressive Relaxation, 96, 131
Promotion, how to get, 160, 162
Psychoanalysis, results of, 3
Psychoimmunology, 24

Psychological victims, 114
Psychology
early history of, 2-5
humanistic, 4-5, 12
Psychosomatic medicine, 18-19
Psychotherapy, use of for phobias, 137-38
Pyridoxine. See Vitamin B$_6$

R
Raise, how to get, 160, 162
Rape, hotlines for, 98, 99
Raynaud's disease, 94
Reality therapy, 6, 7
Relationships
adult child/parent, 62-66, 72-73
importance of, 59-81
parent-child, 66-69, 72
Relaxation
benefits of, 9, 36
for phobias, 139
for sleep, 32
learning, 87
use of biofeedback for, 94
use of self-hypnosis for, 92
Resentment, effect of on energy, 27, 30
Respect
mutual, in conflict resolution, 150
role of in parenting, 68
Respiratory system
effect of emotions on, 20-21
effect of music on, 85
Rights, enforcing own, 148-49
Risks, 151
Rolfing, 89
Rules, importance of, 72, 147
Runaways, hotlines for, 99
Running, benefits of for depression, 52

S
Satisfaction, importance of, 36
Schizophrenia, 42, 44, 56
Sedative-hypnotics, 32
Sedatives, possible side effects of, 52
Self, 7
being good to, 103, 129
inner, finding, 7, 154
learning to like, 8, 103, 120
Self-actualization, 5
Self-compassion, 87
Self-confidence, building, 117
Self-control, 87
Self-help group, how to find, 13
Self-hypnosis, 92-94
Self-induced healing, 27
Self-pity, vs. self-compassion, 87
Self-reliance, developing, 117
Selfishness, enlightened, 156
Senior citizens, hotlines for, 98
Serotonin, effect of on sleep patterns, 32
Sex
effect of drugs on, 80
problems with in marriage, 79-80
Shame, patterns indicating, 108-9
Shiatsu, 88
Shyness, 102-4
Siblings, relationships between, 63
Single parents, hotline for, 99
Sleep
effect of on health, 30, 36
patterns of, effect of depression on, 30-32
steps to help, 32-33, 36
Sleep disorders, 30-32

Rodale Press, Inc., publishes PREVENTION®, the better health magazine.
For information on how to order your subscription,
write to PREVENTION®, Emmaus, PA 18049.